Dad,
from
Marion and George
September 30, 1934

Valentine's Manual of Old New York

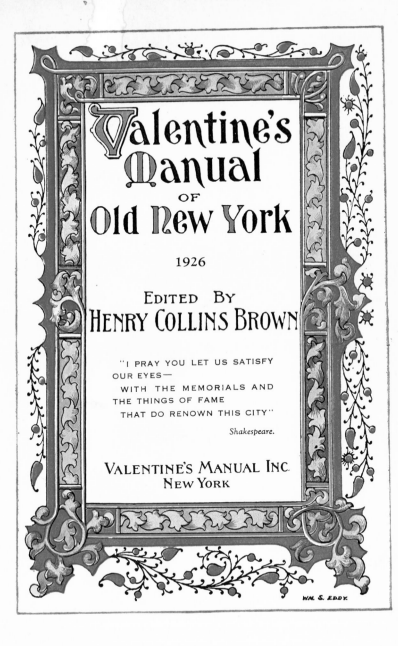

Valentine's Manual
OF
Old New York

1926

Edited By
Henry Collins Brown

"I PRAY YOU LET US SATISFY
OUR EYES—
WITH THE MEMORIALS AND
THE THINGS OF FAME
THAT DO RENOWN THIS CITY"

Shakespeare.

Valentine's Manual Inc.
New York

W.N. S. EDDY.

Press of
THE CHAUNCEY HOLT CO.
New York City

1626   New York   1926

"Many, Many Happy
Returns of the Day"

FOREWORD

THE closing glamorous years of the Nineteenth Century should have enjoyed the genius of a Pepys or an Evelyn. Failing that, the record must be set down by a scrivener who can make no pretence to aught that would enhance his narrative save the plain truth plainly told.

Perhaps the historian of the future may turn eagerly to these modest pages for a glimpse of the everyday life of the average inhabitant of our Island at that time. In no other place in the world, I venture to say, would it be possible to treat of so recent a period as if it had already passed into history. Yet that is exactly what has happened to New York of the Seventies. And, believing the record to be of permanent value, it has seemed wise to me to leave behind the testimony of an eye witness, and the contemporary sketches by the artists of *Harper's Weekly*.

It is quite possible that here and there my memory may have played me tricks. Memories do such things. A year or a month may occasionally stray, but on the whole, the picture I have painted of the city of my youth, will be found historically correct.

I also feel certain that many old New Yorkers will live over again in these pages the scenes of their younger days. It is for them, especially, I have written. "The thoughts of Youth are long, long thoughts" and it pleases me to believe that perhaps I may here and there touch a sweet and tender chord of yesterday. If so, my reward will be greater than I dared to hope and for this I shall always remain grateful.

Remember me to all the folks. Write soon.

THE AUTHOR.

CONTENTS

CHAPTER I

CHAPTER II

CHAPTER III

CHAPTER IV

CHAPTER V

LIST OF ILLUSTRATIONS

[xv]

[XVI]

[XVII]

Valentine's Manual of
Old New York

"The City then contained about a million inhabitants. The towers for Brooklyn Bridge were only just beginning to rise. The figure with the tall hat is John A. Roebling, builder of the Bridge. (1873)."

THE LAST FIFTY YEARS IN NEW YORK

By Henry Collins Brown

CHAPTER I

HARLEM BOATS – LAMP LIGHTERS – BROWNSTONE FRONTS –
THE FIRST TELEPHONE – THE FIRST ELECTRIC LIGHT –
THE BOB-TAIL CAR – BROADWAY STAGES – COMING OF THE
ELEVATED – "FRENCH" FLATS – THE GRECIAN BEND – CON-
GRESS GAITERS – POCKET TOOTHPICKS – REIGN OF THE
WHITE COTTON STOCKING – SASHES ON PIANO LEGS –
PAINTED COAL SCUTTLES – WAX FLOWERS – HIRED DRESS
SUITS – "SURPRISE" PARTIES – AMATEUR ELOCUTIONISTS

OF the City itself, as I knew it in the Seventies, scarcely
a vestige remains. At this time it comprised about
a million inhabitants. The most commanding feature,
viewed from the Bay, was the spire of Trinity Church,
and the tallest building for any purpose was the new
Post Office in City Hall Park. The Towers for Brooklyn
Bridge were only just beginning to rise, and travel to our
sister city was entirely by means of ferryboats. Fulton
Street on account of this was perhaps the busiest cross

street in the City, and the famous Fulton Market did a roaring retail business. The streets presented an incredible contrast with today's thoroughfares. The Street Cleaning Department was a temperamental Government function that existed principally for the reward of the "Boys." Only the principal thoroughfares received any systematic attention. Perhaps the personal habits of the citizenry in general were largely responsible for the unsavory condition of the highways. The genial custom of householders in the poorer districts of depositing refuse in the gutters for the nourishment of peripatetic pigs, dogs, goats and other local fauna, still persisted. Ragged small boys, such as have been perpetuated by Horatio Alger, swept the crossings for penny perquisites and these, aided and abetted by the kindly elements and by occasional spasmodic municipal exertions, made the streets tolerable for the passage of humanity.

As for roadway traffic, it was immense. Horse-drawn drays, carts, vans and wagons innumerable kept New York below Canal Street in a perpetual "traffic jam." The only visible police control was by the celebrated "Broadway Squad"; massive men whose functions appeared confined to the Chesterfieldian task of escorting timid ladies across the thoroughfare.

Transportation was then, as it is today, our most vexing problem. We were still in the days of the stage coach and the street car. "Hill horses"—an extra team to assist in dragging the overloaded cars up the many steep ascensions on the way to Harlem—were still plentiful. The Third Avenue line ran a "Special Drawing Room" car to meet the fastidious demands of the aristocratic families living along the East River. An extra fare of 10c. was charged for this exclusive accommoda-

One of the famous "Broadway Squad," 1880.

tion. On the west side many of the Sixth Avenue cars
bore signs "This Car for Colored Persons Only."

The most important, because the speediest, communication between downtown and Harlem was undoubtedly by
way of the Harlem Boats. A line of beautiful white
steamers, *Sylvan Stream, Sylvan Glen, Sylvan Dell, Sylvan Grove,* and others were the rapid transit of the day.
They were speedy little craft and on pleasant mornings
the sail on the East River was a delightful experience.

These boats were crowded morning and evening. At
130th Street they connected with the *Emily* and the *Tiger
Lily* which took you to points on the Harlem River—
Fordham, Highbridge, Morris Dock, Kingsbridge, Marble
Hill, Fort George, Spuyten Duyvil. It was the continu-
ation of a delightful trip beginning at Peck Slip and its

beauty lingers pleasantly in the memory of the old New York. On Sundays they took us to many shaded nooks and pleasant woods along the East River and their final disappearance left a void which has never found a satisfactory substitute.

The fastest commercial vehicle was the butcher's two-wheeled cart, driven by a diabolic youth in a white apron at the rate of eight miles an hour. The best pavements the City could boast, even on Fifth Avenue, were of Belgian block which, under the thousand iron tires moving on it, resounded with a mighty roar. These pavements laid under contract with a magnanimous City Government, were soon a series of hills and hummocks and in the neglected poorer quarters the Irish teamsters had no reason to feel homesick for the "Rocky Road to Dublin."

Street lighting was almost entirely by gas, and the lamplighter, hurrying in the twilight with his torch, was a familiar figure. Few there were to see him in the early dawn, quenching last night's flame, except that urban disturber of the peace, the milkman, whose whoop announced the morning milk, then delivered directly from the can.

There were still many street pumps in active use throughout the city. The one that I remember most particularly was in the downtown section, on the corner of Trinity Place and Cedar Street. I have frequently seen it surrounded by groups of children from the parochial school at this corner, and in warm weather watched with delight the pleasure they derived from the cooling water that gushed from the spout. I do not know when this pump disappeared but I should imagine it lasted well into the Nineties. The only other one I recall definitely was on the corner where the Custom House now stands. This was still "Steamship Row," occupied by the offices

Painted by James Bard   Original in Collection of New York Historical Society

One of the popular Harlem Boats, 1879.

of the various Atlantic Liners. This pump, however, disappeared at least twenty years earlier than the one on Trinity Place. Further uptown, on both the East and West sides, they were by no means infrequent, and in the early Seventies could be counted by the dozens. As the Croton Water System improved and expanded, the need for the street pump became less and less, and I imagine today there is scarcely one in existence on the Island.

The architecture of our residential districts was largely the production of job carpenters and a few God-gifted plumbers. They revelled in what was known as brownstone fronts. Long rows of these atrocious structures afflicted the City for many years. Traces of this awful visitation are still numerous on our side streets and a few survive on the Avenue. In its devastating effect architecturally it may be likened to the early visits of cholera, which appeared with painful regularity, until we organized a street cleaning department to supersede the pigs which formerly functioned in that capacity.

Nor were our streets beautified by the files of telegraph poles that stood mile after mile along the principal thoroughfares. These unlovely utilities were not levelled to the ground until many years later during the administration of Mayor Grant.

As for business buildings, the "cast iron age," may be said to have dated from this period. Builders of armor plate and iron clads, thrown out of work by the ending of the Civil War, were perforce turned to the arts of peace. The result was the erection of such a melancholy set of buildings that many persons thought it would have been much less harmful to let the war go on. Specimens of this distressing era are still to be seen in the wholesale dry goods district, notably the building at Broadway and

Broadway between Liberty and Cortlandt Streets showing Benedict's
Corner at right, first of the "Cast Iron" fronts.

Cortlandt Street which I believe had the honor of being
the first iron-clad monitor to bedeck Broadway. Their
original claim of being fireproof was soon proved a fallacy
and dealt a severe blow to their popularity.

Aside from these cast iron fronts, there was little of
note in the buildings of the business district. The Stock
Exchange, Drexel, Morgan and Co., the Custom House
and the Treasury Building were the only possible exceptions from endless cheap looking structures that had
already served their day and generation as warehouses,
cheap hotels and boarding houses. Wall and Broad
Streets were shabby in the extreme. The office building
as we know it, hardly existed. Most of the heat was supplied by ancient Franklin stoves, the coal for which was
stored in a box situated in the hall. There is still one

of these buildings doing business in Nassau Street today with this same archaic heating apparatus and there may be more. Great excitement was occasioned when the old Exchange Place building announced that it had installed an elevator. It may be remarked in passing, there was no instance of a worker in the financial district belonging to the gentler sex, with the possible exception of the cashier at Delmonico's.

At this time there was a place on Third Avenue near 63rd Street where the old horse car barns subsequently stood, called the American Institute Fair. Many of our old merchants still proudly display the gold medals and "Certificates of Merit" awarded them as being the best ever in their respective lines. This fair was quite a venerable institution and gave yearly exhibitions. It has recently been revived. An old-time program lying before me shows that Alexander Bell was exhibiting here a contrivance which he called a telephone and for the small sum of ten cents you were permitted to talk from one end of the hall to the other. I squandered a dime for this and remember holding a hollow thin disk to my ear and speaking through it and hearing a voice from the other end. It attracted no attention and was considered on a par with the dozen other insignificant catch-penny devices which invariably accompanied any public exhibition of this sort.

A few days later Mr. Bell was announced to speak at Chickering Hall on his new fangled invention and promised at the same time to give a practical demonstration of his machine. I was too young at that time to enjoy a scientific lecture so I was not present personally. But I had curiosity enough to look up the newspaper

Bronx River. West Farms.

Confluence of Spuyten Duyvel Creek And The Hudson.

Morrisania from Harlem R.R.

Spuyten Duyvel Creek. Kings Bridge.

West Farms Village.

Pleasant places to which we went on the old Harlem Boats.
Now all covered with apartments, etc.

accounts of the meeting for this article and I attach the report as it appeared in the *Times*.

"At Chickering Hall last evening, before 300 persons, Prof. Alexander Graham Bell lectured on the speaking telephone. At the end of the lecture Prof. Bell stated that he had intended to give what he believed would have been interesting and instructive illustrations of the power of the telephone, but unfortunately his improved instruments had not arrived from Boston and he would have to content himself with displaying a telephone of inferior power. This was connected by an ordinary telegraph with an improved telephone in New Brunswick, N. J., thirty-two miles away, and this in turn was attached to an ordinary organ, upon which a number of simple tunes would be played and the sounds transmitted to New York by means of his instruments. He then telegraphed to New Brunswick and shortly after, from a little box on the stage and from other instruments in different parts of the hall, came the music of the song known as 'The Sweet bye and bye.' This was followed by 'Home Sweet Home,' and afterward, by 'Hold the Fort,' sung by a strong baritone voice and plainly audible. After this Prof. Bell and Mr. C. W. Field asked a number of questions through the telephone. They were all answered satisfactorily by those at the end of the wire in New Brunswick."

In a rather depressing building on Pearl Street another "crank" was working on an impossible idea. His name was Edison and he was telling folks that he was going to provide them with a light that needed no matches, would have no odor or heat and could not be blown out. You can imagine the cordial encouragement given in those

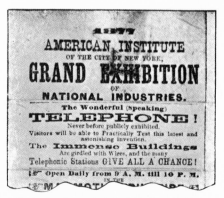

First advertisement of the Telephone in New
York, in program of American
Institute Fair, 1877

LIST OF SUBSCRIBERS
Central Office System
OF THE
BELL TELEPHONE COMPANY OF NEW YORK.

The complete Telephone book in 1876.

days to such a brainless idea as that. Presently, however, the office of the *New York Times* then at the junction of Park Row, Nassau and Spruce Streets was equipped with this new fangled light. To the surprise of everybody the unexpected happened, and the incandescent light took its place among the inventions which were among the first to mark the last half century in New York as the most fruitful period in the history of mankind.

Not long after, Bradford Lee Gilbert, working on an idea which he said came to him in a dream, erected a building at 52 Broadway of skeleton steel construction— the first successful skyscraper. Though only eight stories high the new type demonstrated that buildings so constructed could reach any height desired within reason. And the city began at once to develop up in the air instead of along the ground.

The vast majority of our buildings, however, were unpretentious in character and not over two or three stories high. Many residences had the old style sloping roof with dormer windows, such as you see in lower South Street today. Giant shade trees still adorned City Hall Park, Union and Madison Squares; many were yet left all through our downtown streets. A pear tree at the corner of Third Avenue and Twelfth Street, planted by Stuyvesant two hundred years ago, existed up to within two years of my story. Union Square was still a beautiful flower market in the spring and squirrels scampered out to the Broadway edge. Awnings in front of Broadway stores extended in an almost unbroken line from Fulton Street to Grace Church. Wooden canopies with iron stanchions, carriage blocks, old stoops, hitching posts, and street hydrants on Broadway still impeded the progress of the pedestrian.

There was an atmosphere of half-village, half-town, that began as soon as you struck the Bloomingdale Road at Broadway and Twenty-third Street. The old city was undeniably pretty and homelike, but as I remarked before, scarcely a trace of that remains.

Street cars drawn by two horses were practically the sole mode of conveyance. Stages ran on Broadway, which had no street cars, also on Madison and Fifth Avenues, etc.

Some lines maintained a service known as "bob-tail cars," a primitive form of one-man control now once more in favor among the economists of our traction systems. These were half-portion cars without conductors, the drivers of which were provided by the company with small change in envelopes to expedite the collection of fares, which were deposited by the passenger in an illumi-

Awnings, canopies, etc., extended all the way up Broadway
to Grace Church.

nated box behind the busy "Knight of the Dashboard."
There were many heated disputes regarding the performance or non-performance of this essential ceremony.
There is a case on record in which a young man, claiming
to have been "short changed," proceeded to collect the
deficiency from incoming passengers to the intense morti-
fication of the driver who summoned a policeman. The
abstruse legal problems involved were argued in General
Sessions and the young man admonished, in the future,
to seek his remedy in less summary proceedings.

It was the driver's custom when fares were dilatory, to
rattle the fare box and tap the window glass, with a most
urgent violence. It was sometimes impossible for the
driver to single out the delinquent, perhaps an active
young man who had boarded the car unnoticed while in
motion. The ensuing period, during which the fare-box
bell rang incessantly, was one of great embarrassment to
the passengers each of whom stared fixedly forward lest
a sideward glance might be termed an accusation of his
neighbor and an unlooked for encounter result.

An unrestrained and passionate desire for heat in these
vehicles in winter was answered by a liberal allowance of
straw. By some occult form of reasoning this commodity
was supposed to possess this desirable property and every
car was equipped with a bale or two, loosely spread on
the floor. On wet days, the virtue of straw was further
enhanced by the addition of mud. This combination of
wet straw and wet mud was supposed to answer every
aesthetic demand of the day, and was accounted an unquestioned luxury by a simple and confiding public. It
had its advantages from an economic standpoint as the
straw was subsequently a prominent item in the menu
of the stables.

Feeding Squirrels in Union Square, 1882.

Lighting was furnished by means of dismal, violent smelling oil lamps, one at each end of the car, and a resplendent central fixture generally in a condition of smoke and disrepair. There was a good deal of camaraderie among the heterogeneous long-riding passengers, especially when composed of mellow Irishmen and complacent Germans, warmed by unrestricted alcohol, and an occasional Chinaman or two as universal butts.

The Broadway stages were started and stopped by means of a leather strap attached to the driver's leg which served notice of a passenger's intention to alight. Fare was deposited in a box within view of the driver and small change was made through an aperture behind him. These gentlemen possessed unrivalled talents as "short change" artists, it being difficult for an aggrieved passenger to discuss finance with a pair of legs—all of the driver that was visible from the inside of the bus.

One of the old Broadway Stages

A flock of these busses careening up Broadway from one side to the other resembled nothing so much as a Blue Fish fleet in our day leaving Canarsie Bay. They swayed wildly and gloriously on their mad career. Ever and anon one soul more adventurous than another, would essay the perilous feat of cutting a competitor out of a fare. A terrific volley of profanity would follow a successful sortie of this nature, followed up not infrequently by a savage attack with the whip. This playful performance in some way or other made an irresistible appeal to the risibilities of the spectator on the sidewalk and was greeted with unstinted applause from the impromptu audience. Small boys who had a fondness for sitting with the driver (a weakness encouraged by the driver, who always pocketed the fare) were sometimes the innocent victims of these conflicts and their discomfiture added greatly to the already enjoyable performance from the sidewalk point of view. Yet these men were doubtless the forebears of the present staff of the Fifth Avenue Coach Co., selected solely for their politeness and collegiate bearing, each one of whom rejoices in a name plate so that you can address him as Mr. Flaherty, Mr. Rigolletti, or Mr. Kabowski, as the case may be.

The rapid growth of the city focused public attention on the imperative need of immediate and increased transit. It was seen that more and better forms of transportation were needed. The streets were already congested beyond reason with stages, street cars and business traffic. They could hold no more. Blockades were numerous and it was no trouble, in the rush hours, to walk faster in the downtown section than a stage could travel. Something

A flock of stages on Broadway near Houston Street, 1876.

had to be done, so Mayor Wickham appointed a Rapid Transit Commission—the first of its kind.

Long before the initial meeting, newspapers were filled with the same unending complaints regarding the inadequacy of facilities as we read today. There we have the same old letters from "Vox Populi," "Constant Reader," "Tax Payer," etc., giving wrathful expression regarding the stupidity, criminality and general cussedness of those responsible for the deplorable conditions. However, the actual appointment of a Commission by the Mayor was an earnest that the authorities were alive to the situation and his action was received by the public with a sigh of relief.

To the credit of this Commission be it said that almost within a year from their appointment practical relief was assured by the building of the Third and the Sixth Avenue Elevated lines and the extension of the Greenwich

Street lines. The Commission promised to provide cars to carry "15,000 passengers daily." This was supposed to be far in excess of any possible requirement and was hailed with delight by the community. During the progress of their deliberations the Commission was not exempt from the usual amount of abuse and were charged with being in league with iron manufacturers, steel mills, and other big "interests," and that they would not permit any inventor to submit an idea or consider suggestions except from personal friends. A great deal of this talk was nonsense, just as it is today.

Early in their meetings they made one significant decision. They unanimously agreed that "underground bores would be out of the question." They generally favored the elevated plans which were finally adopted.

The first elevated on Greenwich Street was operated by means of a cog-wheel system. The trains started and stopped with all the violence of a collision. On the trial trip, one of these sudden jerks dislodged the "store" teeth of the president and nearly choked him.

In raising money by the sale of stocks the new railroad met with one serious objection—no one would climb the stairs. However, enough venturesome spirits were ultimately found to purchase the bonds at a low price even in spite of this drawback and construction was soon afterward successfully accomplished.

The original fare on the Elevated Railroad was 10c. In 1884 the light travel on Sundays induced the management to reduce it to 5 cents from 5:30 A. M. to Midnight on that day. The movement was hailed with genuine satisfaction by the public and the *Tribune* said—"Even those who take the elevated road to reach places of worship rejoice that the reduction will enable them to increase their contributions when the plate is passed around." One pious woman remarked, "If every five cents saved on Sundays through this action of the Elevated Railroad companies were thus disposed of, the heaviest debts on church edifices would speedily be lifted."

The competing surface car lines, however, took a more cynical view of the situation, probably alarmed at the possible loss of business. James W. Foshay, President of the Broadway Line, said: "This reduction may take some passengers from the surface roads who could not afford to pay the ten cent fare heretofore charged. That is the only way I know of, in which the income of the elevated roads will be increased by this action. *Travel on Broadway on Sundays is almost a blank.* We might almost as well keep our horses in the stable on that day. In the winter

In heavy snowfalls six and twelve horse sleighs ran on Broadway in place of street cars.

time I don't believe it pays to run the elevated trains on Sundays, but it has to be done for the convenience of the public."

The final curtain was rung down on the picturesque stages by Jake Sharp who appeared in 1884 with a franchise from the Aldermen to operate a line of Street Cars instead of Busses. Many members of this Board on their first uptown trip concluded to pursue the journey as far as Canada. Others made a stop-over at Sing Sing.

So ended a link in a chain that bound us to a period not so very far distant when these vehicles ended their journey amid leafy bowers and dusty country roads—as far north as Fourteenth Street. Of the final disposal of the old stages a contemporary furnishes the following interesting account:

"The march of civilization and Jacob Sharp has driven the omnibus toward the setting sun. Last week there was a sale of the stages that formerly rattled through Broadway. They have been dispensed among the rural towns all the way from the Hudson River to the Mississippi and however glad we may be to welcome the Broadway cars we cannot witness the slow but sure retreat of the omnibus toward the Pacific without a feeling of sadness.

"Once the omnibus owned our streets and in its proud defiant way ground timid pedestrians under its wheels and bumped unoffending carriages and carts. Now, like the Indian, it is fast disappearing and has become an object of curiosity and contempt to staring countrymen.

"To take an omnibus from Broadway and set it down in Oshkosh or some less surprising and more probable town is to completely crush its spirits. There are to be met here and there throughout the country, stages that still bear the legend, 'Broadway, Eighth Street and Tompkins Square,' or 'Broadway, Amity Street, Sixth and Seventh Avenues to Twenty-eighth Street,' but they are shabby and demoralized. Their paint is old and worn, and their varnish has vanished forever. They are weak in the springs and their hinges are failing. The degraded omnibus is sometimes used to convey passengers from a railway station to a hotel, or to carry a Sunday School picnic to the grove where rheumatism awaits the teachers and cholera morbus is ready for the pupils, but it knows no longer the pleasures of picking up passengers from the sidewalks or the wild joy of racing with a rival.

"When the omnibus is compelled to leave the city it leaves its driver behind it. Thenceforth it is condemned to be driven by casual countrymen. No man except a New York omnibus driver knows how to drive an omnibus. He alone understands how to shave a lamp post or to keep in front of a rival and take his pavement. Only years of experience can enable a driver to master the mute language of the 'strap' and to know by the slightest pressure on his knee whether the strap is pulled by a pretty girl who should be allowed to dismount close to the sidewalk, or by a fat man who should be dumped in the middle of the street where he can minister to the rational pleasure of the public. Divorced from its natural driver the omnibus loses its interest in life. It feels degraded when a countryman climbs to the driver's seat and takes the reins in his incompetent hands and places the strap across his dull and ignorant knee.

"Then the omnibus in the country misses the pavement. It no longer rattles as it rolls over the sandy road, while on the other hand, it bumps rudely through mud puddles and across railway tracks. It misses the small boy who once stole rides on its steps and the metropolitan friends of its original driver, who delighted to sit beside him on the roof and submit their boots to the study of the passengers. There are no theater doors before which the omnibus can loiter at night until some irascible passenger slams the door furiously and calls out, 'Go on, or I'll report you!' The omnibus exiled to the country, no more resembles the omnibus of Broadway than the Indian of Saratoga resembles the Indian of Cooper's novels. In its dirt, decay and melancholy it is the most depressing of all vehicles. . . . It is the law of nature that the stronger vehicle must push the weaker to the wall, and the omnibus and the horse-car cannot dwell together. We are a busy and a careless people and the misfortunes of the omnibus sit lightly upon us. But some day the metropolitan traveler will get into a stage at the Milwaukee railway station after a long day's ride, and as he looks at the dim kerosene lamp he will recognize on the glass case the familiar words—'VA NOSIDAM & YAWDAORB' and he will drop the tear of sensibility in the damp straw of the fallen Broadway stage."

"All the Fulton Ferry stages have pictures on each side panel and in two instances yesterday buyers paid a slight advance for the picture. One stage had a design representing W. H. Vanderbilt driving Aldine and Early Rose, and it sold for $47.50, while one upon which Robert Bonner was represented speeding Dexter sold for $55."

It was said that Elihu Vedder, Will Low and E. H. Blashfield were the painters of some of these scenes.

With the building of the Elevated Roads began the construction on a vast scale of what were then known as "French Flats." These afforded undreamed of conveniences to former dwellers in old-fashioned houses, in the way of door openers, dumbwaiters, electric bells, and in some of the better class, steam heat and hot water.

Old-fashioned housekeeping in New York had but one compensation—Bridget, Lena or Christina at $10 a month, one night and Sunday off. Private dwellings meant stoking several stoves all winter, running up and down stairs to answer the door-bell, perpetual coal fires in the kitchen range for laundry and bathing purposes, pumping water by hand for all purposes above the second floor. Tin bathtubs encased in wood. Wash basins ditto; Baltimore heaters that provoked a strange prejudice against Baltimore and for which coal had to be carried in hods from the lower regions. All this caused a hegira to the newfangled flats and the upper West Side and Harlem began to assume the aspects of boom towns. Although the aforesaid Bridget, etc., etc., found their tasks easier, the new places had their drawbacks. The sweet personal contact with milkman, butcher boy, baker and policeman that had been so conducive to matrimony, was now in the romantic past. The tender confidences of the areaway were perforce changed to the raucous calls of the dumbwaiter shaft. The nights off became more frequent and the "general houseworker," instead of entertaining below stairs, must fain find her gallant at the "Ball of the Gasfitters Union, Gents 25c., Ladies Free."

With the flat house came that strange domestic animal, the janitor. The fantastic combination of menial and tyrant has become a figure too familiar to dilate upon, further than to say that in all cases in which he is endowed with a uniform and cap he expects a mere tenant to address him as "superintendent."

The nomenclature of these flats was redolent of baronial, manorial and ofttimes ducal antecedents. Buckingham, Warwick, Beaufort, Wiltshire, Fountainebleau, Versailles, were some of the names emblazoned on these glorified tenements. It only required the presence of the inevitable garbage can to complete the implied connection.

One of the New York newspapers offered a prize for the "most artistic design for furnishing a flat." Amateur decorators from such artistic centers as Oil City, Penn., Lisbon, Ohio, and points adjacent who had spent a lifetime trying to neutralize horsehair "parlor suits" with Navajo blankets, Japanese screens, Persian portieres and other international embellishments were among the contestants. The winner, a Brooklyn lady, included among her specifications the following:

Bedroom—Brass bed. White maple furniture. Toilet set, pale green. Pictures edged with pink ribbons, bows at upper corners.

Bathroom—Woodwork, pale sea green, large mirror in silvered frame. Suspend from ceiling Turkish lamp in front of mirror. Two small corner shelves for toilet articles with Oriental curtains.

Kitchen—Frying pan clock over range.

These frying pan clocks are still discovered extant among articles of vertu at "Rummage sales."

"Shanty town," east and west of Central Park,
superseded by "French Flats."

Another lady stipulated that "Pet engravings will be framed with old gray fence boards."

Another plan for a kitchen exacted "a hand towel on a roller," proving that a practical turn of mind is not incompatible with strong artistic leanings.

There was a vivid Oriental feeling in the Harlem of that period that delighted in the languid atmosphere of the Shahs and the Sultans and expressed itself in "Turkish Corners" and similar dreamy devices. A proper Turkish corner required a pair of spears, supporting a canopy of brilliant hues, and if possible a small arsenal of side arms for a background.

A lady, who only missed the prize by exceeding the number of words named in the conditions, was inspired by these mystic Eastern influences to offer the following:

Library—As one enters a library the effect should be cosy and luxurious. Nothing can give this atmosphere of comfort so well as the soft blending of colors of the Orient. In one corner have a divan two feet wide. Pillows of different sizes should go with this covered with silk in Oriental blues and reds. At one side place a Cairo stand with brass tray holding a Turkish coffee pot. This can serve as a smoking table as well and will give an artistic finish to the whole room. In the corner, over the divan, suspend from the ceiling a Moorish lamp of carved brass. A candle placed inside of this when lighted will give an Arabian effect, very picturesque. The chairs can be of rattan with two or more dark wood ones mixed in. Those *in colonial style* with claw feet are the most artistic. The seat of these should be upholstered in Turkish coverings. Cover the windows with Syrian cotton curtains and drape a Turkish curtain over these. If there is an open fireplace drape the mantel with two India cotton table-cloths. Other drapings in Japanese or Turkish embroideries hung on the walls make a rare and artistic room. Have book shelves of oak. On the top shelf put bric-a-brac. A Chippendale desk should stand in one corner, with brass trimmings, and bamboo curtains hung at the doors complete this very Oriental and artistic library.

The hectic desire for "draping" evinced by the inventor of the above mentioned symphony was merely an expression of a taste which ran riot at that time. There is only a casual reference to books, and even these are evicted from the top shelf by "bric-a-brac."

Looking north on Broadway from Vesey Street about 1870.

At this time there was a faint trickle of a new stream of foreign immigration though it gave not the slightest indication of the avalanche that ultimately was to follow. Here and there appeared an Italian organ grinder, sometimes accompanied by a monkey but more often with some bright olive-complexioned boy with fascinating black eyes, not more than seven or eight years of age. In some peculiar manner the public conjured up for itself a fantastic tale to the effect that these harmless organ grinders were blood-thirsty bandits from Sicily and that the little children with them had been stolen from sunny Italy and thrown into a life of pitiless cruelty and unrequited labor. In fact *Harper's Weekly* went so far as to draw a full page picture of the alleged cruelty that was practised on these helpless innocents and our newly arrived visitors were everywhere regarded with grave suspicion, not unmixed with savage hostility. As a matter of fact there were no grounds for the foolish talk.

They settled first in the Irish quarter but the Irish were so secure in their numbers, their political influence and their great importance economically, that little or no attention was paid to the swarthy skinned denizens whose appearance at that time was so insignificant. In a short time the Irish contractors cast avaricious glances in the direction of the cheaper Italian labor and presently riots of no small magnitude were a frequent occurrence between the newcomers and the Irish already established. The ever handy sharp bladed shovel was of course an instrument of deadly import in the hands of enraged men and many serious results arose from these conflicts. Even during the lull in hostilities there was not the slightest thought in the head of any Irishman that the tide of Italian immigration would shortly rise to such propor-

The early popular idea of the Italian immigration.

tions as to entirely engulf him and all his connections, than there was that the moon would fall.

In what was once the stronghold of the Irish below Fourteenth Street there is now scarcely a trace of the former Celtic population. Even if they are there now they are so wholly and completely swallowed up by the swarthy skinned Latin as to be hardly discernible. In the section on the West side south of Vesey Street was another peculiarly Irish neighborhood. It was composed almost exclusively of longshoremen and dock workers along the North River. They held together for many years with a tenacity unusual even in this City of fluctuating populations, but within the past decade practically no sign of the former inhabitants is left. While their places have not been taken by Italians, the newcomers are of a kindred race but wholly from Central Europe, Armenia, Macedonia and Syria predominating with a liberal sprinkling of Italians from Northern Italy.

If the Irish on the lower East side had practically absorbed the town, the Germans stretching farther north and east were also a formidable body. Combined, these two races made up virtually three-fourths of the entire population of the Island and on their particular holidays the rest of the town bore the same aspect as Yom Kippur produces today. It is not at all unlikely that the German and Irish descendants today are even greater in numbers than they were at the time of which I write, but in comparison with the hordes that have come from Italy, Russia, and Poland, their numbers are negligible. The German barber, baker, lager beer saloon and grocery store were practically ubiquitous. Four lager beer saloons to a

This view shows Fifth Avenue and 42nd Street in 1850. Chauncey I
This gives a startling idea of how near we still are

SERVOIR

as eight years old when running water was thus introduced into the City.
tive village.   The Public Library now occupies this site.

corner was a fair average. The Irish were in every hotel, saloon, contracting business, while the police force was almost wholly recruited from the ranks of this virile nation. They individually could not be ignored. They stood out with a vigor and an aggressiveness that could not be mistaken. The same sections of our City as they appear today, apparently bear no trace of the former overlordship of the Irish and the Germans. A wholly different race has taken possession in such countless numbers that our friends of former days are completely absorbed.

Having glanced over the City from its outward and visible aspect, let us now enter its homes and recall some of the more intimate details of everyday life as it was lived in these endearing old days.

A brief glance at the family album of that date reveals a race of men and women of strange and grotesque

"Started at Last." Incident of street car travel when breakdowns were frequent.

appearance. It cannot be that they were typical New Yorkers. This charming young lady with the high chignon, the dinky little hat, the Grecian bend, the enormous bustle and the long trailing skirt, cannot possibly be cousin Kate whom you clearly recall as the belle of the day? And this austere looking gentleman with a gold watch chain shining brilliantly in the colored photograph and an enormous mop of hair plastered tightly over his left eye in an all compelling curve—this cannot possibly be Uncle Dan? But it is, and the huge high hat held with difficulty in his hand was known in those ribald days as a "stove-pipe." Uncle's hair was liberally soaked with pomade or highly scented hair oil. People living in the country (above 59th Street) called it "Bears' grease." Special tidies were provided, called "antimicassars," so that the raven soaked locks would not ruin the delicate horsehair or ingrain upholstery a g a i n s t which he was wont to rest his head in his hours of ease.

"Uncle Dan" (aged 23)

In matters of attire we differed strangely from the styles of today. The men wore paper collars; shirts that buttoned up the back; a wide silk sash with tassels hanging down the ends, preceded the leather belt—a London idea—with polo caps and blazers. They also wore as much hair on their faces as they could raise, and the less wool there

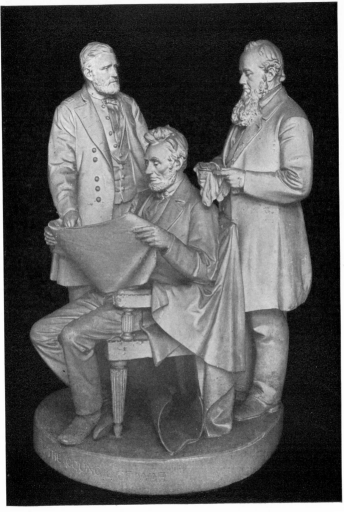

The Conference—Lincoln, Seward and Grant. One of these
John Rogers statuettes was in every household

was on the top of the head, the longer and bushier were the whiskers. They carried their lunches to business. They wound up their watches every night with a key, pounded their "stylographic" pens to bring down the ink; bought meal tickets; their "spring bottom" pants were "skin tight"; their shoes were elastic or "Congress" gaiters; and they wore flat, pancake derbies.

But the last word in ultra-fashionableness was undoubtedly the pocket toothpick. This was an indispensable adjunct to the man who would be well dressed. It was usually worn attached to the watch chain just as we would wear a charm today. They were expensively made in solid gold and silver. All were beautifully chased and many were set with diamonds and precious stones. Every jeweler carried at least a tray of them in various designs.

Other items of an intimate personal nature worn by the fair sex were also highly prized, though a more enlightened age has doomed them to oblivion. In fact even in this liberal age it is embarrassing to name them. Bosom pads stuffed with horsehair and also of inflated rubber to give a more artistic finish; breast plates of wire; and corsets of such unyielding properties as to resemble ancient instruments of torture. Enormous half sections of woven wire suspended from the rear, produced the bustle. Altogether the costume of a lady of fashion with her high neck, long sleeves, trailing skirt and skimpy hat was a precious sight. Present-day styles are exactly the antithesis of the Seventies. A glimpse of a young lady's ankle, discreetly covered by a leather "high-top" boot, was the limit of public indulgence. Only by something short of a horrible disaster was more of her "limb" ever exposed and on these rare occasions much excitement and great confusion always followed.

White cotton stockings were universally worn. These were later embellished with horizontal stripes, in red, yellow, green, and other delicate pastel colors, producing a refined effect, which was considered the acme of artistic achievement. Our worthy forefathers had, of course, nothing like our present-day first-hand observation in this direction; so to avoid any misjudging on this point, let me say that this detailed information comes from the contemporary catalogs of the dry goods people.

In the matter of interior decoration we certainly were a law unto ourselves. Current photographs entitled "Room in the house of a Fifth Avenue Millionaire" are

Parlor in "Millionaire's" home, 1876.

something the like of which was never before seen on earth or in the waters under the earth. Moorish fret work was the prime motif. Scarves of every conceivable size and color were laid over everything. Huge satin ribbons of undoubted width tied around piano legs; Pampas grass in vases. Bric-a-brac, painted coal scuttles, three-legged stools, whisk brooms tied in baby blue; forget-me-nots, antimicassars, foot stools, gigantic portfolios, wreaths of hair in small frames, stereopticon views, wax flowers, chenille curtains with wonderful fringe, autograph albums; all helped to complete the reposeful picture. The "Cosy Corner," that last word in oriental luxury, was a later development and created a horror all its own. But if we add the inevitable group of statuary made by the indefatigable John Rogers, our picture of the room in the Seventies is complete. Mr. Rogers produced many unquestioned works of art and his product was to be encountered in the homes of the lowly as well as the great. His most popular subjects were "Weighing the Baby," "Checkers Up at the Farm," "Neighboring Pews" and that crowning masterpiece of the poet of the suburbs, "Speak for Yourself John"—in which the immortal scene between John Alden and Priscilla was faithfully reproduced for his host of admirers the country over.

A Baltimore heater, resplendent in shiny nickel, occupied the place formerly reserved for the grate fire and the andirons. Where the grate fire still lingered, the space in summer was hidden by a "fire board," usually a gaudy lithograph printed by the immortal firm of Currier and Ives depicting a scene in Central Park—preferably the

"Fire Board" showing scene in Central Park.
Currier & Ives Litho, 1870.

lake covered with wooden swans; or one showing the goat carriage which the children used to ride with mother stroking the goat in loving fashion while a couple of Sanfords and Mertons looked on. It was all very idyllic and exactly the scene which drew such excited commendation from the gifted pen of Frederica Bremer.

Perhaps the most popular decoration at this period was the Rubber plant. It flourished luxuriantly in hovel and palace. It seemed particularly at home in one of these old halls formerly paved with tile and in which all the tiles were more or less wobbly. The first seedlings may have been sown in New York but the plant reached its highest development in our sister city Brooklyn. There it grew in glorious profusion and occupied the most prominent place in the parlor. In cases where a bay window was available it reared its glossy green leaves in riotous verdure. So multitudinous was its presence that a rubber plant and a baby carriage became symbolical of the City of Churches and the combination furnished endless merriment for the paragrapher and the cartoonist. It was thoroughly in keeping with the "golden oak" furniture and the cast iron hat stand with the prongs made to represent the horns of a deer.

Those of us who boasted anything in the way of a lawn—and there were still quite a few houses well set back from the street—had a peculiar weakness for the zoological productions of the firm that manufactured the hat stand. Huge reclining Newfoundlands, St. Ber-

Sitting room, Fifth Avenue home in the Seventies.

nards; majestic looking moose; timid looking deer, that
couldn't run if a stick of dynamite was set off under them;
ferocious lions and all the other Natural history specimens, were crouched or stood in artistic poses—not
knee-high in the damp, lush grass, but stark and naked
in the closely cropped lawn. Sometimes the menagerie
was further embellished by heroic figures of mythological
origin—Mercury, Hebe, Juno and Venus. Garden houses
modeled after the Temple of Love in Versailles—a long
way after—and other chaste and gladsome examples of
the Monitor-and-Merrimac school of art were also seen in
the habitat of the Big Game. It was a large and tolerant
age. We are prone to laugh at it now. But what of the
wood handicraft now so proudly displayed on the Estates
of our Best People—the Cigar Store Indians, the carved
figures from the bow of some half forgotten clipper, or
the booby hatch of a long lost merchantman?

There was another phenomena at this time which deserves passing mention—the almost universal belief in
the efficacy of blue glass for whatever ailed you. Exactly
how this craze began I do not now recall but I do remember that its virtues as a cure-all were on every tongue.
The idea spread from a single pane, inserted in the usual
window light, till the whole window was blue. Then
special rooms were built after the modern sun parlor idea
in which the roof and sides were all blue glass. In this
solarium the patient was expected to repose, allow the
sun's rays to filter through the blue glass and fall upon
his alabaster skin. It was especially recommended for
rheumatism and, as is customary, some marvelous cures
were popularly ascribed to this newly discovered specific.

The patent medicine men were in a panic. The nostrums which they sold were already guaranteed to cure everything but suicide and a broken neck; but the blue glass crowd went the limit in cures, and made no exceptions whatever.

In time, however, the craze died down and disappeared completely. For years, however, reminders of this strange manifestation remained in the shape of odd looking additions to houses; a lingering pane of blue glass here and there but that was all. It did no harm and possibly some good. Perhaps it was the progenitor of the present violet rays. At all events it left a worthy successor, as the Blue Glass Parlor was undoubtedly the precursor of the light and airy Sun Parlor as we know it today.

Wax flowers popular decoration in the Seventies.

One of the early manifestations of a congested population in New York was the folding bed. This ingenious piece of furniture was designed to camouflage its real purpose by assuming, during the daytime, various alien shapes such as that of a wardrobe, desk or chiffonier. But the only one who dwelt in a state of illusion was its owner. Everybody else knew it was a folding bed, but the etiquette of the times forbade discussion of the subject. It was perfectly obvious that the bookcase in the library of an over-crowded apartment that had the capacity of Dr. Eliot's five-foot book shelf, was a folding bed. Likewise, that the large cheval glass in front of an apparent cupboard concealed another of the genus, but these innocent fictions were taken as a matter of course.

There was one type of folding bed, however, constructed with weights, that had a disconcerting habit, when its equilibrium was disturbed, of folding up like a jack-knife to the intense amazement of the occupants. For a stout gentleman to find himself suddenly awakened and standing on his head in bed was only a small inconvenience compared with the imminent danger of asphyxiation that the situation afforded. There were a few cases of premature burial recorded in this connection, and this type of bed began to be regarded with the suspicion that it combined the functions of the ancient Moloch with its inducements to repose. It consequently declined greatly in popularity and is now largely extinct.

There was another solemn rite sacred to these days—New Year's calls—with which we celebrated the beginning of a New Year. It was a custom, I understand, which came down to us from our Dutch forebears—those immaculate souls now preserved in an odor of sanctity which endows them with all the virtues and graces denied them in the flesh. At all events the ceremony incidental to these festivities included an enormous amount of eating, drinking and sprinting—particularly drinking. There has come down to us also from the early records of this city, competent evidence of the occasional disastrous results

of the unrestrained holiday merriment in the following
item:

CORONER'S VERDICT (1786)

"THAT THE SAID TATUM'S DEATH WAS OCCASIONED BY
THE FREEZING OF A LARGE QUANTITY OF WATER IN HIS
BODY, THAT HAD BEEN MIXED WITH THE RUM HE DRANK."

Those of us who were specially favored of this world's
goods indulged in the luxury of a carriage for the
day. The carriage could hold six. On ordinary days
it did duty as part of a funeral cortege. Its cost was
$5.00, except on New Year's when it was advanced
to $6.00. This was divided pro rata among the oc-
cupants. It was considered very *recherche* to have
only four in the coach.

Weeks before "der tag" much patient thought was
bestowed upon a very vital detail—the calling card.
These were the product of a genius who deserves immortality. Some of them bore charming winter
scenes with real snow produced by ground glass.
Others were decorated all around with beautiful silk
fringe in all the colors of the rainbow. They were
masterpieces of decorative art and a basketful of
these strange devices would be today of extraordinary
interest. They were greeted with exclamations of
wild delight by the recipients; we were supposed to
leave one card apiece for the young ladies upon whom
we called. As a rule the ladies received in groups, and
as long as you knew one of the group that was sufficient to justify a call. Custom decreed that you must
break bread with your hostess and partake of some

New Year's Calls in the days of Stuyvesant.

liquid refreshment. Lemonade was the most favored beverage but wine became popular toward the end and I think the Demon Rum had considerable to do with the final disappearance of the custom.

It was not unusual to make ninety or a hundred calls which, of course, meant madly rushing in and out and no small amount of fatigue when a heavy snow fall intervened as sometimes happened; our Colonial friend Tatum, just mentioned, fell asleep in the snow. The men boasted of the numbers of calls they made and the ladies counted up the total of their cards. All the old sociability and neighborliness which I imagine was the original charm of the custom gradually disappeared during the hectic period of its closing days.

The Hokey-Pokey Man selling ice cream.

Clang! Out of the way of the cable car!

Then one year there was no calling, and no observance whatever. There was apparently no prearrangement or anything else. The practice simply ceased. Baskets were placed on door knobs to receive any cards that callers might leave. But the houses were closed—and so ended with all its faults one of the oldest and pleasantest customs on Manhattan Island.

Forty years ago every young lady owned an autograph book. This was generally in appearance a miniature red plush photograph album with gilt edges and the loveliest robin's egg blue paper interspersed with salmon, gray, pink, buff, and a few other shades. It was the custom of her friends and acquaintances to indite verses, tender, facetious or admonitory in this treasury of mementoes. "Be good, dear child, and let who will be clever" was a favorite sentiment of a reprobate old uncle or cousin. Similar incongruities fell like pearls from the pens of spinster aunts. Gawky puppy-lovers wrote carefully studied verses taken from "Gems from the Poets," in flowing Spencerian hands. Every visitor was primed with a rhyme or a couplet in anticipation of the inevitable "Oh Mr. Jinks, won't you write something in my book?" Whereupon you would dash off impromptu:

> You ask me to write something original
> But I don't know where to begin,
> For there's nothing original in me,
> Excepting Original sin.

or this:

> The inner side of every cloud,
>   Is bright and shining.
> Therefore turn your clouds about
> And always wear them inside out,
>   Just to show the lining.

Perhaps you felt more ambitious than usual with the following result:

> The days of pleasures past,
> And think of joyous hours and all
> In after years when you recall
> Have flown away so fast.
> When some forgotten air you hear
> Brings back past scenes to thee
> And gently claims your listening ear—
> Keep one kind thought of me.

Here, however, was the one great standby:

> In the tempest of life
> When you need an umbrella,
> May it be upheld
> By a handsome young feller.

A signature was a portentous thing in those days. A gentleman with an elegant set of Galway whiskers, a plush coat, and cameo cuff buttons was not inclined to execute his cognomen in any meagre or cramped fashion. The name of "Alonzo B. Cheesecake," was written far into the night in violet ink on an azure blue page, to obtain the inimitable flourishes beloved of the "business college."

The old autograph album is a tender memory nevertheless. We may look at some of the old verses differently today, but when they were fresh on the page they produced many a delightful thrill.

A fruitful source of domestic strife in those days was the harmless and necessary Dress Suit—particularly in families where there were two boys of about the same age. When these boys happened to be invited to the same party on the same evening, unpleasant complications were sure to ensue. Generally speaking, this item of sartorial splendor, being in the nature of a luxury, was owned in common, but which one owned it, under such circumstances as I have narrated, often became a mooted question. This dispute came up so often, that the head of the family fled the scene precipitately when it threatened.

The custom of hiring this mark of social importance was at this period quite general, and signs to that effect were everywhere displayed. But the disbursement of three dollars was quite a formidable financial undertaking, hence the stormy scenes to which I have alluded and which, by the way, were not always confined to dress suits. In families I have known, where there were as many as four boys, the first one up was always the best dressed.

The hired dress suit was considered perfectly good form among the exclusive circles of the East Side and these garments were usually worn with all the grace and elegance of a coat of mail. Truthfully speaking the fit was on a par with this medieval garment but that in no wise dimmed the lustre of the occasion. The absence of this confection, fit or no fit, was frequently the cause of bitter heart-breakings among the swains who lacked the necessary three iron men. The success of a ball or a dance was invariably gauged more or less by the number of full dress suits worn by the beaux and belles. When I speak of this custom being more or less general, I do not, of course, include Elisha Dyer Le Grand B. Cannon, Lispenard Stewart, Frank Sturgis, or Berry Wall. These men were conceded to own their dress suits outright.

Our pleasures in those days were simple but no less enjoyable on that account. One of the most popular social diversions was the Surprise Party. Some morning you would receive a note written in long hand—this was

"The children's friend."   Policeman escorting children across Broadway.   (1877).

before the days of elaborate engraved stationery—penned somewhat after this fashion:

"Dear John:

You are respectfully invited to attend a surprise party to meet at the residence of Miss Flora Bancroft, No. 22 East Eighteenth Street, on Thursday evening at eight o'clock P. M.

Yours respectfully

The Committee

P. S. Please furnish oranges."

This last line was changed in each invitation so as to provide a variety of edibles.

Armed with your votive offering wrapped in an unostentatious parcel, you made your way on the appointed night to the place of designation. When all had gathered, the entire party proceeded to the home of the young lady who was to be surprised. Occasionally we would be fortunate enough to preserve the secret and burst in upon the young lady in the delightful, though unromantic pastime of helping mother wash up the dishes. Frequently, however, the secret would leak out and the object of this social attention would be all dressed, ostensibly on the point of going out. She, of course, remained to entertain her guests. This bit of harmless fiction in no wise detracted from the pleasure of the evening. We generally managed to have a good time in either event. I have since attended many more important functions than a Surprise Party but I doubt whether I ever had any more real pleasure. Music for the dances was usually supplied by several volunteer players from the group—most of the young ladies in those days played the piano—and the Polka, the Quadrille and the Waltz were enjoyed to our heart's content. There was none of this tango or jazz music, and dancing in a space the size of a nickel was unknown in my day.

Decoration Day. Scene at the flower market, Canal Street, 1880.

At these parties there was invariably present that curious person known as the Amateur Elocutionist. Outwardly this terrible creature gave no hint of the devastating power lurking within her bosom. She lulled you into false security by dressing in the most simple and guileless of costumes—white-dotted swiss with her immature hair tied with a baby blue ribbon, hanging down her back. It was only when the company took temporary leave of their senses and asked her to recite, that you were able to sense the terrible tragedy soon to follow. "Curfew Shall Not Ring Tonight" was one of her favorite instruments of torture, but "Bingen, Fair Bingen on the Rhine" was a good second. "Robert of Lincoln" was a bird piece, in which a lot of alleged chirping was let loose with a whistling bout in between. "The Charge of the Light Brigade" was delicious, and the fine frenzy rolling in her eyes when she reached the part where the six hundred went over the top, was only equalled by her grief-stricken sobs announcing the fact that when they rode back they were not—not-the-s-i-x-h-u-n-d-r-e-d ! "Cannon to right of them, cannon to left of them, was there a man dismayed?" Not that you could notice it. They succeeded in giving the impression that the famous charge was not a military mistake at all, but was a pre-arranged massacre for the benefit of future elocutionists.

There were several other pieces which I do not recall. Comic relief was furnished by some such local composition as "Pa Shakes Down the Furnace While Ma Hangs Out the Wash." In later years Rudyard Kipling gave this school a new lease of life by his "Gunga Din" and "Shooting of Dan McGrew," and Sam Bernard popularized "The Face on the Bar-room Floor."

Bob Burdette, a well-known humorist on the *Burlington Hawkeye,* was another partner in crime of the amateur elocutionist. Forsaking journalism for the lyceum, he had a piece of his own which was avidly imitated—"Wine and Water." As usual, Wine was the villain of the play, and Water, the hero. In all these parlor pieces the high moral tone was the dominant note. So in this famous poem, Wine is supposed to be bragging of the ruin he has wrought, while Water recites, with due modesty, how his life has been spent undoing the harm done by the fizz water. A better idea may be gained from the closing stanza of the poem itself.

> "I cheer, I help, I strengthen and aid,
> I gladden the heart of man and maid;
> I set the chain wine-captive free,
> And all are better for knowing me.
> These are the tales they told each other,
> The glass of wine and the paler brother,
> As they sat together, filled to the brim,
> On the rich man's table, rim to rim."

Broad Street showing Drexel Morgan Corner and adjoining old warehouses, etc., 1876. (see page 9)

Another favorite pastime that seems to have vanished is rolling the hoop. I remember when every child had a hoop and there were various sizes, some a great deal taller than the owner. Sometimes these hoops would break and I recall a chromo that was once very popular entitled "Mending the Hoop" in which a little girl was tearfully viewing a hoop which an old man was trying to repair. Some of these hoops were of iron and were guided by what you would take for a poker in the days of open fire grates. These pokers were used not only to speed the hoop but were skilfully used in guiding it and also to bring it to a halt. Oh yes, rolling a hoop was a great sport at one time.

Nor do I run across groups of children playing various games that were always accompanied by singing and more or less acting. One was:

> "Little Sallie Waters
> Sitting in the Sun
> Crying and weeping for her young man.
> Rise Sally, rise, wipe off your eyes,
> Turn to the East and turn to the West
> Turn to the very one that you love best."

This was played by a dozen or more girls who circled around one who sat in the center of the ring until the song said "Rise, Sally, rise."

Whereupon she would rise and finally choose one of her companions as the one "She loved best" who would thereupon take her place in the ring.

Another equally popular, was entitled "Jenny o' Jones," and involved quite a little movement. One girl sat in a corner and a dozen or less other little girls, all holding hands, would advance and retreat, singing meanwhile:

"I came to see Miss Jenny o' Jones,
Miss Jenny o' Jones, Miss Jenny o' Jones,
I came to see Miss Jenny o' Jones
And how is she today?"

The first verse elicited the information that Miss Jones was not very well, whereupon the group fell back, singing:

"I'm very sorry to hear it, to hear it, to hear it,
I'm very sorry to hear it, to hear it, to hear it,
I'll call another day."

Miss Jones lingers through several stanzas until finally the sad news is communicated that Miss Jones is dead. All the children then burst into cries of mock grief and then another girl is chosen while the same performance is repeated ad infinitum. Ada Rehan gave a delightful rendition of this childhood rhyme in a play called "The Country Girl" and it was easily among the best things she ever did.

I don't think boys today have the variety of sports they had in my day. All that boys play today are ball games. Where do you see a boy today lashing a top or snapping the whip, always the first sign of spring in old times? Boys of today go in for men's games. Kite flying that made Ben Franklin famous is almost obsolete. Nowadays, boys disdain the simple kite. Marbles have attained a position of semi-professionalism. I always had a pocket full of "realers," "glasses," "alleys" and "agates." There was a wonderful variety of tops from the penny whip tops just mentioned, to a rainbow-tinted beauty that had a mechanical arrangement to revolve it. Boys matched to see whose top would spin the longest. There were lots of indoor games, too, before people went to the movies, such as indoor croquet, parchesi, and bagatelle.

The famous "Pigs in Clover" game was an obsession of the late Eighties. It concerned five little leaden pellets which were manipulated in a glass-covered round box. The object to be obtained was to assemble the pellets in a cavity in the middle of the box. This philosophic occupation engaged the attention of a large proportion of the population of the country.

The 13-14-15 puzzle, which raged a short time before, rivaled the present cross-word craze. It involved some mathematical skill akin to the etomological attribute of today's puzzle.

The return of the harmonica to popular favor reminds me that this was the favorite instrument of the street boy of the Eighties in the creation of home-made melody. Then there was the accordion and the concertina, whose strains came floating on summer nights over backyard fences for the benefit of all and sundry. There were a great many more amateur musicians then, than there are today. The mechanical musical devices of the days of Moody and Sankey were limited to the hand-organ and the Swiss musical box. The perforated paper rolls of the hand-organ are still in use in the modern electric pianola.

The musical box existed in many degrees of pretentiousness from the child's toy that looked like a caviar tin and played the "Sweet Bye and Bye" as you turned its little handle, to the elaborate rosewood cased mechanism, with chimes, that played a repertoire enumerated on an ornamental cardboard under the lid. The musical box sometimes assumed the shape of a cart or wagon that played a tune as the wheels turned. There were also a large number of musical toys on the market, such as

"Snap the Whip."

zithers, zylophones, toy pianos, drums, trumpets, etc. There was a great sale for whistles and they were found attached to riding whips, pop-guns, and even to baby corals.

Und dot leedle Cherman Band with its doleful oompah! oompah! seems also to have disappeared. Time was when it could be heard and seen in almost every block or as the cigar store has it one "always in sight."

And the street organ! Only recently I read of the death of the author of "The Sidewalks of New York" bringing back vividly the day when almost anywhere you could see children dancing to the strains of "Sweet Violets" or some other masterpiece of the hurdy-gurdy while an amused policeman leaned against a lamp post and smiled.

"Oompah-Oompah"—Dot Leedle Cherman Band

Rag-pickers at work on the scows.

The Rag Picker—once a flourishing industry in this city; the junk man, with his string of discordant bells and his strident cry; the old clo' man; the "hot corn" man; the hokey-pokey man, and many others are all now as silent and invisible as the Dodo.

Toboggan slide, 110th Street and Fifth Avenue, at old Polo Grounds, 1880.

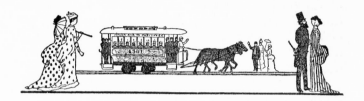

CHAPTER II

WINTER sports are now principally indulged in at
the country clubs, but forty years ago there was no
lack of skating, hockey, lacrosse and even tobogganing on
Manhattan Island. In fact, there was a great toboggan
slide built at the Polo Grounds, on Fifth Avenue and 110th
Street, in imitation of the famous Montreal slide. There
was also a great deal more interest in ice-skating than
there is today and the park lakes were crowded on winter
evenings with ruddy skaters. The comic press had no
end of fun writing of ice skaters, the favorite butt being
some showy performer who comes to grief by the various
misadventures which only a cartoonist could invent.

Ponds were located in what are now congested retail sections. There was a sizeable pond on Fifth Avenue between Thirty-seventh and Thirty-eighth Streets; Beekman's Pond, between Fifty-ninth Street and Sixtieth Street; Alexander McMillan's, at Forty-sixth Street, site of Windsor Hotel; the New York Skating Club, at Fifty-ninth Street, site of Plaza, and later corner of Fifth Avenue and Seventy-second Street.

An obsolete institution that flourished mightily in the days when dimes and nickels were counted as money, was the "Tonsorial Parlor." More than a mere hair cutting establishment, the tonsorial parlor ministered to man's gregarious nature. The art of conversation as brought to a high perfection on cracker boxes in country stores, was, in New York, fostered in the old-time barber shop. We fear it is now a lost art. The modern barber is a mere mercenary with his eye on the clock. And besides he has none of the encyclopedic qualities of his professional forebear. The latter was usually a German or American of that stock. His opinions on politics, sport, the drama, art and current topics in general were voluble to the point of verbosity. He was the repository of state secrets which he transferred to the ears of the discriminating. He was leisurely, as was most becoming in our only example of a "gentleman's gentleman." Haste was indecent except when specially requested by the client.

The "tonsorial parlor" was heavy and languid with all the perfumes of Araby. The customer arising from one of its plush covered chairs, carried upon his person, olfactory evidence of his visit in a weird aroma of occult essences compounded after a fashion that only years of barbering could bring to perfection. Conspicuous among

Skating in Central Park. 1882.

the signs displayed in the more advanced establishments was "A Clean Towel to Every Customer." Other decorations included a chart depicting the various styles of trimming the beard, among them the "Galway," "Vandyke," "Burnsides," "Dundrearys" and "Muttonchops," all greatly in favor as masculine embellishments.

The *Police Gazette* was an indispensable adjunct to any barber shop that had any pretensions to class. Its front page was invariably adorned with a huge woodcut depicting some buxom female clad in "tights," varied occasionally by a lady in short skirts, exposing much less of the lower extremities than we now see in any of today's society columns. In those days, however, a rigorous censorship was maintained over the exact height of the skirt and if it exceeded by so much as one poor scruple of the proscribed brevity allowed by law, the luckless publisher found himself at once entangled in the meshes of Mr. Comstock's Society for the Suppression of Vice. Its well-pawed pages testified to its soothing effect on the

Shaving mugs and mustache cup, 1880.

Telling her Fortune

Bargaining for a Horse

Cocoanut Game

A Gypsy encampment right on Broadway near 57th Street; a picturesque feature of New York life in the early '80s.

righteous patrons of the tonsorial parlor and time thus spent passed all too swiftly for those whose waiting ears heard the unwelcome words—"you're next."

The other outstanding educational feature of the hirsute emporium was Mr. Keppler's *Puck*. This gaudy publication enjoyed a barber shop popularity that was the mainstay of its enormous profits. The well-drawn cartoons, the genuine merit of the pictures themselves, served to keep this publication in the forefront of money makers for many years. When Keppler passed away and the brilliant Bunner was no more, *Puck* ceased to wave its magic wand. Perhaps the less leisurely habits of the customer and the introduction of safety razors had also something to do with the change in barber shops when *Puck* made its final exit.

Patrons in these barber shops easily became acquainted with each other and the waiting crowd on a Saturday night and Sunday morning was a sort of informal club. Honorary membership was conferred on those distinguished patrons who rejoiced in the possession of a private shaving mug, handsomely decorated with its owner's name and perhaps the additional ornament of a design representing his occupation. A cutlery dealer, for example, would display a pair of shears, depicted in a delightfully realistic manner. A trophy of this kind always brought to its owner extra indulgences, such as an additional squirt of bay rum on the scalp, or a dab of high-priced French "cosmetique" on a beautifully curled Imperial mustache. After closing hours many of these shops became rendezvous for pinochle and penny-ante players, and so continued their functions as social centers.

Making cigar store signs. Painting the figures.

Many of these barber shops ran tobacco counters as profitable adjuncts and the striped pole became identified with the tobacconist's Indian. The fate of these tobacco store Indians is almost as deplorable as that of the aborigines themselves. There were hundreds of them in the city forty years ago, and today they are as scarce as clipper ship figureheads. And we may remark in passing that many of the Indians were the handiwork of the artisans of the figureheads. While the Indians were greatly in the majority as cigar-store signs, there were other figures in use that will be remembered. There was a grinning, dancing darkey of the West Indian type, with a

[73]

Cigar store Indians now eagerly sought for by Collectors.

banjo. This type of figure was clearly of European origin, the dandy West Indian negro being far more familiar in France and England at that time than the tatterdemalion cotton picker of our Southern States. There was also a rather infrequent, very wooden young lady in a jaunty hat and trailing skirt, who, with as much coquetry as her constitution would allow, extended to the passerby a bundle of wooden cigars. There was, too, her male escort, a cheerful young man wearing a high hat, tan coat, skin-tight trousers and spats. This was the effigy of the "dude," the subject of an immensely popular song, "I'm a dude, a dandy dude."

Mr. Pickwick was also to be met with in alien neighborhoods, whose inhabitants must have wondered as to the origin of the genial stout gentleman in gaiters and shorts, beaming on the passerby. This figure was reminiscent to Dickensians of the "Little Wooden Midshipman" of "Dombey and Son."

These unoffending emblems of trade frequently became the objects of hostility on the part of inebriated gentlemen, who misconstrued their gestures. The mortality among Indians with upraised tomahawks on St. Patrick's Day, was only equalled by the broken knuckles of their assailants.

Among other archaic means of making a living in that happy time, that of the "soap artist" is not without interest to the aesthetically inclined. The embellishment of saloons, cigar shops, etc., owed much to his talents. He would pay seasonal visits to these establishments and decorate their mirrors in the medium of tinted soap with the most elegant designs. His "Merrry Xmas and Happy New Year" done on a bar mirror was rated by the German saloon keeper only a degree lower than a Michael Angelo ceiling. His spread eagle for the 4th of July was voted by the patrons of Mike Casey's "Wines and Liquors" as the most realistic representation of that bird in the whole range of art, equalled only by the counterfeit $10 bill by an anonymous craftsman hung in a frame over Casey's till. The soap artist was a boon to the saloon porter in the summer time in the way of labor saving—the decorated mirrors requiring no cleaning.

Another "fly-time" benefactor was the man who appeared at the beginning of the summer with the material for covering the elaborate chandeliers and mirrors in saloons, confectioners, bakeries and other resorts of the sportive fly. His flynets in pink and green and blue and yellow, ingeniously swathed around the convolutions of a gas pipe, were regarded as symphonies in decoration and, when happily combined with tinfoil, the consensus of opinion was that art could go no further.

The famed "free lunch" of those golden days must reappear in the light of the present period of "cover charges" and similar iniquities as a preposterous fable. If so, many a "bum" of the Eighties has been physically nourished on fables. The free lunch varied in scope and quality with the class of patronage, but it was an indispensable adjunct to every beer saloon, whiskey shop, cafe, gin mill, wine stube or other dispensary of alcoholic beverages whatsoever. Some of these lunches were spread out on long counters and consisted of innumerable varieties of viands and condiments. Where workingmen were apt to congregate, hot soups, stews, and chowders were served. It was only necessary to buy a glass of beer for five cents to enjoy this refection. And many a penniless tramp has assuaged the pangs of hunger by pretending to be a customer. Indeed the "free lunch fiends" were recognized as a big nuisance to the bartenders of that mellow day.

If the free lunch was sumptuous on ordinary days what can be said of it on such festive occasions as Thanksgiving, Christmas and New Year's, particularly the latter? The great uptown hotels had wonderful spreads of turkeys, hams, salads, soups and cheeses, provided by a personal boniface and not a managing director of a "chain" hotel. The good cheer of such a time was in startling contrast to the present system of "so much for so much." Even the cheaper places made extraordinary efforts in gala direction and if the "strapped" had no other day of rejoicing, they had it then.

A word must be said of that terrible instrument known as the "free lunch fork." This was a weapon, now obsolete, that served the common use of the patron of the lower class saloons. Its receptacle, when not in use, was a goblet of greasy water that stood on the lunch counter. Its superb qualities as a germ carrier were recognized by the Board of Health, which, long before the saloon made its final exit, placed it under the ban.

In the Bock Beer season spry and festive goats on gaudy posters proclaimed the arrival of New York's favorite spring beverage. Competition was keen and huge muslin signs, emblazoned with a picture of an elongated glass or "Schooner," as it was called, conveyed the welcome intelligence to the thirsty wayfarer that here he could procure "the largest Schooner of Beer in the city for 5c."

At a theater the other evening one of the scenes recalled these sinful and degenerate days. Time: The Night when the Brewery Mortgage was paid off. All hands were in the back room. An old familiar object was rolled on the stage. It was a keg of "suds"—only that and nothing more. Sobs and cheers shook the building and stopped the show.

Among the many quaint and picturesque features of New York City life in the Eighties, none was more interesting than the Sunday morning eel market of Catherine Slip. This was founded as long back as the 18th century by the Canarsie fishermen and did a flourishing business for years. It was an open-air market, held on the sidewalk of the east side of Catherine Slip, between Cherry and South Streets, and along South Street to

Market. Its chief object was the sale of Canarsie eels and many an old-fashioned resident of New York would go without his favorite dish of fried eels or eel pot pie if the Catherine Slip market was abolished and he could no longer buy them on a Sunday morning at this particular place. So strong was the force of habit and tradition that although attempts had been made to establish Sunday morning eel markets elsewhere in the city they had all failed and for the sake of procuring eels where their fathers and grandfathers before them were accustomed to buy, purchasers rose long before daylight and traveled from distant parts of the city and even from Brooklyn and Jersey City.

The great advantage of buying in the market was as one of the venders put it, "here they sees their eels alive, and sees 'em skun and knows what they's a-gettin'." Besides live eels, a good business was done in dried and smoked eels, many of which were bought by Chinese, who might have been seen in numbers at the market.

In early years, mountebanks and strolling musicians frequented this Sunday morning market, and "dancing for eels" was a performance that attracted crowds of spectators and afforded endless amusement. The performers were negroes who would come from great distances to exhibit their skill, the better of two competitors in each dance receiving a live eel as a prize. These eel dances were abolished on account of the noisy crowds they attracted.

Next in volume of trade to the eel venders, were the oyster men who, with the hatches of their sloops brought ashore and supported on trestles so as to form tables, retailed oysters and clams at one cent a piece to be eaten on the spot. A free lunch of pilot bread was thrown in,

The Eel Market on Catherine Street, 1880.

and the oyster men showed their knowledge of human nature and especially of the class to which their customers
belonged by describing their bivalves as "real Coney Island clams up from Coney Island this morning," or "Fresh
Rockaway Oysters, just in from Rockaway." By these
simple means, fond memories were revived and the shell
fish thus localized were eaten with a relish that would
be lacking had they hailed from Little Neck, Blue Point,
Saddle Rock, or other shores known only by hearsay.

Adjacent to the eel market on South Street was one of
fruit and vegetables and beyond this another for second-
hand clothing, hats, and odds and ends of every description. Of these latter, the average price was ten cents
although "genuine Japanese lacquer waiters, right from
Japan" were sold for six cents or two for ten, and another
familiar cry was, "Here you are now, Jumbo only three
cents." The Jumbos offered were small brass elephants
intended for watch-charms which met with a ready sale.

Then there was a man exhibiting tapeworms preserved
in alcohol and offering for sale a worm specific, guaranteed equally efficacious in removing corns; and a peripatetic dentist was present ready to extract teeth or sell
spectacles. Another familiar figure was an alleged sailor
of Hebrew physiognomy who offered any quantity of
lace at ten cents a yard and confided to you in a low
tone, that he had smuggled it over on his last voyage and
is now so afraid of being detected that he is willing to
sell it at less than cost in order to dispose of it quickly.

By nine o'clock the police began to clear up the market
and by the time the church-goer appeared nothing remained of it but the heaps of refuse being swept up by
the street cleaner.

Oyster boats along West Street, 1880.

An early New York institution common to the days when there were epicures on Manhattan Island, was the oyster house. In place of the rotisseries, spaghetteries, cafeterias, coffee potteries and what-nottaries that now cater to the inner man, the oyster house was the great middle-class refectory. "Oysters in Every Style" appeared on the signboards of every restaurant large and small, and certain eating houses made the bivalve a specialty. Another peculiarity was quail eating contests whereby a wager was made that a quail should be eaten once a day for thirty days. These contests excited much comment in the daily press, and progress was closely followed by the public. The oyster house was the favorite resort for an after-theater snack, and Darby and Joan of the period usually repaired there after an evening at Wallack's or Daly's to discuss the drama. Darby today, fleeced by speculators, robbed by cabmen, black-mailed by coat boys, flayed by restaurateurs, and gouged by waiters, may well envy the simplicities of Dad's courting period. The oyster house had no cover charges, no music (?), no cabaret "artists," nothing but "Lynn Havens," "Blue Points," "Cape Cods," and "Rockaways" opened at the counter by a skilled mechanician whose speed and dexterity excited the admiration of laymen.

The popularity of the oyster house among theater parties led to the establishment of some more pretentious resorts for their entertainment. O'Neill's, at Sixth Avenue and Twenty-second Street, and Bristol's, a few doors below, will be remembered by frequenters of the nearby theaters, and by the sporting fraternity that had a strong hold there. These were the precursors of the "lobster palaces" of the upper tenderloin, but the real old-time oyster house was a plain unvarnished institution that made up in excellent fare for its lack of gilding. Dorlon's in Fulton Market was really a celebrated place. All the old Harper firm used to lunch there, and many famous men accompanied them. Among its late survivors was the "Oyster Bay" on Broadway, just below Forty-second Street. A very excellent resort was Carroll & Regan's, on Sixth Avenue facing Bryant Park. It was a large spacious resort with a grill in front at which a conjuror in a white apron used to transform raw shellfish into epicurean delights. Carroll & Reagan's main dining hall used no tablecloths and its cutlery was of the camp outfit variety, but the prices were consistent with the lack of display, and no one ever found fault with a soft shell crab and a mug of ale served here on the bare board. There was a small annex at which the more fastidious might dine with white napery and silver, but its users were

looked down upon by the regular frequenters as "jays."
Old man Reagan, who had an acquaintance with shell food
of an occult and mystic nature, presided here during later
years, and might have been seen summer and winter in
shirt sleeves and a straw hat overseeing the comfort of
his patrons.

There is little compensation in our modern marble halls,
with their crystal chandeliers, their canned victuals, their
stock sauce and their standardized cuisine for the gastronomic excellence of fresh food cooked to order—of a
beef cut from the joint, of oysters and clams opened to
order, and of a grill in plain view of the patron. People
of small means lived well in those days. Food of all
kinds was plentiful and wholesome. The miserable ounce-
weighing and the petty frauds of modern shopkeeping
were hardly known. "One for good measure" was the
motto in business. Small householders bought foods by
the peck and not by the pound as in our own hair-splitting,
cheese paring times. Nature was bountiful and the independent shopkeeper found it profitable to throw in an
extra handful and gratify his customer. He was not an
automaton worked from a central office and compelled
to account for the last grain entrusted to him.

Many of the proprietors of the resplendent lobster
palaces of the Nineties learned their trade as waiters in the
humbler oyster houses of the previous decade. Shanley's
began thus. George Boldt, millionaire partner of the
Waldorf-Astoria, was a waiter in Parker's, a renowned
sporting resort which stood on Broadway at just above
the position of Saks' central store-door. Parker's was a
sort of minor Delmonico's, and flourished exceedingly for

many years. Its clientele gradually declined, however, and it fell into the hands of Charley White, the pugilistic referee, who later resigned it to Jim Corbett who had at that time not yet turned to the stage as a permanent profession.

The cheap restaurants of New York were of a very miscellaneous character, and those of native type, it must be admitted, of a very inferior grade. They were usually conducted by ex-waiters who had acquired some experience in "running the front," but whose knowledge of foodstuffs and their proper methods of conversion into edibles was practically nil.

The bill of fare in such an establishment was not enshrined in a single document, but appeared in separate items on numerous placards, hung like the banners

Many housewives visited the markets personally, bringing home their purchases in baskets.

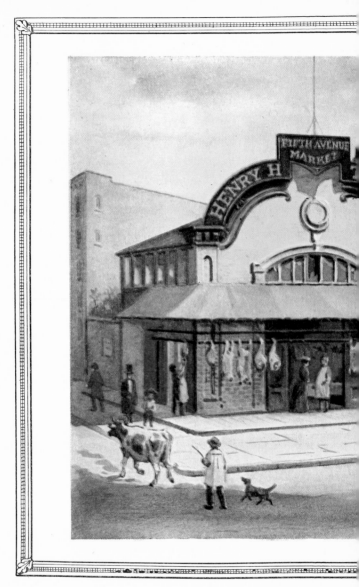

"Ye Olde Willow Cottage

As late as 1905 this quaint old reminder of the
which it derived its name, was a familiar
was conducted by Tom I

AVENUE AND 44TH STREET

ket at 44th Street, with the solitary tree from
n the Avenue.   The old inn at one time
mous old-time pugilist.

Can you imagine Sioux warriors making purchases at a Broadway dry goods store for themselves and squaws? (1877).

in a baronial hall, within easy view. Sometimes these
were of a highly ornamental character and were a
strong influence in the choice of food. A patron yearn-
ing for pork chops would discern the legend "liver
and bacon" gloriously emblazoned in gold on a Prus-
sian blue background, while "pork chops" appeared in
a displeasing combination of yellow and red. An instant revulsion of feeling, based on aesthetic grounds,
would seize upon the customer, that only an instantaneous plate of liver and bacon garnished with fried
onions, could assuage. These signs, however, were
sometimes of a deceptive nature and an embittered
client for "Corned Beef Hash" alluringly set forth in
heliotrope and silver, has often had occasion to sigh,
"The world is still deceived by ornament."

There were some noteworthy exceptions to the general run of these "joints," among them Oliver "Hitchcock's" and "Dolan's" on Park Row. Hitchcock's in
particular enjoyed a patronage remarkable for the
tremendous difference in the social status of his patrons.
To the uninitiated, his clients were popularly supposed to
be confined to "owls"; conductors and drivers of the
Third and Fourth Avenue horse cars whose runs ended
here; bootblacks, newsboys and riff raff generally. As
a matter of fact Whitelaw Reid, John Hay, Bret Harte,
Isaac Bromley, Horace Greeley, Mark Twain are only
a few of the celebrities that might have been seen sitting
there in the early hours of the morning. Years afterward
when Mr. Hay was Ambassador to London you had
only to mention the magic words "Oliver Hitchcock"
and all formality, all the stateliness of the dignified
minister, would melt into an engaging smile.

There has been a considerable change in the gastronomic habits of New York in the last fifty years. The large sirloin steaks and porterhouses once so prominent and so common on bills of fare, are almost obsolete, and articles of vegetarian or farinacious nature have superseded them. Such common edibles as spaghetti and macaroni were all but unknown in the Eighties except among the Italian immigrants that were then beginning their invasion. It was their coming and the establishment of Italian "table d'hote" in the city, at first mainly patronized by opera singers and traveled Gothamites, that brought about the change. The pioneers of the business were Moretti and Riccadonna and Morello of Union Square, where one might have met Campanini, Trebelli, Ravelli or Brignoli of the glorious old "bel canto" days at the Academy of Music. The skill of the Italian in these humble and inexpensive viands and the variety of the dinners attracted native attention and an evening at the theater was frequently preceded by a dinner with "vin ordinaire" and regarded as a novel experience, almost equivalent to a trip to "Little Italy." Bohemians were early attracted to these places and resorts like "Maria's" on Twenty-first Street, were the scenes of boisterous conviviality.

Of course New York has known French cooks and cooking since the days of Brillat and Savarin, but the French cook was identified with the "haut ton." Mrs. Vanderbilt's $10,000 French cook was a newspaper sensation of the time—but the Italians brought their gastronomic art within democratic bounds. The French menu was associated in the American mind with elaborate sauces and difficult recipes. The Italians brought

a simple and palatable menu to local notice that has
since widely flourished.

Among other foreign restaurants that were once
patronized by the general public were the Hungarian
restaurants around Second Avenue. A notable example
of these was "Little Hungary" on Houston Street,
where President Roosevelt was frequently entertained
while Police Commissioner. One of Little Hungary's
principal allurements was the unlimited flow of native
wines that accompanied a dinner there, and the Hungarian band that still further entranced the enlivening
proceedings.

Although the "Cries of London" have been perpetuated
in picture and story there has been no historian to preserve
for posterity the cries of the old-time waiter in some of
the all-night "beaneries." This individual was a character.
He looked like a disappointed prize fighter—perhaps he
was. His ritual was to wipe off the table with a dubious
towel, place before the guest an incredibly thick tumbler
of ice-water and stand at surly attention. His ability
as an equilibrist was remarkable, as manifested in the
number of dishes he could carry at once, whether
filled or empty. These dishes were of a shock-proof construction and usually were broken only in melees which
were not infrequent in such premises. But there was
nothing about the waiter more interesting than his language in transmitting orders to the kitchen. The traditional "beef and" originated with him, and is still heard
in the "one-arm" lunchrooms, but other cabalistic calls are,
we fear, as extinct as the dodo's notes. "Slaughter in
the pan," indicated beefsteak. "Red Mike wit a bunch
o' violets," indicated corned beef and cabbage. "Drop one
on the brown," was a sententious call for browned hash

Bowling was a popular indoor sport

with a poached egg. "Eggs in the dark," meant eggs fried on both sides, while the poetical term, "White wings, with the sunny side up," was translated as eggs fried on one side, and "A sheeny funeral with two on horseback," was roast pork and boiled potatoes. "Chicken in the bowl," was a requisition for chicken soup. Coffee was never mentioned by name but was referred to by the cry of "Draw one," or "Draw one in the dark," for black coffee. To order tea in one of these restaurants was a mark of eccentricity. All in all this strange language deserved attention from philologists that it never received.

To order an unaccustomed dish in one of these places was the cause of a pained astonishment on the part of the waiter. There is a story of a guileless Briton who strayed into "Beefsteak John's" and ordered a traditional meal including marmalade, water cress, tea and sundries. The amazed servitor was staggered, but only for a moment. Pointing to an organ grinder, about to begin operations, on the sidewalk, he bellowed to a colleague, "Hey Jimmie, tell the ginney to play 'God save the Queen'—the Prince of Wales has came."

A vanishing institution of New York life is the boarding house beloved of O. Henry and many lesser chroniclers of the local scene. The boarding house flourished mightily in the days when homes and business places were within easy distance of each other. They were of various degrees of quality from those providing sustenance and shelter to poorly paid working-people, to pretentious establishments in the abandoned homes of the aristocracy. The boarding house was a prolific source of inspiration to the comic papers of the *Puck* era. The austere boarding house mistress, the "star" boarder, the robust butter, the maiden lady boarder, the lone oyster in the stew, the lordly floorwalker—who posed as someone else—all these were the infallible resources of late nineteenth Century "comics," not forgetting the prune that still survives as a stock *"jeu d'esprit."* So tenaciously did this "humorous" convention take hold that in certain genteel quarters not far remote from a shirt sleeved and sword swallowing ancestry, the prune was regarded with horror as a plebian emblem betraying an entire ignorance of strawberries in January.

A contemporary description of the boarding house landlady will reveal many points of resemblance to our present "furnished room" purveyor. "She shows you through the rooms, and informs you of the genteel character of her boarders. She never takes anyone that she doesn't know all about. She prefers nice people to common people even if the latter have money. She has been well reared herself, and would have been wealthy still, if poor, dear Mr. Dobbs hadn't gone on the paper of his friends and lost his entire fortune. She gives you a biographical account of all her boarders; declares you ought to know them; that you would be delighted with them; that her house is like a home; that she has frequently thought of giving up the business, but that her boarders wouldn't let her. Her young men, she believes, really love her, and would be quite inconsolable if she should ever give up. She ventures the opinion that they would marry if they couldn't board with her.

"You reflect which of the two evils will be the greater; conclude to enlist under the petticoat banner of Mrs. Dobbs; and disregard matrimony and fresh butter forevermore."

When Shenstone wrote his immortal lines at the Henley Inn:

> "Who e'er has traveled life's dull round,
> Where'er his courses may have been,
> May sigh to think he still has found
> His warmest welcome at an inn."

he wrote not of the twenty-storied caravanseries, with two thousand rooms wherein the traveler became a member to be ticketed like a trunk, and represented to the landlord as a colored card in a rack. This, then, is the fate of the twentieth century New York hotel dweller. But two-score years ago it was not altogether so, although there were some big houses of five hundred rooms in which already the transient guest was becoming a trifle nebulous. There were, however, a large number of hostelries in which the old-fashioned boniface held forth—the landlords of the "fill the flowing bowl" type. The Hitchcocks, Darlings, Brockways, the Lelands, the Cranstons, Clarks, Hawks, Wetherbees, Fords, Shaws and Earles. Many ancient houses of early nineteenth century vintage still existed, their very walls redolent of early hospitality.

We were still in the age when women were classed politically with criminals and idiots and our kindly attitude toward the gentler sex obliged to travel alone, is a sweet and beautiful retrospect. After dark no first-class hotel would receive her unaccompanied by a male relative. Even then she was compelled to come and go through a dingy door on the side street, labelled, "Ladies' Entrance." She might just as well have worn the scarlet letter as to walk through the main corridor. In order that she might not pollute the pure atmosphere created by the masculine guests, she was huddled into a dark room in an obscure and inaccessible part of the building ostentatiously labelled

"Ladies' Parlor." No sunlight or cheerfulness was ever allowed to penetrate this padded cell and visitors were constantly under the supervision of a lynx-eyed chamber-maid who dusted chairs ceaselessly and thus artlessly performed the duties of a chaperone. A generation was to elapse ere the town was electrified by the news that Mrs. John Jacob Astor had peremptorily declined to leave the Waldorf upon the night clerk's refusal to provide her with accommodations. She had been guilty of arriving after sundown. The hotel capitulated and the whole country rang with the sensational tidings next morning.

To avoid the charge of rank favoritism, Mr. Boldt announced that thereafter a certain floor of the hotel would be open to provide for these strange wayfarers. Other hotels read the handwriting on the wall, and gradually this archaic restriction was finally removed. But it took time, and is nothing to brag about.

Before the days of the telephone, hotels had annunciator boards to indicate the room number of a guest calling up the office for service. Then, later in the Eighties, someone invented a machine to do away with fifty per cent. of the toil involved in a journey to find out what was wanted and a later journey in supplying it. This machine was in use in most of the hotels of the early Nineties.

In each room in the hotel was a dial with a movable arrow like a clock hand. On the dial was printed the names of everything a guest would be at all likely to want —all the drinks that were ever heard of, paper, envelopes, telegraph blanks, "help," a doctor, police, chambermaid, messenger boy, eggs, toast, milk, soup, oysters, breakfast, dinner, tea—in fact every eatable in common demand, a city directory, playing cards, cigars, cigarettes, chewing tobacco, a barber; in short everything in a list of one hundred or one hundred and fifty necessaries. The guest pointed the arrow to the name of whatever he wanted and by pressing a button registered his demand on the dial behind the clerk's desk.

It was discovered, however, that notwithstanding the wide compass of the dial there was always something a guest wanted that did not appear on its catalogue. Then again the dial was prone to get out of order and a guest calling for ice water was on occasion surprised with a service of hot tea. The dials were not long in use before they were superseded by the telephone.

Among these old-time hostelries were the Astor House, with its famous rotunda restaurant, in which one could always meet at lunch celebrities of politics from the neighboring City Hall, a Postmaster, perhaps, or a few judges from the adjacent law courts. French's Hotel, on the site of the present "World" Building; Nash & Crooks, Lovejoys, the United States, at Pearl and Fulton; the Stevens House, on lower Broadway; resorts of old-fashioned visitors to town; Noakes, and Smith and McNells, on Greenwich Street, where the farmer and produce merchant found convenient domicile, and the Cosmopolitan, on Chambers Street, handy to the Boston boats, were a few of the downtown houses.

Further uptown were Earle's Hotel, at Canal and Centre Streets; the Metropolitan, at Prince and Broadway, an imposing "brown-stone" edifice, housing the famous "Niblo's Garden." At Bond Street still stands the "Grand Central" of Stokes-Fisk notoriety, and at Waverly Place stood the historic New York Hotel, and below that the St.

The Astor House Rotunda, 1888.

Nicholas, a hot bed of Southern sympathizers during the Civil War, and long patronized by visitors from Dixieland. At Eleventh Street and Broadway stood the St. Denis, noted for its cuisine and a favorite with lady shoppers during the heydey of the "Ladies Mile," as was to a lesser degree the Sinclair House at Eighth Street.

Union Square was a center of well-known houses, such as the Morton House of early "Rialto" fame, always thronged with actors; the Union Square Hotel, the sedate Everett House, also of culinary renown, The Clarendon with its mid-century memories of Thackeray, and the Prince of Wales, and the stately Westminster, with its later recollections of Dickens. Westward, at Fifth Avenue and Eighth Street, Clinton Place, its early name, still stands the Brevoort, beloved of the Briton, where one could generally meet an ambassador, or a Cunard captain or two discussing uninhibited "hot scotches."

Approaching Madison Square one encountered the more modern houses, chief among them the dignified and historic Fifth Avenue, the New York headquarters of the Republican party, with its seat of the mighty, the famous "Amen Corner," in a recess of the lobby. Then to the north, the Hoffman House, renowned for its cafe, whose habitues constituted a "Who's Who" in sport, politics, the stage and Manhattan fast life in general. Adjoining it was the Albemarle, a reserved and exclusive house of English flavor, from one of whose windows Mrs. Langtry witnessed the burning of the Park Theater, on Broadway and Twenty-second Street on the night of her intended American début at that house. "I watched the flames approaching a billboard bearing my name in front of the theater and felt it an omen of better fortune to come when

French's Hotel, where the World Building now stands; Nash & Crooks in the old Times Building; Lovejoys in Chambers Street; Hitchcock's and Dolan's on Park Row

they were quenched before consuming it" said the "Jersey Lily" later, in an interview with the famous "Tay Pay" O'Connor.

Across Madison Square, and facing Delmonico's, was the "recherche" Brunswick where the Coaching Club used to foregather and on brilliant spring mornings take aboard guests for a run to New Rochelle. All this gayety and vivacity gave Madison Square a truly Parisian aspect, with its trees verdant in foliage and the smart equipages of society rolling up and down the "Avenue." This aspect was enhanced at 27th Street by the Victoria Hotel in the French style of architecture, favored of Grover Cleveland, when called from the capitol to the metropolis. Northward of Madison Square, hotel life mainly centered on Broadway, excepting for the semi-private residential hotels favored by a large class of permanent guests. The Windsor, at 46th Street, was the one great transient house that the Avenue boasted—the early home of Andrew Carnegie and Edwin Booth. There were a number of unpretentious hotels on Fourth Avenue, among them the Ashland House and Putnam House, not far from Madison Square Garden, and contiguous to the horse marts, then a very thriving feature of the city's business. These houses were headquarters for out-of-town horsemen, and also derived considerable patronage from the circus and sporting fraternity concerned in Madison Square Garden's activities. Farther up Fourth Avenue was, and still is, the Park Avenue Hotel, a converted home for young women, built by A. T. Stewart. This philanthropy which proposed to put working girls on a level with inmates of a reformatory was not widely popular and the structure was leased as a hotel. Opposite the Grand Central Station was the Grand Union Hotel, conducted by that noted humorist, Simeon Ford, and his art-loving colleague, Shaw, among the last of the old school bonifaces. The Murray Hill Hotel, opposite, was one of the city's first fireproof hotels. On the corner of Lexington Avenue and Forty-second Street, was the Vanderbilt, the headquarters of the redoubtable John L. Sullivan.

Broadway, from Madison Square to Forty-second Street, was a succession of houses of good cheer, notable among them being The Gilsey House, whose presiding genius was mine host Breslin, a typical old-school boniface, whose name is perpetuated near the scene of his ancient hospitalities in a modern hotel structure. At Thirty-first Street, the Grand Hotel still recalls some of the city's French influence of the Seventies. Two houses of a lower grade were the Sturtevant and Coleman, of sporting and theatrical flavor.

About Thirty-fourth Street on Broadway the hotels were of a miscellaneous character. The Marlborough catering to the sons and daughters of the Old South, its most distinguished patrons being Mrs. Jefferson Davis and her daughter, Winnie ("the daughter of the Confederacy"), was at Thirty-sixth Street. At Thirty-eighth still stands the Normandie, a dilapidated shell of its former splendor when it was run by General Earle, son of the founder of the Earle's Hotel on Canal Street. Perhaps the most distinguished political patron of the Normandie was the late Governor David B. Hill. The Oriental, at Thirty-ninth Street, was favored of the stage, while at the Gedney House, at Fortieth Street, might be met the stars of the prize-ring, including such worthies as Charley Mitchell, the Slavin brothers, George Dixon, Tom Shar-

The Rossmore (right) and St. Cloud (left)
at Broadway and 42nd Street, 1876.

key, and others. The Rossmore, at Forty-second Street,
and the St. Cloud, facing it, marked the ending of the
city's central hotel district, with the exception of the Barrett House, at Forty-third Street, for many years the
only hotel on what was then Long Acre Square.

The era of the modern New York hotel begins in the
early "Nineties" with the construction of the first Plaza
Hotel, and the Holland House. For many years the
antiquated fittings and out-of-date "conveniences" of the
best hotel of New York had been a byword to travelers,
who had been entertained in the splendid new houses of
the fast-growing western cities. London, too, slow-going
and not much given to gorgeous Babylonic caravansaries,
had its Metropole, Savoy and Victoria Hotels, more pala-

tial accommodations for the visitor than any New York could boast. With the coming of the great Fifth Avenue houses, however, New York attained its present pre-eminence in collossal and magnificent houses of public entertainment. The Imperial Hotel, built by the Goelets in 1890, was the most sumptuous hotel Broadway had ever known, and was the impelling motive in the con-struction of its later rival, the Waldorf, around the corner, which was the climax in the overpowering magnificence of its time. "Why don't you put your boots outside the door to be blacked?" asked the wife of a well-known English visitor, newly arrived at one of those glamorous hostels. "I'm afraid I'd find them gilded in the morning," he replied. It seemed, indeed, that the hotel builders of that period were determined to pile Ossa on Pelion in their efforts to dazzle the Yokeldom of the na-tion with their "Royal Suites," "Bridal Chambers," "Palm Gardens," and other allurements to fat wallets. Our mod-ern hotels are somewhat less exuberant in ornament, going in more for "period" decorations, and "cover" charges—a practice that would have created a riot in these simple days of which I speak. There was never any charge for bread and butter, these edibles being supplied in generous quantities and taken for granted.

The gorgeous ready-made hotels of the Nineties brought a reaction against the unaesthetic state of af-fairs that were not in the least consoling to the plain traveler who didn't care to eat his breakfast eggs in a Louis 16th room. The glamorous Fifth Avenue group called in that curious product of a frontier civilization known as the "interior decorator." "Bridal Chambers," "Royal Suites," "Palm Gardens," reproductions from

Venetian palazzos, baronial halls, and Rhine castles gave these hotels the atmosphere of a furniture dealer's warerooms. There was a dearth in New York then, as there has been ever since, of plain middle class accommodations, devoid of flunkeyism, for the average citizen. The "suites" were overburdened with an enormous amount of decorative gimcracks ostensibly "in the period." It did not then, and has never since, struck the New York hotel-keeper that a more homelike, less flamboyant style of innkeeping might appeal to a large public. A small merchant from Keokuk eating a plate of porridge in the "Pompeiian Room" attended by a waiter who is probably the absentee landlord of a chain of East Side Apartments, is certainly a pathetic figure.

Another pleasant custom of the guests in those days was the practice of sitting out in chairs on the sidewalk after supper. The Broadway Central, the Continental, the Ashland, and the Grand Union were particularly noted for this. When the fire engines went past the old Ashland, which was near an Engine House, there was always a wild scurrying to get the chairs out of the way. And at the Grand Union, a real, old-fashioned southern darkey used to appear nightly and whistle old plantation melodies: "My Old Kentucky Home," "Darling Nellie Gray," "Old Black Joe," in a manner that touched the hearts of his hearers and also their pocketbooks. He was accompanied by a clever banjoist and their collection never contained anything but silver.

It was a real genuine old homestead custom, and I was sorry to see it disappear.

CHAPTER III

INTERNATIONAL RIFLE MATCHES – ROWING – ARCHERY –
CROQUET – CRICKET – IS BASEBALL A NATIONAL GAME?
THE QUESTION RAISED BY "HARPER'S WEEKLY" – PEDES-
TRIANISM – TENNIS – SLEIGHING – TROTTING – CONEY
ISLAND IN ITS EARLY DAYS – SUMMER VACATIONS – BLACK
EYE CURE – SUNDAY EXCURSIONS – PLAYERS AND PLAY-
HOUSES.

IN no department of everyday interest has there
been a greater change than in the range of sports.
Baseball in the "seventies" was by no means the
wholly absorbing sport it is today, and in other respects there is a vast difference.

Where we now have endless accounts of golf, tennis, basketball, boxing matches and so forth, none of
these was mentioned then. The sporting page of
those days was almost wholly occupied by the comings and goings of the American Rifle Team and by
the scores made by the various regiments at Creedmoor. In fact it is quite impossible for the present
generation to realize the tremendous public interest

taken in the series of international rifle matches between Ireland and America. Nor would it be possible, we think today, for any visiting sporting company, no matter of what character, to be received in just such an elaborate manner as was accorded the American Rifle Team arriving in Belfast. They were met by the mayor and members of the Corporation. A procession was then formed, aided by numerous brass bands, and a triumphal entry made in the Irish city among the plaudits of an enthusiastic multitude. The papers were filled with columns of news regarding the movements of individual members of the team, as well as of the team itself. The "crack shots," Col. Bodine, Major Fulton and Col. Gildersleeve, were personages of the most exalted importance; their comings and goings were the subject of the most minute description in lengthy cablegrams. I do not recall when first the popularity of rifle shooting began to decline. Apparently it no longer exists as a sport. It seems strange that it ever loomed so large in the day's news, so completely has it vanished. But in its time it was certainly the most talked-of sport in existence.

Another sport that almost equalled the rifle shots in public interest was rowing. The Hudson River men stood out most prominently, particularly the Ward Brothers, of Newburgh, and Ten Eyck, of Albany. Edward Hanlon, of Toronto, was another famous oarsman, and there were many others.

In the summer the grand intercollegiate boat race was held at Saratoga Lake. Whether from motives of economy or for other reasons, all the college boat

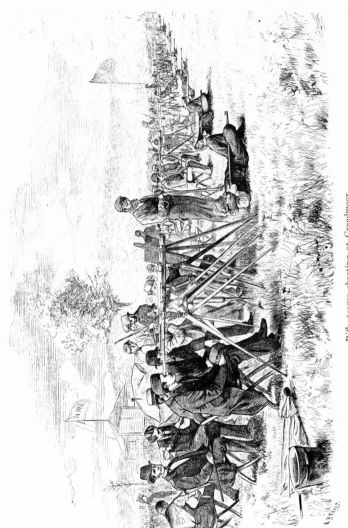

Rifle teams shooting at Creedmoor.

races were held at one time, and in this year (1875) thirteen boats left the starting point representing the following colleges: Yale, Harvard, Amherst, Bowdoin, Brown, Cornell, Columbia, Princeton, Dartmouth, Hamilton, Union, Wesleyan and Williams.

The great vogue of rowing caused to spring up along the Harlem River a large number of boat clubs devoted to the sport. Some of them which had their origin at that time have survived to this day. But the sport itself possesses little or no interest for the general public, compared with former days. In the time of Hanlon and the Ward boys nothing else was talked of. Their pictures adorned the *Police Gazette* and even staid old *Harper's Weekly* deigned to follow suit. But rowing, like shooting, has succumbed to the tennis racket and the baseball. There is now no fascination in this one-time popular sport.

Other games that came in for attention were Archery and Croquet. Both Central Park and Prospect Park, in Brooklyn, had many devotees of both sports and in comparison croquet probably created as much furore and produced as many thrills as a tennis tournament of today does at Forest Hills. Many matches were prolonged far into the night when the moon permitted and there were few back yards or front lawns that did not at some time of the day provide their contribution to the reigning craze. One sees croquet played occasionally by elderly persons at a summer resort. But even that is rare. It is not recommended by the doctors as beneficial for the old and feeble as was formerly the case, so we must class croquet as among the lost arts. Archery is in the same class,

First Spring Meeting, Archery Club, in Central Park. 1880.

although it would not be strictly true to place Archery in the same category with Croquet in point of popularity at any time. While it was affected by a few, it never reached the standing of Croquet, and its tenure of existence was brief and without incident.

With the English game of Cricket, however, the case was entirely different. For a long time it was a

"They played croquet far into the night."

Drawn by Harry Ogden

First National Lawn Tennis Tournament, St. George, Staten Island, 1880.

toss-up which was going to prove the Great American National Game — Cricket or Baseball. In the early stages of the controversy a large section favored Cricket because of its greater gentility. In fact *Harper's Weekly*, which in those days was the court of last resort in all sporting matters, was not sure that Baseball was entitled to be even considered mentioned as a possible national game. It is quite interesting to read its views at this time, as it undoubtedly reflected those of a substantial portion of the general public. It said:

"Whether baseball is a better or a worse game than cricket we do not now propose to inquire; but it is really worth while inquiring whether the former is or is not as popular among us as is *commonly* reported in the newspapers.

"In New York, it is well known, there are several baseball clubs which play periodically. The same thing is true of Boston, Philadelphia, and perhaps one or two other cities. But is baseball so popular that it is a regular and well-understood diversion in most of the counties in most of the States of the Union? Do young men naturally learn baseball in Massachusetts, in Pennsylvania, in Wisconsin and in Louisiana? Could a baseball match be got up in every town of ten thousand inhabitants throughout the country? We leave it to those who are better acquainted with the sporting fraternity than ourselves to answer these queries. For our part we regret to say that we doubt very much whether baseball be a popular game at all in the interior, or in any part of the country except in a few great cities. We see no evidence that either baseball or any other athletic game is so generally practiced by our people as to be fairly called a popular American game."

Nevertheless, Baseball continued to grow in popularity, and despite the visit of an "All England" team, Cricket declined steadily. It retained, however, its hold in Philadelphia and also for many years on Staten Island. But early in the eighties it disappeared completely from the fields occupied jointly by the base-

Champion baseball team, 1876.

ballists and the cricketers around New York, and was heard of no more. Strange to relate, it is still played on the same fields on which its first popularity was won fifty years ago, and to this day you can still see a good Cricket match either at St. George, Staten Island, or in Philadelphia.

There was a great rage in the early "eighties" for pedestrianism; in fact "heel and toe" matches were on a par with modern boxing contests—Gilmore's Garden, later called Madison Square Garden, held six-day races that excited intense interest everywhere. Contrary to present conditions in the ring the champions in this line of sport were usually Britons. Charles Rowell was one of the great names on the long distance track. The six-day races attracted huge crowds, including a large vicious element. Pick-pockets, shell-workers, three-card monte men and the various crooks and sharpers attendant on such assemblages held high carnival. Tramps and pan-handlers spent the entire period of the race inside the Garden sleeping on the benches. Overcoats and other articles of apparel disappeared from their rightful owners with miraculous swiftness and without hope of redress. It was necessary for contestants to walk a certain number of miles to be "in on the money" and some of them were deplorably unequal to the task, besides lacking the proper nourishment to attempt it. It became painful to watch these haggard wretches limping wearily hour after hour, day after day, around the course, and eventually the affair became a public scandal which culminated in a "Ladies" contest in which eighteeen females were entered. The present laws, such as govern bicycle races, were the outcome of these abuses.

Rowing and sculling claimed considerable attention from New Yorkers in those days and professionals like Ward, Hanlon, Ten Eyck and Bibby often rowed in local waters. Another aquatic celebrity was Capt. Paul Boynton, who for a time ran a tavern called "The Ship" on 29th Street and who invented a kind of life preserver in the form of a rubber suit that was guaranteed unsinkable. The Captain cast himself overboard from a steamer near Queenstown and made a successful landing.

There was a sort of rage for tennis in the early eighties but it was too exotic for the youth of the day who was especially prejudiced against the brilliant blazers affected by the devotees of the net. There was also considerable riding on the old high-wheel bicycle, and there is a test case on record in which the rider was arrested on the charge of scaring horses.

Snow laid in our streets for a long time in these days and every vehicle took to runners. The uptown drives and

The Six-Day "Go-as-you-please" Walking Matches at Gilmore's Garden
(The Old Madison Square). Charley Rowell leading.

Sleighing in the Eighties

Central Park were alive with sleigh riders. In the early morning and all through the forenoon happy fathers might have been seen taking an airing behind the staid family horse, harnessed to the family sleigh. The fair young lady with the "bang-tailed" pony, russet harness and "natty" cutter was also noticeable. The Country (sic) swain from Westchester County with his best girl helped swell the crowd and was not the least joyous of the merry-makers. The "swell" young man with his Russian drosky drawn by three horses decorated with red plumes was the observed of all observers, while the fashionable man reclined lazily in the regulation sleigh with an English "tiger" drawing the lines over the prancing steeds.

In the afternoon and evening the butcher, the baker, and all kinds of tradesmen who possessed horses that worked through the working days helped make up the holiday

Third Annual Meet of the American Wheelmen, Riverside Drive, 1883.

gathering. The proprietors of the road houses were joyous and their smiles were only curtailed by the position of their ears, and as they went to bed with the prospect of a continued run of sleighing they dreamed of fortunes that the best of modern Utopias could not hope to realize. To say that "Gabe" Case was happy would be but a faint expression of his condition, and his 250 pounds could not shake sufficiently to express his satisfaction. "Gabe's" was not the only house that was well filled by any means. John Barry of the "Romantic" had his hands full, and stated that he had never had such a run of custom. At "Judge" Smith's, his stabling facilities were tested to their utmost mostly with family parties. At "Gabe" Case's a banjo and guitar helped to make music. Charley Johnson of Harlem, sixty-three years old and weighing 200 lbs. was so carried away by the reels and jigs as to renew the pastimes of his youth in executing pigeon-wings and double shuffles with such grace and skill that "Gabe" flushed in a way that showed the poisoned barb of jealousy had pierced his soul.

Wm. H. Vanderbilt was out behind his famous team Early Rose and Aldine. He drove up as far as McCombs Dam Bridge, turned around and without stopping returned home. Nathan Strauss at different times took a spin behind Majolica, Majolica Maid and J. D. Ripley. As he passed Alderman Hugh J. Grant driving a chestnut pacer he shouted a challenge for a brush down the road. Shepard Knapp was one of the first to go up the road and one of the last to turn his horse's head homeward. Frank Work was out in the morning with Regina, and in the afternoon with Edward. An old man driving a black

Sleighing in Central Park, 1886.

gelding harnessed to a Portland sleigh, painted yellow, made the frequenters of Seventh Avenue open their eyes as he let his horse out for all there was in him. He didn't linger long enough for anybody to ask his name and nobody could keep within hailing distance. Edward Stokes was out behind Lyman. Myndert Starin drove one of the youngsters bred by his father and the colt showed good mettle. Newbold Morris slashed along with Captain while A. de Cordova drove out behind Dejanera.

There were no such extended summer vacations as are now customary. In the early Seventies my best recollection is that there were none at all, except for the fairly well-to-do and even they were loath to spend more than a week or two in downright idleness. The hours for labor were from 6:30 and 7:00 a.m. to 6 p.m., and for store and office workers from 7:30 to 6.00. And that went for every day in the week. Few so-called legal holidays were observed. The banks, that were ostensibly closed, kept their forces practically intact and only a few business houses closed their doors. Such firms as were liberal in this respect were considered eccentric and were looked upon by their neighbors as "putting on airs."

Nevertheless, the desire for a less strenuous existence gradually spread, and the custom gained new recruits every year. With no particular prearrangement, most of the houses began a system whereby each employee in the office force received first an entire week in summer with pay, and finally two weeks. These two weeks were usually spent papering a couple of rooms or fixing the kitchen stove which was generally in need of repair owing to Bridget's weakness for starting the fire with kerosene. The pleasing fiction that we were holidaying in the coun-

Mr. Frank Work's "Dick Swiveller" and "Edward," and
Mr. Wm. H. Vanderbilt's "Early Rose" and "Aldine."

try, did no one any real harm. Those of the force who were engaged in the manufacturing end received the same privilege, but with the important difference that no pay was included, as they were paid for overtime.

The Saturday half-holiday was another plant of slow growth. It started among the office workers themselves, who voluntarily arranged that one-half the force would stay while the other half "knocked off." This applied to alternate Saturdays in July and August only. It was some time before the idea of everybody going off on Saturday afternoons was generally adopted and there were always some who persisted in keeping open. However, it finally became a universal custom and the new plan was soon seen to possess merits hitherto unsuspected. Office hours also began to shorten. First to eight o'clock in the morning. Then to 8:30. Shortening of the day at the other end was more difficult of accomplishment, but gradually it became 5:30 and then 5:00, where it has since remained. With the latter as the closing time, the opening dropped to 9:00. This was quite an economic gain and was not attained without exasperating delay. The growth spread over practically twenty years or more before it was the universal custom.

The present custom of closing entirely on Saturday during July and August, among the dry goods shops, is of quite recent introduction and is not yet a general rule by any means. "Week ends," and the lengthening of the summer vacation from two to three weeks and in many places an entire month, would have shocked the business world fifty years ago and started a universal cry of Confiscation, Socialism, and all sorts of direful predictions.

The Drive. Central Park at four o'clock. 1883.

The reader of Monday morning's newspaper is pretty sure to encounter during the open season an extended record of the fatalities and casualties of the Sabbatarian joyrider and speeder. He must not suppose that the recreationist who considers his holiday spoiled if he does not beat a railroad train to a grade-crossing has no spiritual ancestor. He has. But the ancestral diversion was of a different type. A headline in a New York paper forty years ago to the effect that there was a "Huge Crowd at Coney Island—No Arrests Made" would have been a journalistic curiosity by reason of its sub-title. In the palmy days of political chowders, barge picnics, moonlight excursions, barbecues and other nautical and pastoral festivities, their sanguinary incidentals called for the services of the war correspondent. The following headlines appearing on Monday mornings during two months in the summer of Eighty-five are illuminating:

"Killed in a Sunday Riot, Attack on a Bohemian Liquor Shop." "Burning a Sleeping Man in Kerosene." "Brutal Assault in Brooklyn." "Ruffians on Elevated Trains." "Ruffians Assault an Excursion Party." "Riot at a Long Island Picnic." "Death From a Blow." "Dead for Fifteen Cents, How Two Sailors Ended a Spree." "Probable Murder With a Bottle." "Shot for Refusing to Drink." "Cutting Affray in Jersey City." "Hit on the Head with a Bottle." "Result of a Drunken Brawl at Woodside, L. I." "Pistol Shots on Two Barges, Fighting Among Pleasure Seekers."

The foregoing is only an index of holiday relaxations. Scanning the week-day "Local Jottings" we find sundry matrimonial endearments emphasized with the domestic axe, tenement house fires resulting from misdirected kerosene lamps, "mixed ale" parties which usually culminated in the parties becoming mixed, besides the ale, and an innumerable list of disconcerting items reflecting the contemporary "hearth and home."

A typical account of a Sunday "outing" in 1885 is the following; and as a photograph of the times is worth reading:

"Yesterday was a festal day for that highly respectable portion of the Community that makes The Allen's Bleecker Street den its headquarters. The frequenters of this temple of revelry self styled the 'American Mabille' have organized themselves into an association for mutual aid in the pursuit of pleasure and are known as the Thomas Albers Association.

"The association, which rejoices in Mr. Albers' name and protection, chartered the barges *Grinnell* and *Harvest Queen,* along with the tug *Robert Hoe,* yesterday, for a trip up the North River to Spring Hill Grove. The expedition left the foot of Clinton Street, East River, at 11 a.m. with 400 of the roughest characters to be found in the city. Beer flowed freely, and had its usual influence on the ordinarily lamb-like dispositions of the pleasure seekers. The committee withdrew into the cabin of the *Harvest Queen* (happily named) to divide the spoils, otherwise known as the receipts, and came near getting into a quarrel among themselves as two or three members came out several dollars short. This matter was smoothed over, however, and they rejoined their comrades on deck. Off Spuyten Duyvil a slight man with light hair and mustache, dressed in the full uniform of the 11th Regiment, tried to jump overboard from the *Harvest Queen.* A crowd rushed to prevent him, and after a scuffle he was pulled back. As soon as released he dashed over to the *Grinnell* which was lashed to the *Harvest Queen,* and endeavored to carry out his intention again. In the resulting scuffle somebody's temper gave way and slugging began in dead earnest.

"The fighting soon extended over both barges and on both decks. The band kept on playing. Capt. Temple, commanding the tug stopped his boat by the barges to see what the trouble was, and in the rush of frightened men and women for this haven of refuge, a girl and two men went overboard, but were picked up safely. On board the barges the center of the fight surged up one side and down the other. Knives were used indiscriminately. James McCarthy, of 324 Cherry Street, was terribly cut about the head and hands.

"The Captains of the barges reversed their colors as a sign of distress, and the tug with its load of refugees steamed down to 148th Street, where the police patrol was lying. Captain Smith, in charge of the patrol, immediately started to the rescue. Meanwhile, on board the barges, Albers, with his trusty lieutenant, Joe Burroughs, and others of the committee, was doing his best to quell the riot. Somebody whacked him over the head and down he went at full length on the deck. This was too much for his Christian fortitude and self-control. Pulling his revolver he fired two shots, inflicting a deep wound in the shoulder of a boy, Robert Crawford, of 229 Monroe Street, and cutting the scalp of Wm. McKenzie, 329 Madison Street.

"Half a dozen fellows who were badly cut and bruised were taken on the patrol. Albers was captured after leaping into a boat and pulling for the New York shore with all his might. So general had the row become in the half-hour during which it raged that the only man who escaped injury was the drunken militiaman who caused the disturbance. During the mêlée on deck, a party of ruffians raided the 'lunch counter' below, kept by Thos. K. Albers, who shot two of his assailants in defense of his property."

A fracas at Elm Park between Orangemen and Hibernians—1875.

A familiar sign along the Bowery and on Sixth Avenue years ago was "Black Eyes Cured." This was usually a euphemism for painting a discolored optic, but there was one expert at least whose process was really medical and scientific. This was an Englishman, a former trainer of prize-fighters, who used fomentations, notably one of buttermilk and a secret mineral, and certain emollient roots, besides, in some severe cases, sweating the patient. This business was enormous in those frolicsome days. Interviewed by a reporter who asked what was the best season for cases, he replied:

"Business is pretty good all the year through, but is best about the holiday season. I had a special importation of twenty pounds of roots for the recent holidays. Then the picnics and excursions with the incidental beer make the summertime a good season for me. But winter is best. The week after New Year's I had all I could do, day and night. I don't know that keeping resolutions to swear off made people any crosser and fuller of fight than usual, but I know there were lots of black eyes in the community that week. One thing amused me a little. I had two men here under cure. One lay there on the bed, the other there on the sofa. A boy came in and wanted me to go to Bleecker Street to attend a man, and directly a messenger came for me to go down to Bond Street to cure a fourth man. As soon as I could get away I went down and treated the Bleecker and Bond Street cases, at the same time going from one to the other and back again, to watch the treatment. They were two saloon-keepers who had been fighting together and each one thought he was the only one hurt. When both men were cured and each knew that he had bruised the other, both were quite happy and contented. I get from $3 to $5 ordinarily for curing a black eye here, if it is not a very bad one, but sometimes as high as $50 for an awful case, or where I have to go a considerable distance. I also listen to explanations, which I never contradict. The abrasion made by a fall on the stairs, the marked line of contusion from a door, the cut of a seal-ring—one of those big knuckle-duster rings that brutes and loafers carry—the plain bruise of a blow are all plain as print to me.

"A man came in here one day with a lady who had a bad black eye, and began telling how she got it, when she interrupted him, saying, 'No; you did it and there's no use in your saying it was a fall.' He had no more to say, but he looked as if he would have liked to black her other eye if he dared.

A Target Company at Lion Park, who shot all day and came home half shot at night. Steady customers of the Black Eye Cure man.

"Charity cases? Oh, yes, many of them. Where I was satisfied that a poor young clerk had no money to pay and might lose his employment if he showed up with a black eye, I have never refused to help him. But when it comes to charging I can do what I like, for I've got a monopoly. Druggists and doctors send me lots of cases for they know that I can do what none of them can, and that I never fail. No cure, no pay."

Despite its advance in the scale of grandeur, the early Coney Island was a far more fascinating resort than it has ever been since. It had been a real beach for most of its length, only partly obstructed by "concessions." The principal ways of approaching the island were by the Iron Steamboat Co. and by the steam-cars from Bay Ridge. Tickets to Coney Island were sold on the Manhattan "L" stations for the Bay Ridge Lines. The terminal of one of these, the "Sea Beach," at Coney Island, was an exhibition building from the Philadelphia Centennial, which continued as a kind of miniature fair, containing glass blowers, crayon artists, astrologers, quack doctors, etc., besides a bewildering variety of catch-penny machines, from model locomotives to the recently introduced phonograph.

The Island itself was a picturesque congeries of shanties, pavilions, clap-board hotels, fishing huts, bath-houses, etc., mostly assembled in what was known as the West End. The outstanding features were the old and new Iron Piers; the Observatory, a tall iron tower near the piers; and the great wooden elephant hotel, a caravansary built to resemble that eccentric beast. This was the most noted feature of the place, and "seeing the elephant" passed into popular slang.

Coney Island then abounded with fake side-shows, fortune tellers, soap-game swindlers, monte men, crooked roulette wheels, tin plate games and every conceivable fraud ever invented. These games were pursued with brazen effrontery upon the open highways, and even boys in their teens were fleeced without mercy.

Bill Tweed is credited with having made his escape from Norton & Murrays Point (now Sea Gate) where a boat conveyed him to a sailing vessel anchored off-shore. The first bathing-houses of any description were the rude home-made affairs erected by Norton & Murray, who were the pioneers of this famous resort.

One of the delights of Coney Island bathing was the probability that one's clothes or valuables would be missing from one's bath-house on emerging from the water. They were extracted by hooks passed over the tops of partitions. In later times this was circumvented by a wire screen laid over the top of the rude compartment dignified by the name of bathroom.

The predecessor of the "hot dog" at Coney Island was clam chowder. The qualities of this sustaining comestible varied from a mysterious compound sold for five cents and served on rude counters, to the very excellent article on the bill of fare of the Manhattan Beach Hotel.

There is hardly a trace in the suburban settlement now called Manhattan Beach to recall the days when that famous resort was the chief center of metropolitan, better class, summer recreation. The great hotel with its huge veranda teemed with celebrities of the stage, sport, and the gay life of the city generally. The famous P. S. Gilmore and, later, J. P. Sousa, and Levy, the cornetist, held forth there with band concerts in the attached music hall.

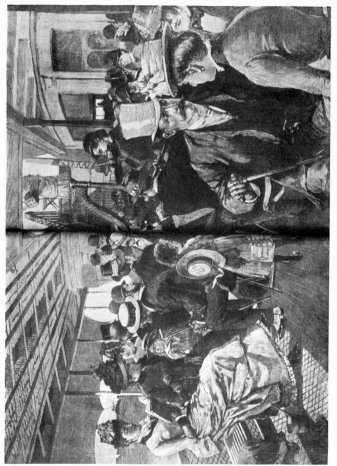

On the way to Coney Island, 1886.

A "swan dive"—vintage of 1880.

For many years Pain's fireworks gave pyrotechnic spectacles such as "The Fall of Babylon" and "The Destruc-
tion of Pompeii" in a great amphitheatre adjacent to the
hotel. The Sheepshead Bay races brought large crowds
to spend the evening at the beach, which presented a scene
of great gayety and animation on such occasions. At the
extreme easterly end of Manhattan Beach was the Oriental Hotel, particularly noted as the seaside retreat of the
celebrated Tom Platt, "The Easy Boss" of the Republican
party, and originator of the Amen corner in the Fifth
Avenue Hotel.

He was Senatorial colleague of Roscoe Conkling.
Platt's political methods were subtle and Machiavellian in
contradistinction to the bludgeoning tactics of his cruder
Democratic opponents. He is generally credited with the

All there was of Coney Island in the Eighties.
View eastward from the Observatory.

"coup" that placed the intractable Roosevelt in the Vice-Presidential chair, hoping thereby to insure the latter political oblivion; only to see him elevated to the Presidency upon McKinley's assassination.

Among the earliest users of the electric light in skyline advertising was the great structure above the old Erie "Cow-catcher" at Broadway and Twenty-third Street calling attention to "Manhattan Beach, Swept by Ocean Breezes," sometimes burlesqued "Sweat by ocean breezes," an allusion to the temperature when a land breeze was blowing. Our picture gives an excellent idea of Coney's early days and its size compared with the present.

Between Brighton and Manhattan Beaches spread a desert of sand and seaweed that separated the two resorts by a barrier negotiable only by the tiny Marine Railway. This was a curiosity of transportation, probably not equalled throughout the entire railway mileage of the United States. The Manhattan Beach authorities assuming certain apocryphal rights in the connecting territory operated a shuttle road about a quarter of a mile long, with a rolling stock of an engine and one or two cars, as traffic demanded. The fare on this unique extortion was five cents each way. The owners explained by stating that their object was to keep the Coney Island rabble from encroaching on Manhattan Beach.

New Jersey used to be considered a sort of "hinterland" for the sophisticated denizens of the metropolis; a kind of no-man's land where the harassed Manhattanite would flee when the legal pressure of his own beloved burg bore too heavily upon him. Hoboken, provincial Hoboken, the butt of the minstrel end man, the laughing

Fireworks at Manhattan Beach. The Last Days of Pompeii, 1885.

stock of the variety halls—was a very haven of refuge when the lid was down in New York. It was a limitless fountain of never-ceasing Pilsner or Wurtzburger, and as the hart panteth for the cooling spring, so did the parched Gothamite seek the sanded floor of the Hoboken beer garden.

Further back in this outlaw's paradise was Guttenberg, the dear old "Gut" on whose classic course many a "good thing" came home at long odds, and many a favorite had his head nearly pulled off for being in too great a hurry. Union Hill, where Germans used to foregather for target shooting — and lager — to steady the aim; Fort Lee, where one could find French chicken dinners and *vin ordinaire a la* South Fifth Avenue. Meyers Hotel in Hoboken was a famous house in its time known to all the officers of the German liners. It was a great stopping place for Germans from out of town on their way back to visit the Fatherland. Taylor's in Jersey City was another famous house for travelers from the West and South. Our neighbor in those days loomed large in the doings of old New York.

There was also a "River Walk" running under the Palisades which provided a delightful place for a stroll on moonlight nights. It is now covered with massive coal docks but in those days was one of the most charming retreats that could be imagined. Its memory is cherished by many old timers who recall its sylvan beauty and the dancing water.

Mankind may be divided into two classes, those who enjoy fishing and those who don't. There were large numbers of the former in New York years ago who used

angler

to go down to the sea in steamboats, with hook, line and sinker, for a day's sport in angling. Certain superannuated excursion boats—the *Al. Foster* will be remembered—were employed to carry these enthusiasts to what were known as "The Fishing Banks." It was necessary in order to become a passenger, to rise at an unearthly hour in the morning, for the boat left her wharf shortly after daylight, with a grim, resolute company carrying baskets and fishing tackle for the business in hand. The baskets going out usually contained eatables and drinkables—especially the latter—for the day, and there is a story told of one fisherman inquiring of another—who had been delegated to provide the fare—as to the contents of their baskets, "I got half a dozen sandwiches and two quarts of whisky." "What are we goin' to do with all the sandwiches?" complained the first.

Arrived at a favorable place in the Lower Bay, the boat would stop and hundreds of lines be cast overboard. If the catch was good, all was well, but if not, there were bellows of "Move the boat" from the disappointed anglers who were disposed to regard their ill-luck as a conspiracy, for some ulterior motive, on the part of the captain and the crew. A goodly proportion of the passengers were made up of frugal Germans, who indulged in bitter lamentation when they failed to obtain their equivalent, in fish, of the price of passage. "It's a schwindle on der Cherman peoples" one of these was overheard to say on landing at the Battery with a light basket. Lines cast from the upper decks rarely succeeded in landing a prize. It was considered bad form for the Izaak Waltons on the lower decks to allow the ascent of a perfectly good fish beyond the first deck; and many an expectant fisherman hauling in found nothing but his neighbor's tackle on his hook. The novice often became seasick; and the state of the decks was not calculated to alleviate his distress. Altogether a trip to the fishing banks was a very charming affair—for those who enjoyed it.

The rocky formation of upper Manhattan was regarded as a special dispensation of bountiful nature toward patent medicine men. Upon the rocks, through which many Harlem streets were hewn, were emblazoned the virtues of pills, porous plasters, liver pads, hair restorers, spring tonics and all the vast catalogue of nostrums incidental to a credulous public. The broad driveways of upper Broadway, Seventh, Lenox and Jerome Avenues where those who drove might read, were particularly well favored mainly with reminders of spavin cures, horse liniments, ointments, and other veterinary remedies. One of the ubiquitous advertisers of the Eighties was St. Jacob's Oil, whose newspaper publicity was of a particularly indigenous type. The unsuspecting reader of the news was apt to light upon matter of this description: "The bark *Mary Mullins* was towed into port yesterday in a water-logged condition. Her commander, Capt. Silas A. Judd, seen by a reporter, said, 'We were five days out of Fayal when the ship struck a hurricane and sprung a leak. All hands were called to the pumps and for three days and nights worked to stem the onrushing tide. As the men went off duty their muscles were rubbed with St. Jacob's Oil and to this I ascribe the almost superhuman power that kept us afloat.'" St. Jacob's Oil was not only an emolient for man, but according to the testimony of Buffalo Bill, that appeared in one publication, was an efficient alleviator of the discomforts of horses and buffalo, not to mention Indians and camp followers.

The Coaching Parade leaving Brunswick Hotel—1883.

Indeed the belief in external remedies in those days was almost an article of faith. The druggists sold acres of plasters, tons of ointments, and gallons of liniments and embrocations. These plasters were counter irritants of such agonizing properties as to reduce the original pain of whatever intensity to a mere inconvenience. Some of them could be removed only by the corroding hand of time; others took with them in parting, a broad and generous section of cuticle as a souvenir of their sojourn. Similarly there existed a childlike faith in exotic remedies, particularly those of the untutored savage—"Indian Blood Syrup," "Kickapoo Bitters," "Commanche Herb Tea"— which were held in high repute by many residents of the Island of Manhattan. Of the more sophisticated remedies, such tonics purporting to contain large percentages of celery, and other health-giving garden produce, particularly barley corn, were hailed with delight by our bucolic friends and consumed enthusiastically.

These barn decorators and mountain-side painters, and other practitioners of the gentle art of defacing the landscape were then in the heydey of their glory. One adventurous spirit desiring to achieve immortality as one of the Hudson River School of Artists, essayed to paint the face of the Palisades with "Pearline for Easy Washing," but fortunately was brought down by a game warden who mistook him for a buzzard.

New York used to be a great manufacturing center for road vehicles. The American light wagon was renowned throughout the world for its strength and adaptability. The Brewster buggy was a classic on wheels. Our smooth automobile highways were unknown and the rough roads even in suburbs made it imperative that a cart or a carriage should be rugged. At the same time lightness was

Tandem Parade, Central Park. 1881.

in demand for the latter on account of the universal employment of the fast trotter not alone for pleasure, but in many forms of business. The American driver exacted a speed almost equal to that attainable on horseback.

The New York carriage-maker also turned out a large variety of sleighs as the following ad of 1884 will show:

SLEIGHS!
Of the Best Class
IMMENSE STOCK OF ELEGANT SLEIGHS
Vis-a-vis Family Sleighs
Victoria Family Sleighs
Cabriolet Family Sleighs
Canadian Rumble Sleighs
French Style Rumble Sleighs
Russian Four Passenger Sleighs
Four Passenger Portland and
Albany Sleighs
Portland and Road Cutters
Chimes, Bells, Plumes, Fur Robes, etc.
Lowest Prices for Prompt Cash

A rather intimate glance of the city is afforded by the contemporary guide books of that day There is something naïve in the lack of formality which is the dominating characteristic of all these periodicals. In one respect they have a special value; they give a "close up" of the city which is obtainable in no other way and aid us materially in reconstructing a period of which hardly a trace remains. In addition to their services as guides, the authors assumed an attitude of paternal solicitude toward the stranger that is refreshing in these present material days and of which the following is a fair sample. It is evidently addressed to the "Saturday night" ablutionist of the rural districts.

"N.B.—If you have come in town, travel-soiled and weary, and have another day for sightseeing, you will wish to proceed directly to your hotel; preface your first meal by a rapid bath; it wonderfully revivifies. There are barber shops and bathrooms in all first-class hotels. At other houses a bedroom with water and towels answer the purpose; in fact, this refreshment will be well worth the time, in the rest it will give you and the zest it will add to your first venture at sightseeing, even if you have but a few hours to spend in the metropolis."

In fact there seemed no limit to the friendly counsel which these guide books bestowed upon their patrons. Nor did their exertions end with their physical admonitions. They cheerfully went beyond this and included also their moral well-being, as may be inferred from the following cautionary signals:

BEWARE—
On approaching and coming into the city, of the good-natured civilities of persons you have never seen before. Gratuitous offers of assistance or advice, or good-fellowship, are suspicious, to say the least. Do not be persuaded to go anywhere with these casual acquaintances. If you are an utter stranger, you will find the "Handbook" your best and most trustworthy friend. It will not mislead you. While it is not necessary to particularize every place in the metropolis that is respectable as a stopping-place, or as a resort for amusement, it leaves unmentioned such as are in the least doubtful, and which ought to be avoided. Some which are notorious and extremely insidious are briefly specified under this heading, while the newspapers give daily accounts of the innumerable ways of entrapping strangers in the city.

BEWARE—
If you are at a loss in the street of accosting anyone but a policeman; him you will know by his uniform—blue coat and cap, and brass buttons. If you do not see a policeman, step into the nearest store or hotel and make your inquiries.

BEWARE—
Of the purlieus of the city. They are only to be visited under the escort of a police officer.

BEWARE—
Of Mock Auctions in stores, and of the pleasant-faced man who invites you to look in.

BEWARE—
Of Panel Houses. A sliding panel is let into the walls of some double houses, through which thieves enter unperceived and have you at their mercy.

BEWARE—
Of Saloons with "Pretty Waiter Girls." They are among the most dangerous in the city.

BEWARE—
Of all who accost you in the street, particularly if they want your advice about a pocket-book they have just found, or a roll of money which they have picked up. Such persons have a very innocent and inexperienced air. Distrust them—don't stop to listen to them.

BEWARE—
Of visiting fashionable gambling-houses "just to see what is going on."

BEWARE—
Of giving street beggars or organ grinders more than a few pennies.

BEWARE—
Of walking in the evening, except in the busiest thoroughfares of the city.

BEWARE—
Of exposing your watch, pocket-book, or jewelry in the streets, lecture-rooms, theatres, or in omnibuses or cars. You should suspect anyone, man or woman, well or ill-dressed, who *crowds* or presses against you; the contents of your pockets are in danger. Ladies, keep your pocket-books in the bosom of your dress.

BEWARE—
Of hack-drivers' extortions. (See index for "Hacks and Hackmen.")

BEWARE—
Of passing under a building in course of erection or repairs. It is worth-while to cross the street twice to avoid it.

BEWARE—
Especially in the evening, of persons who ask you what time it is. They have designs on your watch.

BEWARE—
Of leaving any considerable sum of money or any valuables in your trunk, or of carrying them on your person. There is a safe in every hotel where you can deposit such things without charge.

BEWARE—
Of talking about your business before strangers.

BEWARE—
Of even the *orderly* "Dance-Houses." A sadder story of New York life cannot be written than that connected with these places.

Other items of contemporary interest are:

"It is much the custom in New York for gentlemen, and often ladies, to go themselves to market to make their purchases for the day's requirements

"A peculiar feature of New York is the multiplicity of fashionable hotels and boarding-houses. These are sustained to a great degree by the 'respectability' of the metropolis. This is partly owing to the want of good servants (a great want), partly to the fact that only persons of large incomes can pay the enormous rents for private houses, it being a rule of 'good society' that every family must live in a *whole house* (if they keep house at all); and fashion, arbitrary here as elsewhere, compels people hoping to maintain their position to live in a large and handsome house, however small their family may be. Hence, hotel and boarding-house life has been reduced to a fine art.

"It is getting to be much the custom for families who are so fortunate as to own splendid houses on the Avenue, and who lack somewhat the means to support these establishments, to live almost wholly at their suburban residences, which, as a rule, are very fine, and come in the city to a hotel at their convenience and pleasure, while the town house, with all its rich furniture, is let to a 'fashionable' boarding-house keeper.

"Fashionable New York usually quits for the country in June, and returns in October. Before the Civil War the city was none the less gay for the flight of its inhabitants to cooler regions. The Southern planters came North with their families, flocking like tropical birds of brilliant plumage to the hotels, fluttering along the walks, and keeping the sultry streets full of life and brightness. They come still, those who can; but they have no longer the inclination or the means for the former display."

They were also unstinted in their praise of our weather:

"The climate, though variable, is extremely healthy. Fogs never obscure the heavenly blue skies, and such weather as Nature sends has a poetic beauty, whether in sunshine or storm. Here are found the exhilaration of the Russian winter, the balmy influence of the tropical summer, and the incomparable spring and autumn peculiar to the northern United States.

The following reference to the early days of the English sparrow will recall a situation that is all but forgotten. Some years before my story begins a plague of caterpillars descended upon New York. It would probably appear ridiculous to the average reader to imagine that there ever was a time in this great city when people walking in the streets would be covered with caterpillars dropping from the trees. Nevertheless it is true. And travelers in those days spoke of the beauty of our trees and the "grateful shade" in summer provided thereby. With this explanation the following paragraph will be better understood.

> "The parks and squares are delightful breathing spots. Unenclosed and beautifully paved, they are peculiarly inviting. They are planted with trees, and have beautifully kept grass plots and admirable walks and inviting seats. They are filled with English sparrows (imported for the protection of the trees against the caterpillars); and in Madison and Union Squares are ingeniously contrived miniature buildings for these little birds, placed among the branches of the trees, which represent different business departments, as 'The Post Office,' 'The Custom House,' 'The Exchange,' &c., &c., &c., and it is very amusing to see the little creatures enter these different edifices, their busy, hurried air irresistibly giving the idea that they really know where they are going and have a purpose in it."

Some idea of the gradual lengthening of the summer vacation season may be gained from the following:

> "The most fashionable period at the chief summer resorts is the last week of July and the first two weeks in August."

As a matter of fact few persons indulged in the luxury of even so much as a week. Although a vacation was frequently talked of it was a custom more observed in the breach than in the performance. Our present custom of "week ends" would have been anathema in those days.

The opening of the Metropolitan Opera House in 1883, was an epochal event in social and musical circles. It was the result of lack of room at the old

The old Opera House—Academy of Music—
On Fourteenth Street, 1880.

home of opera, the Academy of Music, for the newcomers in society anxious to "keep up with the
Jones's." The opera house, although erected by subscription among the wealthiest citizens of the city,
was built with strictly utilitarian views. That part of
the house not devoted to stage and auditorium was
used for apartments and rented for stores. Nor were
the former exclusively used for operatic purposes.
The Patriarchs, The Assembly, the Charity Balls, were
given there, not to mention more democratic routs
such as the Old Guard, The Arion, French Cooks and
Circle de l'Harmonie. The high jinks at some of

Ball in aid of the Russo-Turkish war sufferers, in the old
Academy of Music, 14th Street.   December, 1877.

these latter caused much concern to the stockholders
on the mornings after, the golden horseshoe being
considerably tarnished by the revelers. The fact was,
the deficit on grand opera was a serious question to
its sponsors, and they were not too particular regarding the means of avoiding too great a discrepancy.
Consequently, amateur boxing and wrestling bouts
were also held here, and on one glamorous occasion
at least, there was police interference. A formidable
professional wrestler known as "The Terrible Turk"
was matched with Ernest Roeber, the local champion.
The house was filled with a typical audience of rough-
necks to see the bout. Roeber, although an expert
wrestler, was no match for his gigantic opponent and
was rapidly being pinned to the mat when Bob Fitz-
simmons, one of his seconds, and no novice in such
devices, jumped into the ring to save his principal
from the stigma of defeat. This was a signal for the
police who, with drawn clubs, cleared the stage of the
howling mob of partisans ready for any extreme.
"The Terrible Turk" departed from America soon
after with considerable earnings, but, distrusting
banks, he carried his funds in gold coins in a heavy belt
upon his person. Unfortunately he set sail on the
ill-fated *La Burgoyne* and it was reported by survivors of its wreck, that he was dragged down by the
weight of his money belt.

The first season at the Metropolitan was a disastrous one and brought Manager Abbey to bankruptcy.
The second season it was decided to put on German
opera on the theory that the large German popula-

Flower Show at the Metropolitan Opera House.
Another scheme to produce revenue.

tion of the city, would support it. But the average German preferred his east-side beer garden with music on the side. The ponderous Wagnerian repertory bored the fashionables in the boxes and what was worse, the performance interfered with the small talk, an important factor in Grand Opera in those days. To appear in an opera box in time to hear the overture was considered bad form. The chatter in the parterre and grand tier during the performance grew to such a nuisance that the babblers were hissed and letters appeared in the papers signed "Opera Goer," "Family Circle," "Standee," etc., referring to these uncouth proceedings. From babbling, the golden horseshoe took to yawning, and unhappy stockholders looked with dismay upon rows of empty benches. Indeed opera-going was merely a fashionable pose in that period at the Metropolitan. The popular taste was not then cultivated to the extent that it could appreciate a corpulent Teutonic Knight in armor, bellowing an interminable recitative to a two hundred and fifty pound hausfrau, or could listen to the Wagnerian catterwaulings of what were termed "love scenes" without astonished questionings. The spectacle of an early Irish King staring speechless at his inamorata for twenty minutes, while an orchestra translated their mental processes in a series of crashing dissonances, was one to which the crude New York playgoer had not yet been educated.

The actors of these legendary romances were anything but romantic in their private lives. Their capacity for good German lager and its concomitants

"Sir Roger De Coverley" at one of the public balls, Metropolitan Opera House, 1890, to reduce the deficit.

was unlimited. After the performance the company would adjourn for refreshments to the numerous beer saloons then adjacent to the Opera House. One in particular on the northeast corner of Broadway and Thirty-eighth Street, was patronized by the famous Lili Lehman, and fabulous tales, rivaling the legends of the Rhine, were told of her powers to absorb the excellent brew obtainable there. Late in the Eighties Messrs. Abbey, Schoeffel and Grau assumed control of the opera and established the more cosmopolitan system that is now in vogue.

Grau assembled an unequaled galaxy of stars, each of the first magnitude, and produced opera largely of the Italian and French schools with an occasional intermixture of the German. Such brilliant artists as Eames, Melba, Nordica, Lehmann, Van Zandt, Calve, Ternina Homer, Scalchi, the deReszke brothers, Plancon, Lasalle, Maurel, Tamagno, Campanini, and many others enlisted under his banner and made his era memorable.

The bright particular stars of his period were the brothers de Reszke. New York opera goers have always set up an idol to worship and Jean de Reszke, the tenor, was elevated to the pedestal previously occupied by Campanini and later by Caruso. He did not possess the melliflous vocal organ of his Italian successor, but far excelled him as an actor and artist, and handled his somewhat circumscribed voice with an amazing skill and discretion. He was of commanding height and figure and exceedingly graceful for so large a man. In romantic roles such as Romeo, Lohengrin, and Raoul in "Les Hugenots" he has never since been approached and one must go back to the mid-nineteenth century Mario for a possible rival. His brother, Edouard, almost his physical counterpart, was a basso-profundo of magnificent range and power. His Mefistopheles in "Faust," has been the standard by which all subsequent singers of that role have been measured. He was also an exceedingly clever "buffo" and his rendition of the "letter song" in "Don Giovanni" was a classic of operatic comedy. The de Reszke brothers were received as social equals in the best New York society. They were of distinguished Polish family and their bearing and manners made them eligible to the highest circles; contrasting in this respect with certain spaghetti and lager beer consuming confreres of a more Bohemian persuasion. It is deplorable to know that Edouard, the former owner of great estates in Poland, died in poverty in a cellar in that devastated region during the German advance in the Great War. There is irony in the fact that the report of his ending was given about two inches of space in the New York newspapers. In his heyday at the Metropolitan, an attack of tonsilitis would have been food for half a column.

"Crank's Alley" was another operatic institution of the "star" period. "Crank's Alley" was the aisle leading to the footlights, down which would troop crowds of hysterical men and women anxious to stand face to face with the mystic lords and ladies of the musical stage. Dozens of these enthusiasts would linger after the audience had dispersed and with salvos of applause recall time after time the painted idols of the occasion to shake their hands and make much of them. These impromptu levees would continue for as long as half an hour after the performance, to the intense disgust of the employes of the house who wished to close up. These demonstrations were principally matinee affairs, in which the famous "matinee girl" of the period—now obsolete—was the prime mover. The "Matinee idol" was the precursor of the modern Valentino and other photographic favorites, but at least the silly girl of the period worshipped flesh and blood and not a celluloid image.

A phenomenon of the musical stage of the day was the comic opera "Pinafore" which swept like an epidemic through the length and breadth of the land. In subject and treatment entirely British this satire on "The Queen's Navie" nevertheless presented to American audiences certain political conditions of their own with which they were entirely familiar, besides being intrinsically comic and set to music that appealed not only to the popular but to the cultivated ear. Owing to lack of copyright protection in America the work was pirated by practically every manager who could scare up funds enough to put it on. It was said that at its height there were more than ninety companies playing it in the United States. New York alone had five theaters giving it at one time, besides burlesques in the variety houses, performances in German on the Bowery and a parody by the San Francisco Minstrels which announced in the papers "Carriages will form in line at the Battery." The popular conception of music, said one contemporary writer, was "Ancient and Modern, Moody and Sankey and Gilbert and Sullivan." Another paragraph stated "Hundreds of prospective 'Buttercups' and scores of ideal 'Deadeyes' infest the dramatic agencies and Union Square is fairly teeming with stars. Humble 'supers' realize the opportunity of a life-time in the call for singers and 'Her

Majesty's Ship' might be manned a thousand times over with the applications of the men who wish to play the congenial role of the 'Boatswain.'" The by-play, "What, Never?" was only one of a dozen lines that passed into universal use and there is a story of a newspaper editor harassed beyond endurance by its appearance in his columns who exclaimed, "Never let those words appear again in this paper." "What, never?" queried a wag in his office. "Well, hardly ever" groaned the miserable man.

Pinafore effected a complete change in the light musical stage of the metropolis. Previous to its advent the rage of the theater had been the characteristically Parisian Offenbach's "Grand Duchess," "Belle Helene" and other risque farces of the boulevards bowlderized, of course, to suit the taste of local audiences, but nevertheless still of a high Gallic flavor. Of domestic manufacture had been the "Black Crook," a phenomenally successful spectacle that held the stage for years, and was the limit of audacity for the times in its display of feminine outlines. "Pinafore" proved that success could be obtained with more refinement and that stage humor did not depend on innuendo. "Patience," "The Pirates of Penzance," "Iolanthe" and "The Mikado" by the same authors followed with undiminished favor, and even French composers contrived to achieve gayety without offense in "La Mascotte," "Olivette," "Girofle Girofla," "The Daughter of Mme. Angot," "Chimes of Normandy" and other delightful operettas. The success of these ventures led to the opening of the New York Casino in 1882 which immediately took rank as the City's Opera Comique and for years presented light opera of the highest class, notably the perdurable "Erminie," besides that of the

Viennese school, such as "The Gypsy Baron," "Merry War," "Fledermaus," "Beggar Student," etc.

One of the indestructible legends of the late nineteenth century stage was the "Florodora Girl." "The Florodora Girl" was the feminine 50 per cent. of a double sextette that sang the very taking "Tell Me Pretty Maiden Are There Any More at Home Like You," and made it one of the slang phrases of its time. It marked a distinct advance in the employment of the chorus in musical comedy by giving a dozen of its most personable members a song and dance "on their own," without principals. The average chorus man of the period was more renowned for vocal vigor than for any thespian graces, being principally employed in the "Drink to the Bride" type of operatic song. In the "Florodora" dozen, however, he appeared clad in the latest Piccadilly raiment with a silk "topper" paying court to an equivalent female of undeniable pulchritude attired in the latest Paris "creation," according to every detail of the New York *Herald's* "Daily Hint from Paris." The song was an instantaneous hit, and soon it was noised abroad that Miss Blank of the Florodora Sextette, was engaged to a scion of a noble house on Fifth Avenue. This began a matrimonial furore among the feminine portion of the Sextette that included admission to "Burke's Peerage." For years it was a fetish of the "Chorus lady" to claim membership in the "Original" Florodora Sextette, and only the implication of advancing years destroyed this pleasing fiction.

The chorus men of the "Florodora" Sextette have all gone down to oblivion. Not one of them married a great heiress or a countess, or figured in a sensational divorce, or lost his diamonds, or got on the first page of any newspaper whatsoever.

Among the merrymakers whose quips set little old New York roaring with laughter were the San Francisco Minstrels who disported in a band-box of a theater on Broadway at Twenty-ninth Street. Messrs. Birch, Wambold and Backus were among the last of the old school of negro minstrels, the one genuinely American contribution to the stage. The San Francisco Minstrels reflected current events in parody, caricature and burlesque to an intimate audience and were hugely entertaining. This is the way the liquor question was handled by Add Ryman the interlocutor of the company in a temperance discourse delivered in a preternaturally solemn manner: "I intend to put down every drop of liquor now in New York and I want all the business men to help me. I have made inquiries of a neighboring barkeeper, and I find that not more than two-thirds of the assemblage who listened to my discourse last night stopped at his place on their way home; the rest went to the beer-shop across the way." All the crazes of the day were lampooned in burnt cork—Pedestrianism, "Pinafore," "Pirates of Penzance" ("Pirates For Ten Cents"), politics; indeed the modern revue is but the minstrels in evolution.

To Charley Backus of this noted troupe nature had been lavish in bestowing a mouth of fearful and wonderful dimension. The contortions of this extraordinary feature used in singing "She Was Always Chewing Gum" was of the most mirth-provoking quality as was Nelse Seymour's song

> "I've a kid that's black and sassy, Baby Mine!
> And you cannot give him taffy, Baby Mine!
> He has bunions on his toes
> And a wart upon his nose
> And we wash him with a hose, Baby Mine!"

London music hall songs were also very popular with New York playgoers. Such songs as "Whoa, Emma!" "All on Account of Eliza" and "La de Dah" became prime favorites.

> "He wears a penny flower in his coat, La de Dah!
> And a penny paper collar round his throat, La de Dah!
> In his hand a penny stick,
> In his mouth an old toothpick;
> Not a penny in his pocket, La de Dah!"

Backus was not an Apollo, yet he wooed and wedded in succession two famous beauties of the time—Leo Hudson, an equestrian performer of note first and then Kate Newton, another lovely woman. His first venture was not a happy one, but his second was most propitious. After the death of his second wife he made a third choice, a widow in private life. Ere long rumor had it that the stork was hovering over his home and the opportunity for impromptu jests were not lost on his blackface colleagues. As the event drew near a necessary "Sairy Gamp" was engaged and Backus impressed on her the day when she was to be on hand.

The day came and with it early in the afternoon arrived the son and heir, but no "Sairy" until late that evening, when she expressed surprise at the unusual hour of the appearance of the little stranger, asserting to the indignant Backus that according to her experience "Sich things allus happened at night," to which Backus retorted, "My good woman, are you not aware that we professionals give matinees?"

The lighter amusement of *hoi polloi* was largely obtained in the variety theaters. As I have remarked, the term "vaudeville" was unknown until the Nineties. The splendid music halls of our present period had no exis-

CARMENCITA
Painted by William M. Chase. In the
Metropolitan Museum of Art.

tence until "variety" evoluted into "vaudeville" sponsored by such etymologists as Koster & Bial and Oscar Hammerstein. Ladies did not attend variety shows in large numbers. There was a good deal of coarse and offensive language indulged in until certain managers, such as Tony Pastor, emphasized their "clean" performances. Even here there was considerable double entendre though it remained for Koster & Bial on 23rd Street to "go the limit" on this. This famous resort and its "cork room" was patronized largely by the "wine openers" and their female consorts of the period. It was here that Carmencita, who has been immortalized on canvas by Sargent, danced. Here, too, appeared Fougere, one of the earliest of the Parisian "Cafe chantant" singers to thrill the blasé "Gothamite." Fougere sang some naughty little Boulevard ditties, which were declared by the press agent to be very devilish indeed and made a dynamic exit by exposing her nether *lingerie* to a breathless audience. Let me say that it was about this time the term *lingerie* was introduced to the New York underwear trade. Although Fougere's songs were in a language unknown to most of her audience there was nothing in her pantomime to contradict the enthusiastic assurances of the press agent.

Carmencita's American début was made at Niblo's Garden, in 1889. She had been a ballet dancer in Spain at a weekly salary of $20. The Kiralfys brought her from London where she was receiving $40 weekly. She did not draw at Niblo's, and it was only when she had been at Koster & Bial's for some time that she danced her way into public esteem and became the most celebrated Spanish dancer that New York has ever known. She appeared also for one night at the Tuxedo Park Country Club at the special invitation of George Griswold of the entertainment committee.

In 1893 Koster & Bial joined forces with Oscar Hammerstein and took possession of the grandiose Manhattan Opera House on Thirty-fourth Street, now the site of a section of Macy's. It was intended to make this a music hall on the lines of the famous Empire and Alhambra in London. At this house appeared Albert Chevalier, the coster singer, and Cissie Loftus, in their American débuts. The house was noted for long engagements and high salaries. Chevalier received $1,200 a week. Sandow, the strong man, played for five weeks at $1,000. Lois Fuller, the first of the afterward famous "butterfly" dancers, was paid $2,000 a week. The Martinette pantomimists received $1,000. Under this policy the house failed. About this time was formed the vaudeville organization called "The White Rats," which endeavored to keep salaries on the high level inaugurated at Koster & Bial's. The Keith and Proctor interests, however, joined interests and substituted stock companies and legitimate plays for vaudeville and employment to specialty performers was reduced seventy-five per cent.

Tony Pastor's at 585 Broadway and later on Fourteenth Street was a famous variety house (vaudeville was an unknown term). It was under the auspices of the genial Tony that Lillian Russell made her initial bow to the public in the Fourteenth Street Theater. Tony was also responsible for the Kernell Brothers, Kelly, "the Rolling Mill Man," and the stentorian Maggie Cline of "Throw Him Down McCloskey" fame.

One of the numerous incumbents of the little hall previously occupied by the San Francisco Minstrels at

Twenty-ninth Street and Broadway, was Alexander ("The Great") Herrmann, undoubtedly the cleverest, as he was the most entertaining, practitioner of the "black art" of magic, in New York's last fifty years. His feats were accompanied by a constant fire of small talk and witticisms which served the double purpose of amusing and at the same time diverting attention from the business in hand. Herrmann was a well-known figure about town, and like the true showman that he was lost no opportunity of broadcasting his fame beyond "Hermann's Theatre" as the little hall of necromancy was called.

Coming down from Albany in the smoking car, surrounded by members of the Legislature, Herrmann bought an apple from a train boy who came through the car at Poughkeepsie. As the boy was passing on, Herrmann halted him saying he wished to ascertain if the apple was sound. Thereupon he cut it into halves, when, behold, in the center of one of the divisions lay a shining silver dollar! Herrmann picked another apple from the basket and handling the astonished boy a second nickel, disclosed a second dollar when he divided the apple.

"Those are fine apples; I'll take the lot," exclaimed Herrmann. "No you won't!" ejaculated the boy, rushing from the car to the station platform, where amid the laughter of the crowd in the smoker and the jingle of the two dollars Herrmann tossed to him as the train moved onward, the lad sat, splitting his remaining apples, in a vain hunt for more coin.

One evening two of his friends, boasting of their intention to detect Herrmann in one of his tricks, took seats close to the stage; and Hermann, surmising their purpose, no sooner appeared than he handed each a twenty-dollar gold piece, saying, confidentially to them, that they should hold the coins in their closed right hands, and guard them carefully, as he intended to take the money from them without their knowledge, if he could.

The investigators nervously clutched their coins during the entire entertainment, occasionally examining them furtively, but oblivious to all else that was going on; when Herrmann had concluded his tricks, including the one his friends were to detect, they sheepishly handed him the money, as he blandly smiled at them and said, "You are too clever for me; I could not fool you, eh?"

The "Bouncer" in a Bowery Gallery, 1880.

It was to the theater, however, that New York mostly turned for its artistic pabulum and in perhaps no other direction can it show a more astounding development. New York was always a good "show town" from the days of the Park Theater to that of the One Hundred and Sixty-fifth Street Theater. The large polyglot population, to a great degree illiterate, turned to the playhouse for its common diversion. The late "Seventies" were to mark a pronounced development in the art of the theater. Up to that time Wallack's Theater had been the most potent agent in the presentation of the modern drama. Wallack's Stock Company year in and year out had been one of the fixtures of Broadway with an almost unbroken success. It was *the* theater of its time. Into the realm of the stock theaters in the early Seventies had come the young Augustin Daly destined to become the premier manager of the post Wallack period.

With the passing of Wallack's, Daly's Theater took first rank among Metropolitan playhouses. In 1879 Daly acquired the ramshackle old Broadway Theater near Thirtieth Street. His first year's rent was $14,000. The first step in the rehabilitation of the building was to obliterate every reminder of the "Museum" days among whose later attractions was a huge stone image called the "Cardiff Giant" which had been dug up years before on a farm in New York State and exhibited as the remains of a prehistoric man.

The famous Daly company was a result of that able manager's predilection to foster young ambition and the following letters are self-explanatory. To think of John Drew at $30 per week, and Ada Rehan at $35, is enough to make the present managers on Broadway scan their salary lists with pain. But to read the letters:

324 West 33rd Street.

My dear Mr. Daly: I beg to say that I will accept your offer of $30 or $35 per week for next season. Hoping sincerely that it may be in your power—as I am sure it is your inclination—to make it the latter.

I remain, very sincerely,

JOHN DREW.

Dear sir: I wish to formally close the engagement with you for the season of '79-'80. I accept your offer of $35 per week with the understanding that you will increase it as you promised should I be worth more to you which I sincerely hope will be the case.

Yours very truly,

ADA REHAN.

Byron Cottage,
Atlanticville, Long Beach,
July 9, '79.

Today's managers may be interested in Daly's expense account for the first season. Weekly salaries—17 ladies, 14 gentlemen—$1,077. 23 chorus—$248. Stage Hands —$236. Scenic artists—$60. Ushers, etc.—$88, and advertising—16 papers—$300.

Augustin Daly's Theater occupied a unique position in the metropolitan life, not only in the drama, but as a social institution. The opening of Daly's Theater, in the autumn, marked the beginning of high society's activities preceding the Horseshow and the Opera. Daly "first nights" were a roster of society and the rather small and select circle that formed its inner body were sure to meet friends and acquaintances at any performance.

Ada Rehan

But in the drama Daly was by far the best qualified entrepreneur that the New York playhouse has had. Originally a journalist, he was a cultured student of the Drama and to some extent a connoisseur in the arts. His home on Twenty-ninth Street, that served as stage entrance to his theater, was packed with antique furniture, works of art, and a magnificent library principally of dramatic subjects. His stage furniture and settings were formed from this collection and a drawing-room scene at Daly's did not look like a hotel parlor, as at some other theaters.

He brought to prominence such actresses as Agnes Ethel, Clara Morris, Fanny Davenport, Blanche Bates, Mary Mannering and the incomparable Ada Rehan. Miss Rehan, born Crehan, daughter of a Brooklyn Navy Yard mechanic, under Daly's tutelage became, according to the belief of competent judges, the most accomplished comedienne that the American stage has known. Her style was in the grand manner of the early English stage and to see her was to conjure from the past a Woffington or Jordan or other Eighteenth century queen of comedy. Only one other actress of her time could be mentioned in the same breath with her—Ellen Terry. The development of such an artist in the sordid commercialism of the New York stage is an achievement of no small moment, but it was no doubt Daly's ambition to form an organization analogous to the renowned Comedie Francaise. He had the players but America could not provide the plays. In John Drew, "Jimmie" Lewis, George Clarke and Mrs. Gilbert and others he maintained a company of players perfectly coordinating in all its functions.

A remarkable novelty introduced by Daly was a troupe of Nautch dancers from India. There were magicians

"HUGH TREVOR," IN ALL FOR HER.

"CHARLES MARLOW," IN SHE STOOPS TO CONQUER.

"HUGH CHALCOTE," IN OURS.

DON FELIX," IN THE WONDER.

"ADONIS EVERGREEN," IN MY AWFUL DAD.

"ELIOT GREY," IN ROSEDALE.

"JOHN GARTH," IN JOHN GARTH.

"LEON DEL MAR," IN THE VETERAN.

Lester Wallack in some of his best remembered characters.

in the troupe who were accompanied by their cobras, and
their manager wrote to Daly, "One of them is a little
seedy and his charmer is very low-spirited, but we have
hopes, as he still takes his regular rations. They are
enjoying the voyage, as healthy as possible under the
circumstances, snuggled in a bag which is snuggled in
a box. I hope some Custom Officer will put his hand
in there. *I think he will pass the rest of the chests.*"

Daly hired an entire floor of Bangs' Restaurant opposite the theater for the troupe. They were delighted with
it and with the opportunity to sit at the windows and
look out on Broadway. They performed the famous Indian basket trick in a comic opera called "Zamina, or the
Rover of Cambaye," in which Digby Bell made one of
his first successes. A little lad about twelve years old
stepped into a round basket less than a foot in height
and while stooping over a shawl was thrown over him.
This was seen gradually to subside as if the boy were
gradually melting in the basket. Upon the shawl being
replaced one of the men took a long sword and passed it
several times through the side of the basket until the
point showed on the other side. Then the shawl was
again spread over the basket, was violently agitated and
then thrown aside by the boy who stood up smiling before the spectators.

In personal appearance Daly carefully eschewed any
of the outward and visible signs of his profession. Not
for him were the loud checked suit, the flaming necktie
and the moth-eaten fur coat. He was distinctly the es-
thete. Of slight build, pale complexion, long hair and
drooping mustache he looked like the poet of fancy. In
his flat-topped derby and Inverness overcoat he was a
noted figure on the Broadway of his day.

The auction sale of Augustin Daly's effects held May 19, 1900, is full of interest to art lovers and antiquarians as giving an idea of prevalent prices. A portrait of Thackeray by himself in the frame of which there had lain concealed for years a letter from him to Lady Molesworth brought $350. A miniature of Jenny Lind by Inness brought the ridiculous sum of $52.50. An interesting document, the original petition (1842) for the erection of a statue to Washington in New York, bearing the autographs of W. Irving, Chancellor Kent, Fitz Greene Halleck, Henry Browne, Ed. Forrest, Moses H. Grinnell, N. P. Willis, Wm. Cullen Bryant, Sam F. Morse and other well-known New Yorkers sold for the munificent sum of $25. Four Shakespeare folios sold at the bargain price of $7,860. The arms and armor including a full suit for horse and rider (Joan of Arc), a suit of chain armor, a suit of plate armor and eight dress swords brought $312. Relics of Edmund Kean—Shylock's bond, scales and knife, properties used by him and his son Charles—in a glass cabinet sold for $115. A drawing by Watteau brought $17, two by Gainsborough $25 and $30. A miniature of Rachel, full length, by Jerome went for $270; a very remarkable collection, the original title deeds to Nell Wynne's house, Pall Mall, with three signatures by Nell (initials only) sold for $1,100. (Daly paid much more for these.)

Later there appeared on the scene A. M. Palmer, an able, keen and enterprising figure in the world of the theater. Wallack's later period was given to the production of plays of the English stage, conspicuous among which were the Robertson series, including that epoch-making comedy of the cup and saucer school, "Caste." Daly and Palmer went to the Continent for adaptation from the French and German. Clara Morris in "Camille," was the intense and vivid particular star, as also in "Frou Frou" and "Miss Moulton," while Palmer, at the Union Square Theater, made an enormous hit with that model of dramatic construction, "The Two Orphans." "Led Astray," "Rose Michel," etc., also enhanced his fortunes. In the classic drama there was but one name to conjure with, that of Edwin Booth; but his magnificent theater on Twenty-third Street at Sixth Avenue became a failure. Soon lesser lights also essayed Shakespeare with varying success. Let us glance over the following newspaper list of diversions:

SATURDAY, MARCH 19, 1877

Amusements this evening

Booth's Theatre—*Romeo and Juliet*—Geo. Rignold, Marie Wainwright, Frederick Warde.

Fifth Avenue—*Cymbeline*—Adelaide Neilson, Chas. Fisher, J. B. Studley.

Union Square—*Smike*—J. H. Stoddard—J. Parselle, Marie Wilkins.

Wallack's—*Rosedale*—Lester Wallack, J. H. Gilbert, Ada Dyas, Effie Germon.

Park—*The Gilded Age*—J. T. Raymond, Marie Gordon.

Grand Opera House—*The Princess Royal*—Fanny Davenport, John Brougham.

N. Y. Aquarium—Rare and Curious Fish.

National Academy of Design—Annual Exhibition of Paintings.

Heller's Wonder Theatre—Prestidigitation, Music, Humor.

Steinway Hall—Concert.

Central Park Garden—Music and Variety.

Chickering Hall—Lecture by Prof. Graham Bell—The Telephone.

The amount of genuine acting packed in the half-dozen dramatic performances in this programme would balance the equivalent in all the sixty-odd theaters in modern New York. The actors mentioned were products of the old stock system of changing repertoires and were trained in an arduous school. Lester Wallack's professional career comprised nearly one hundred and fifty roles mostly of the standard drama.

Saturday night at the Players' Club, 1890. Booth, Palmer, and Daly in group (standing)

A. M. Palmer presented at his houses such sterling artists as Charles R. Thorne, Sara Jewett, Maude Harrison, J. H. Stoddart, W. J. LeMoyne, Frederick Robinson, Maurice Barrymore, Annie Russell, Minnie Maddern and many others. Of the Union Square Theater a contemporary writes: "There is no other theater in this country which can be compared to the Union Square. The perfection of its stage pictures, the scenic artist, the stage manager, the property man, the stage carpenter and the actors are in such complete accord and under such strict discipline and intelligent direction that they work together like parts of a splendid piece of machinery." Such reading is strange in an age that believes it necessary to go to Berlin and Moscow for stage managers.

Palmer's management of the little Madison Square Theater was marked by the same ability he had shown at the Union Square. The Madison Square was devoted to a more intimate type of drama than the older house. It was the scene of the first of the crook plays so much in vogue today. "Jim, the Penman," the earliest of these, was the greatest success of its type, while "Captain Swift," with Maurice Barrymore in the title role, was one of its most notable successors. The Madison Square was noted for its long runs, one of its earliest productions, "Hazel Kirke," running for over 600 nights, while the later "Trip to Chinatown," had a still longer record. The theater was the first to introduce the novelty of a double stage. An act being concluded, the stage was elevated to the flys, while another stage that had been set below was raised in its place. It also originated the cold air system of ventilation in warm weather.

Of a wider scope were the comedies of Charles Hoyt, originally a Boston newspaper man. Hoyt very nearly reached the dignity of national satire in such plays as "A Texas Steer," "A Contented Woman," "A Milk White Flag," and others of his later period, but he was too genial a humorist to more than lightly roast his erring compatriots. His tenancy of the little Madison Square Theater on Twenty-fourth Street was marked by the run of over 600 nights (phenomenal in its day), of his "Trip to Chinatown," introducing the famous character of "Welland Strong," the hypochondriac—an amusing hit at people "enjoying bad health"—and the song of "The Bowery" which is certainly that celebrated highway's anthem, though considered by its merchants as a "hymn of hate." Among others of Hoyt's vastly amusing output were "A Brass Monkey," a satire on superstition, "A Bunch of Keys," a skit on hotels, and "A Midnight Bell," aimed at the rural hypocrite.

The theater of the early Eighties brought the beginnings of the present school of American drama. The great successes of the New York stage had for years previously been of foreign importation. Of course there had been a crude sort of melodrama and rough comedy of native manufacture, but nothing to approach the finished and artistic work of the British and French playwrights. Bartley Campbell was one of the last of the early school with his "White Slave," "Galley Slave," "Siberia," and best of all, "My Partner." Now came men like Bronson Howard with "The Henrietta," "Young Mrs. Winthrop," "Saratoga," "Banker's Daughter" and "Shenandoah," Gillette with "Held by the Enemy." Belasco and DeMille's "Charity Ball," "The Wife," at the

popular Lyceum Theater on Fourth Avenue, and later
Augustus Thomas' "Alabama," "Arizona," and "In Mis-
souri," Jas. A. Herne's "Shore Acres" and Clyde Fitch's
"Beau Brummel," "Lovers' Lane," "Captain Jinks," "The
Climbers," all of them the forerunners of the present
prosperous domestic drama.

Shakespeare, well acted, always drew the public. Men
like Booth, Barrett and McCullogh played the standard
drama year in and year out. One of the memorable
stars in Othello was Tommaso Salvini, who played in
Italian with English support. A wag of the time tran-
scribed the following:

> *Othello*—Ohi! dessa infida, a me?
> *Iago*—Why, how now General, no more of that.
> *Othello*—Vanne fuggi a la rota del tormenta Mi legasti, Oh!
> tel guiro a meglio assai Ingannato dell tutto azi che
> arlane Legger Sospetto.
> *Iago*—How now, my lord?
> *Othello*—De suoi Furtivi diletti. Quai provae senso.
> *Iago*—Go on, your story interests me much, my general.

Salvini was a man of giant physique and subjected his
"Iago" to such strenuous manhandling that one Irish au-
ditor when asked his opinion of the play replied, "I think
the naygur as good an actor as anny."

Of all the "hick" dramas of the New York stage none
ever equaled Denman Thompson's "Old Homestead."
Uncle Josh Whitcomb was first introduced to the stage
as a character in a variety sketch significantly labeled
"The Female Bathers." Uncle Josh caught on from the
start, was elaborated into a bucolic comedy in an urban
setting and toured the country with great success. It
ran 100 nights at the Bush Street Theater, San Francisco, the old "Forty Niners" going wild over the character of the New Englander.

Old London Streets on Broadway erected on site of Harrigan and
Hart's Theater, now Wanamaker's, 1887.

Among eminent merrymakers of the New York stage of forty years ago old playgoers will remember, with peculiar pleasure, the names of Harrigan and Hart and Charles Hoyt. The first named presented a series of hilarious farces depicting local low life with extraordinary realism. "The Mulligan Guards," "Squatter Sovereignty," "Old Lavender," "Cordelia's Aspirations," and a score of other mirthful pictures of the tenements. Their feuds were enjoyed alike by Fifth Avenue and the Bowery, as were their songs. Among the most popular of them were "Paddy Duffy's Cart," "The Babies on Our Block," "Denny Grady's Hack," etc., etc.

There used to be a coterie of playgoers in New York known as "first nighters." The "first nighter" originally bloomed in the late Eighties and was borrowed from similar institutions in London and Paris. Before this time, dress suits in theaters were rarities, but the "first nighter" felt it incumbent on his importance to adopt formal garb, and the common or garden playgoer quickly followed suit. It was a manager's ambition to have as many distinguished patrons of the drama at his premiers as he could allure, and the newspapers gave as much space to the names of "among those present" as it did to a criticism of the performance. Three names in after-time became a butt of the irreverent chronicler who termed them the "death watch" by reason of their participation in so many failures, but there were some august personages amongst them, and we cannot omit a reference to them. An old record tells us:

"As we pass the first nighters in review, the most commanding, the most delightful figure is that of the old warrior, Wm. Tecumseh Sherman. The front rank he led so well is now exchanged for the front row. The sturdy hand that wielded the sword is raised in graceful recognition of the pretty actress. Gen. Sherman's peculiarities as a first night attraction are unique and immense. He leans forward in his 'fauteuil' and fairly pushes his applause onto the stage. When his hands are idle his tongue wags gleefully with a running commentary.

"Not far from his old comrade and generally in the same row, sits another fighter who enjoys these piping times of peace. No first-class audience at the old Academy, The Metropolitan Opera House, Daly's, Palmer's, or Niblo's is ever complete without this grizzled veteran, and no well-conducted conductor would ever think of moving his baton until the thud of Gen. Sickle's crutch was heard coming down the center aisle."

Club life in New York always came in full force to these gala affairs, among them the members of the Union Club, such as Dr. David Haight, of Fifth Avenue and Fifteenth Street, one of the town's most famous old mansions. Dr. Haight "was a bachelor beau who still finds the greatest ease and pleasure in hearing love made on the stage." Other Union Club volunteers were Gen. William Cutting and his brother, Robert Cutting, Van Horn Stuyvesant, Henry Clews, and John Bloodgood. Then there were the Oelrich boys, Herman, Harry, and Charley "who got more fun out of a good play than the leading juvenile who had to hug the soubrette." Other noted clubmen were Lewis Rutherford de Garmendia Navaro, Hamilton Carey, Mr. Onativia and Tom Howard, leader of cotillions.

The bar sent such legal luminaries as Judge Brady, Judge Daly, Judge Barrett, and Judge Horace Russell whose pronouncements on the drama were as sound as those they delivered from the bench.

Among the "men about town" (these were a noted class when the town was smaller) invariably present at first nights were Mr. Joe Mora (the photographer), Billy Connor of the St. James Hotel, Fred Gould, "Charley" Delmonico, Marshall P. Wilder in his new English clothes, his gleaming hat, his Inverness cape—and Abe Hummell, "who invariably appears for the defense. No matter how many ideas the manager has stolen, or how horribly the Queen's English is murdered, he always makes a plea for the prisoner at the footlights, and usually succeeds in persuading at least twelve persons in the audience that the play is not half as bad as it looks."

There were many lady first nighters, too. Mrs. Stevens, "with a fortune of her own," Miss Otis with a paper of her own, Miss de Wolfe with a delightful talent of her own, "Aunt" Louise Eldridge, and Mrs. Lord with her big diamonds ought to have a special column.

It is curious though, that our cleverest actresses prefer the first night symphony of swallowtails and the resounding encouragement of lavender kid gloves.

The playgoers of every age have laughed at the crudities of the stage of their predecessors, all unconscious of the absurdities of their own. Today's sophisticated audience thinks that "the villain still pursued her" school of melodrama of the past just too screamingly funny for anything, quite insensible to the fact that the villain is still pursuing her as relentlessly as ever, if not more so, in the movies. This attitude of superiority is no new thing. The period of "The Danites," "The Galley Slave," "Siberia," and other blood congealers of the drama was moved to unrestrained risibility in contemplating its ancestral prototypes of the old Bowery such as "Nick o' the Woods, or Bloody Nathan, the Avenger," and other glorious examples of the "Wake Me Up When Kirby Dies" school. The elements that compose melodrama are always the same, only the treatment changes.

Among the more brilliant disciples of the "blood and thunder" drama of forty years ago was N. S. Woods of "Boy Detective" fame. Woods played the "Boy Detective" until he was as old as the fabled *coryphee* of his period who introduced a stage-door admirer to her mature granddaughter. The detective of popular fiction then stalked like Nemesis through the "Old Sleuth" and "Old Cap Collier" series, dear to the heart of the messenger boy, and found his stage counterpart in Woods' personification.

The most delightful thing about the "Boy Detective" was that you never, or hardly ever, knew when he was on the stage. He was in a perpetual stage of disguise. The criminals plotting the kidnapping of the banker's daughter pay no heed to the old woman asleep on the adjoining bench in the railroad station, but as they go off, saying, "tonight at ten, then" the supposed old woman with surprising agility leaps to her feet and cries, "The Boy Detective will be there." But the great scene of the play is in the counterfeiters' underground den. The coiners are assembled and among them a sailor, who is to "shove some of the queer." Now I am not going to deceive my reader, but this very sailor was none other than Butts—that was his name—the Boy Detective, who is on hand to see the law vindicated. He is stealing toward the rickety steps leading upward—and only then does the audience suspect his identity—when he is observed by one of the band who sounds the alarm. "Who are you?" demands the leader of the gang. Standing at the head of the stairs our hero declaims in ringing tones, at the same time producing a pair of six shooters, "I am Butts, the Boy Detective," and the curtain falls amid a pandemonium of whistles, cat calls and shouts from the gallery.

There is no doubt that John L. Sullivan was better acquainted with the rules of the celebrated Marquis. of Queensbury than he was of the laws of the almost equally celebrated Thespis, but this did not prevent Mr. Sullivan from donning the figurative sock and buskin as an interlude in his strenuous vocation of pounding his fellow creatures into insensibility. Mr. Sullivan's prowess in the ring enabled him to achieve this happy result with a certain celerity that was denied his auditors in the theater. These unfortunates at the end of the third act of a dramatic masterpiece called "Honest Hearts and Willing Hands" were in the condition termed by the pugilistic reporter as "groggy"; indeed so much so that large numbers of staggering figures might have been seen emerging from the theater seeking the nearest barroom, therein to be "brought round" and to arrive at the consensus that as an actor Mr. Sullivan was a very fine prize fighter indeed. In the fourth act, however, the playright had very skilfully brought his drama to a happy ending in an exchange of fisticuffs in which Mr. Sullivan with characteristic zeal and in a pair of emerald green trunks upheld the honor of the American flag,

Some of the Gallery Gods

the sanctity of home, rights of labor, Home Rule and other abstract principles dear to the gallery.

John L.'s delivery of the lines allotted to him by the cautious dramatist recalled little Johnnie Jones' rendition of childhood's classic "Cassabianca," allowing for vocal bull power. It also recalled with a singular vividness the elocution of that immortal mariner Capt. Jack Bunsby—"a gruff, husky utterance, which seemed to have no connection with Bunsby, and certainly had not the least effect on his face."

Nor were Mr. Sullivan's green trunks his only sartorial embellishment in the drama. The ingenious playwright had contrived to garb his hero at one period in a white flannel beach suit. Nothing was lacking but the price ticket to convert the King of the Bruisers into a first class clothing store manikin, for Mr. Sullivan's gestures were entirely confined to those essential to the "noble art."

The old pugilists led a precarious existence in New York. The law banned his calling and every policeman's club was against him. There was no state partnership with sluggers as there is today. Public bouts were labelled "exhibitions" and these were under police supervision. When Sullivan knocked Mitchell from the ring at Madison Square Garden, Capt. Williams and his myrmidons immediately cleared the premises of the howling, hooting mob. When Firpo executed the same emphatic gesture on Dempsey not long ago, Mr. Dempsey was hoisted back to the arena, restoratives applied, after which the celebrated North American matador proceeded to demolish the "Wild Bull of the Pampas."

Forty years ago Mr. Dempsey would have been fighting for meagre stake-money in a Long Island swamp or New Jersey meadow, surrounded by a genial band of plug-uglies and assorted blackguards who had been tipped off to the place of meeting. No Superior Court Judge, Wall Street potentate, or Union clubman would have been present to see the interesting ceremonies of "first blood" and "first knock-down" (that is, not for publication). Under such conditions many championship contests were pulled off, among those being McAuliffe's battle with Reagan in the Long Island mud, Sullivan's conquest of Flood on a North River barge, and Corbett's battle with Choynski off the batteaus of Louisiana.

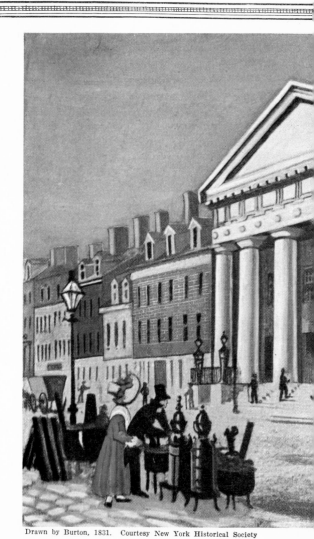

Drawn by Burton, 1831.   Courtesy New York Historical Society

ORIGINAL BUILDING.

Public sentiment against prize-fighting, was a survival of the brutalities of the old London prize ring exemplified by "Yankee Sullivan," Heenan, Hyer, Morrisey, et al. From the days of these worthies until the passing of the Horton Law the pugilistic art was practiced under great difficulties, and it was only the top-notchers who found it lucrative. In one sense it was superior to the modern school. There was no social atmosphere introduced. No bruiser was seconded by his mother. Nor were the prayers of the little tots saved by the receipts of the Babies' Milk Fund broadcast the length and breadth of this fair land. "Ladies" were not present at the ring-side and even such persuasive and delightful persons as Miss Anne Morgan and Mrs. William Randolph Hearst could not have hired the old Windsor Hotel for a "scrap" in aid of anything.

There has been as much humbug in the "uplift" of the ring as there has been in the "uplift" of the stage. The newly discovered "gentleman" boxer, so much in the forefront at present, is no modern phenomenon. He existed as far back as the days of "Gentleman Jackson" who was intimate with Byron and of John Morrisey who went to Congress. The old-time ring had quite as large a percentage of well-behaved, modest representatives as has today's. It is proverbial that the genuine bruiser avoids private brawls, and considering the fact that he was an outlaw for decades, his record is not shocking. In earlier days he was under the patronage of "noble lords" and acquired a passable knowledge of social usages—enough at least to keep him out of trouble. He has always been exploited by managers, showmen, and other experts in the gentle art of "ballyhoo" who have been quick to sense the public relish for the conflicting types of "gentlemen" and "cave man" boxer and the resultant financial returns.

One of the fascinations of by-gone days was the military bands belonging to the National Guard. Such bands as Gilmore's, Gonfula's, Cappa's, Fanciulli's, or Conterno's aroused the enthusiasm of the dense crowds that used to line Fifth Avenue on Decoration Day, or at the famous parades of the Washington Centennial, Columbus Celebration or Dewey's Day. They had stirring marches too while leading the gallant militiamen in dress parade uniform through the cheering crowds. "The Boulanger March," glorifying the general who tried to restore French royalists to the throne, was one of the great musical epidemics of two hemispheres, and did more to advertise that misguided French soldier in America than anything of his own doing. Almost equally popular was the "Father Victory" march which succeeded the "Boulanger" in favor.

The National Guard made a brave showing in those days. Their dress uniforms were gay and resplendent. The city's pet regiment, the "7th," wore gray swallowtail coats and white duck trousers like the West Point Cadets. The "22nd" with the famous "Pat" Gilmore, as bandmaster, wore cream colored tunics. These were the "crack" local regiments and the dandies of the city's militia. Their balls and dances were "classy" social events. The funds for the completion of the present 7th Regiment Armory on Lexington Avenue were raised by a fair which attracted wide attention and was visited by thousands throughout the city.

Street urchins enjoying the Sprinkling Cart

Other public amusements of that time may be recalled by the following. About the year 1884 a rage for roller skating seized upon the normally perpendicular New Yorker and a place was opened known as Cosmopolitan Hall on the site of the present Broadway Theater at Forty-first Street. All classes and all ages indulged in this rather unstable but fascinating exercise. The shrieks of buxom ladies acquiring unpremeditated seats in their then fashionable bustles mingled with the blare of the brass band in the balcony playing "Sweet Violets" and many other incitements to gayety were not lacking while the fad lasted.

The police problem of escaping criminals was ingeniously solved by the writer of the following letter to the Commissioner during the roller skating craze.

[191]

"I desire to call your attention to the advisability of furnishing roller skates for the patrolmen of the City of New York; as it would be almost impossible for a culprit of any kind to get away from an officer in the street who had roller skates on as they can make remarkably fast time with them. Under the circumstances they would have the disreputable at a great disadvantage which would certainly do the public good and at the same time change the phrase 'I'll take you in' to 'I'll roll you in,' yours, etc., John E. Smith, 96 West Twenty-second Street."

Roller skating also reached the six-day craze as the following item of the year 1885 shows:

"Fifteen men clad in fancy colored costumes started on a six-day roller skating match in Madison Square Garden at 12.05 this morning. Long before that hour there had been a steady stream of persons pouring into the Building and when the men began their journey there were about five thousand persons present. For two hours before the start Gilmore's Band furnished a 'Grand Sacred Concert' which included 'Sweet Violets,' 'Only a Pansy Blossom,' and 'Peek-a-Boo.'"

This same Cosmopolitan Hall was the scene of some of the exploits of Prof. Gleason, a celebrated horse trainer and successor of the famous Rarey, who undertook the taming of any horse, however vicious, in public view. There was then a large area of stables and horse salesrooms in the vicinity of the hall and the Professor never lacked subjects for his abilities.

One of the best known characters of the "Tenderloin" was an eccentric negro called "The Whistling Coon." He had none of the darkey's characteristic volubility, but was taciturn and solemn to the last degree. But he whistled like a bird and would shuffle from cafe to cafe, a unique minstrel warbling popular melodies and gathering thereby no inconsiderable coin of the realm. A variety hall song of the period describes him:

"Oh, I've seen in my time some very funny folks,
But the funniest of all I know
Is a colored individual as sure as you're alive

As black as any black crow.
You may talk till you're tired, but you'll never get a word
From this very funny queer old coon;
He's a knock-kneed, double jointed, hunky-punky moke
And he's happy when he whistles this tune."

A primitive "educational" diversion of those pre-cinema days was the cyclorama of battle scenes. The best of these were the work of Philpotteaux, an eminent French master in the art. A building on the northeast corner of Seventh Avenue and Fifty-fifth Street exhibited for successive years "The Siege of Paris," "Battle Between the Monitor and the Merrimac," and "The Siege of Vicksburg." Somewhat later the "Battle of Gettysburg" was shown at the cyclorama on the Southeast corner of Fourth Avenue and Nineteenth Street. Veterans of the war would visit these places in large numbers, with children, and delighted in pointing out the positions they had occupied in the battle. The panoramas were very realistic in their combinations of art and nature. The spectator stood on what was supposed to be a central position in the field—on a platform built over an embankment of real earth, while all around on an immense canvas was unfolded the clash of the contending forces.

An interesting occasion is recorded by the following: "The New Eden Musee was formally opened to the public last Saturday after a private view attended by many society people last Friday evening. The building is very handsome and substantial and runs through from Twenty-third to Twenty-fourth Streets between Fifth and Sixth Avenues. The Musee is intended to be a replica of the Musee Grevin of Paris and Mme. Tusand's of London. A good museum, like Topsy, must just grow; it cannot be made to order. The wax work figures at the Eden are too new to be artistic, so are most of the costumes. For example the Prince Imperial lies dead in a uniform fresh from the tailor's without a wound to show how he died, or a speck of dirt to suggest that he has fallen. The portraits are rather green and most of the personages seem suffering from swelled heads. The Chamber of Horrors is too horrible for people with weak nerves. In a word the Eden Musee is Frenchy when it should be American; but it will become Americanized bye and bye, when we get a popular murderer in the Tombs, and as it is opened to stay, there will be plenty of time for the improvements and additions." Notwithstanding this rather disparaging comment, the Musee became very popular and the "Chamber of Horrors" especially, became one of the goals of the rustic visitor to the city.

The popular murderer alluded to was one of the standard attractions of a certain type of New York femininity. It was one of the delicate attentions of the latter to send floral tributes to atrocious assassins in the guise of philanthropic interest. A Tombs cell embowered in roses, lillies of the valley and other tender blooms became quite an arboreal retreat, with only a locked grating to remind its occupant of durance vile. Henry Clay perfectos and a novel by "Ouida" completed the attendant comforts of this snuggery and consoled its sanguinary tenant for his loss of liberty.

The pioneer of the present prolific school of travel lecturers was Professor Cromwell, who is thus described in a contemporary journal.

"Professor Cromwell has been for years a recognized institution and has been immortalized by Oliver Wendell

Drawn by C. Kessler

"TO EDEN MUSEE, PLEASE!"

This popular place of amusement was in West 23rd Street near Sixth
Avenue, and for many years was the delight of our country cousins.
It departed with the decline of 23rd Street as a shopping center

Holmes in a letter which he proudly quotes at the head of his announcements. 'To sit in the darkness,' said Mr. Holmes, 'and have these visions of strange cities, of stately edifices, of lovely scenery, of noble statues, steal out upon the consciousness and melt away, one with another, is like dreaming a long, beautiful dream with eyes wide open.' "

A successor to Cromwell was John L. Stoddard who varied his oratory with the printed page and issued a series of immense tomes, containing photographs of famous scenes and places which became the successor in countless parlors to the ponderous red plush family album with the brass clasp.

This period might well be termed "The Age of Plush," for there was an immense demand for this material in every quarter. There were ladies' plush coats and boys' plush caps. Parlor furniture was almost exclusively plush. The crayon portrait of Daddy in the best room, usually acquired as a reward for consuming an incredible quantity of a certain tea, had a plush bordered frame. There were plush portieres and window draperies of the same. Theater drop curtains and seats were plush, so were railway car seats, the latter constituting one of the joys of travel in hot weather, especially when complicated with the siftings of soft coal. Pullman cars were padded cells of plush, framed in mahogany in a state of polish only possible under Senegambian supervision. There seemed no limit to the use of this material and its part in utilitarian and decorative purposes was universal. It achieved its greatest success in dolmans and sacques as a substitute for genuine Hudson Seal.

The Civil War was still a very live issue in the Eighties. Many there were who "didn't know the war

Election night, Madison Square, 1888

A torchlight parade in '76

was over." The Grand Army of the Republic was a
very powerful influence in politics and it was only
necessary for the Republicans to nominate a candidate with a Civil War record to insure his election.

The pension scandals and the "bloody shirt" furnished vital issues in politics until the election of
Cleveland in '84 after a bitter and hard-fought campaign. Political campaigns in those days were far
more picturesque episodes than they are now. Immense
parades with thousands in line, torchlight processions,
and huge banners on all the principal streets testified
to the popular interest in politics. The elections themselves were usually attended with great disorder as
there was no secret ballot. The ignorant or venal
voter was handed his ballot by a political henchman

at the very doors of the voting place and was watched as he deposited it in the box. The "machine" was all powerful, the candidate was supported or "knifed" as the word of the leaders went forth. The vote was "delivered" by thousands including "repeaters" and "floaters" and the returns from the "silk stocking" districts were greeted with grins by the heelers of the East Side.

Bonfires to celebrate election; scene in the old Sixth Ward.
When and how did this custom originate?

Drawn by C. Kessler

A "snappy" dresser in the Seventies

CHAPTER IV

FIFTY years ago the department store was just in process of formation in New York. The name was not then known; "Dry goods stores," "Emporiums," or "Bazaars" were the titles applied to the immense establishments that were then spreading the fame of the city as a mercantile center. The modern institution as we know it is an evolution of the old-fashioned "general store" whose merchandise ranged from cellar whitewash to patent roofing, with all intermediate necessities in stock.

Each of these stores was noted for certain lines of commodities according to the antecedents of their founders and proprietors. A store like Stewart's, for instance, was renowned for linens; McCreery's, for silks; Arnold Constable, for British dress goods; Ehrich, for laces, etc.

Curiously enough, the one store left today which is yet strictly mid-Victorian and still sports the celebrated Lamson Cash Carrier system, is noted, of all things, for supremacy in that ungodly article—silk tights for actresses! Shades of Calvin and John Knox! How this rock-ribbed Presbyterian concern should ever have contracted such an unholy alliance with the spirits of evil remains to this day an unsolved mystery. But old Daniel & Son still pursue the even tenor of their way, safe in the righteousness of a valuable and ancient lease from the Sailor's Snug Harbor.

The term Dry Goods implied utter absence of delicatessen, hardware, drugs, sporting goods, beauty parlors, chiropodists, matinee concerts, dentistry, and the million other dependencies of the modern "merchant prince."

The lady shopper of the time was a far better informed customer than is her descendent of today. She was acquainted with the names and qualities of the linens, calicoes, silks, muslins and woolens on sale. She had to be, as there was nothing like the present system of advertised brands. Except in the case of a few of the larger shops the general motto of the storekeeper was, "Let the buyer beware!" A sign frequently met with was, "One Price Only," significant of the bargaining that was common to those leisurely days. There was nothing like the amount of "ready made" that is the principal article of commerce in the shops today. Every well-conditioned household had its seamstress to make up raw materials for feminine wear, and even male apparel was indebted to domestic needlework for shirts and other intimate garb. The home sewing-machine was the greatest benefaction bestowed on the 19th century housewife. There was nothing like the sudden changes of feminine fashion that give impetus to the shopping trade today. A silk dress was a substantial garment intended to do yeoman service as a "Sunday best." Calicoes, ginghams, muslins, etc., were the common garb, while among the more genteel classes the finer cambrics, linens and lawns were in demand. There was a great deal more charm in a dainty, fragrant, freshly laundered cotton gown in the summer time than in the incongruous silk (?) "creations" and "summer furs" that mark the grotesque modes of today. As for "mercerized" fabrics, they were unknown.

The big store then presented some radical differences from today's customs. The most conspicuous

Sport costumes, 1888. Riverside Drive near 80th Street

human object in view on entering the main door was an encyclopedic individual known as a "floorwalker," to whom the stranger turned timidly for direction. This functionary was a sort of mercantile Jupiter, to whom all appeals and complaints were made. He had the bearing of an Apollo, and the grace and gallantry of a Brummel. His most flourishing period was the "Prince Albert," named after the frock coat then the formal afternoon garment which he affected. This, combined with a luxuriant mop covering the whole face, and the brilliantly glossed linen then in vogue, served to make him a personage of uncommon dignity. He has been superseded by the "aisle man" and elevator operator, but will be long remembered.

The varied nomenclature bestowed upon store attendants these days was covered by the one and all-embracing title—"Shop Girl." "She Was Only a Shop Girl at Macy's," was one of the popular songs of the day. Generally speaking, the number of women employed in these stores, compared with the men, was still insignificant.

The strident cry of "Cash," accompanied by an impatient staccato of pencil rappings on the sales counter, was the most musical utterance that could possibly greet the ears of the owner of the "Grand Street Emporium," or the "Fourteenth Street Bazaar." It was the exultant cry of the shop girl bringing home the bacon. It was directed to a diminutive boy or girl of preternatural aspect who appeared, ariel-like, at the summons to convey the spoils to the cashier, and return with change, if such should be forthcom-

Jerome Park on a Race Day, 1886

ing. These human shuttles were of an age that today would bring them under the provisions of the compulsory school act. As a matter of fact they were even then subject to the truant officer, but their pitiable earnings often eked out a family's subsistence, and there was no public clamor for their suppression. Their emancipation, like so many others in the history of mankind, was the result of mechanical invention, the Lamson Cash Carrier, the familiar trolley apparatus of recent years.

An echo of their ancient spirit rappings still persists in the story told of Wm. R. Travers, the famous wit of New York society. Travers was one of an assemblage gathered under the chairmanship of A. T. Stewart to discuss some matters of moment. Stewart tapped on the rostrum with a pencil calling for order, when from Travis' corner issued a voice calling in a simulated female treble—"Cash!"

North of Ireland men and Scots, emulating A. T. Stewart and other extraordinary forerunners, were preferred in the sale of the linens and textiles, for which their native heaths were celebrated. They were valuable to their employers in their knowledge of these goods, and their intelligence in transacting business with the knowing shopper who was not easily gulled by fancy names applied to commonplace material.

As wages increased there was some adverse comment on the tendency of the saleslady to outdo her customer in her general splendor of costume. They even rivalled the present-day stenographers in the financial district, and certain of the higher class shops issued a fiat prescribing a modified form of apparel

Drawn by C. Kessler

THE "BRIMSTONE" MATCH

"Brimstone" or sulphur matches were all we had until the parlor match came in. The latter had a habit of sending sparks in every direction and were kept in a tin box to avoid spontaneous combustion

on the order of the large European shops. This is the general rule today.

The present lot of the department store employee is a vast improvement on that of her early predecessor. In matters of hygiene, mental and physical comfort; and encouragement for a "career" there has been an incomparable advancement. There is no longer need for "Heaven to Protect the Woiking Goil," as Fay Templeton used to sing. That is now attended to by chaperones, nurses, doctors, health examiners, cheer leaders, and lastly, by the moral uplift in the store's own rules which decrees that no employees of the opposite sex shall be seen together within two blocks of the building adorned by their presence.

To a large extent the former excess of male attendants has been reduced. The Scotch and the Irish are in the grocery chain stores or the movies. The entire atmosphere is wholly changed and for the better. No longer is the natural attitude of the salesperson one of suppressed hostility toward the customer. Gone is the ineffable scorn which the poorly attired purchaser invariably encountered; some of us still smart from the dirty look which accompanied some such remark as "we don't carry nothin' so cheap as that." Along with the improvements physically have come equally important changes mentally. No customer today drops in a dead faint when she is greeted from behind the counter with a cordial "good morning" nor does the heaven-born genius on the other side require first aid merely because a patron has said "thank you!" Life in the big stores is once more worth living and all hands are the gainers.

The change of title from "shop girl" to "saleslady" was a gradual yet irresistible trend of the times. The term "saleslady" was not altogether an accurate description as many an intending patron has learned. Her ladyship was wont to discuss matters of personal interest with a colleague at the adjoining counter, and it was sometimes with difficulty that the customer was able to negotiate a purchase. Much conversation concerning social affairs in the lower wards, was inadvertently conveyed to the unwilling listener. This gossip was almost an essential relaxation from the day's toil and consisted largely of "Sez I to him"; "sez he to me"; "ain't he grand?"; "Oh, he's swell," etc. Impatient interruption by the would-be purchaser was greeted with a stony stare and arching of the eyebrows that completely cowed the reckless intruder.

Considerable feeling was also stirred up at this time by the question of properly describing the sexes. For years the ferryboats, then a most popular means of travel, and the highest authority on etomological problems, had summarily settled the question by naming one side of the boat "Gent's Cabin" and the other "Ladies." Gradually the feeling grew that this was not exactly right. All over the city, particularly the east side, where correct form was a religion and not a habit, the male section writhed under the title "Gents." The first adoption of Gentlemen was not, however, attained without the shedding of blood. A Literary and Musical Coterie (they were all called Coteries, though that was also a mystery) brought matters to a crisis. Throwing caution to the winds they boldly announced on their posters, "Tickets admitting Gentlemen and Ladies, 50c." In some mysterious underground fashion—no one knows exactly how—the impression gained ground that this was the latest thing in "side" and the idea was quickly imitated. This really was such a shock to the beau monde of Grand and Hester Streets that when the simpler and correct form of Men and Women, was first discussed, there was not enough snap left in anyone to combat it.

The shop girls or "salesladies" of those days were a motley crew. Many were spinsters of uncertain age; some were widows; most of them kept in employment by sheerest necessity. Their work was poorly paid, their hours long and tedious. Some idea of their situation may be gleaned by the fact that an act of legislature was necessary to provide seats behind the counters for them, when not engaged in serving customers. Many of the stores kept open Saturday nights and for weeks preceding Christmas the days were lengthened almost into months.

There was but one arbiter of ladies' fashions in the Eighties and that was the renowned "Worth" of Paris. "Worth decrees bustles," "Worth decrees balloon sleeves," "flounces, street train, high neck, low neck, no neck, wasp waist"; feminine apparel was a very intricate affair to the plodders of the "Ladies' Mile" on Broadway and Twenty-third Street, and *sotto voce* let me tell you that a young lady in a snug fitting jersey and a "Tam O'Shanter" was not hard to look at on the croquet lawn.

But a word here about "Gent's Furnishings," that happy phrase that had its rise in those pre-pajama days. The term "Haberdasher" was a Madison Square affectation that brought to the mind of Tompkins Square a picture of an effete Briton with a monocle, a double peaked tourist cap, a checked great coat and spats. This apparition inhabited the pages of *Puck* and *Judge* and the burlesque stage from Harry Miner's to Koster and Bial's. "Gent's Furnishings" implied none of this and thus became favored of the outfitter's signboard. It signified *boiled* shirts with solid, impregnable, glossy bosoms, drawn over the head, "choker collars," made up neckties, elastic bows, or others simply hooked on the collar button; underwear of an incredible thickness and bulk, including the highly favored red flannel of the outdoor laborer, red flannel being superstitiously regarded by the wearers as a sure preventive of rheumatism, cholera morbus, chilblains and other climatic disorders. Embroidered suspenders, of a strength calculated to sustain the bronze trousers of Daniel Webster's statue in the Park, were in demand by cautious purchasers. Nightgowns were the universal nocturnal toga, pajamas being an eccentricity of some youthful members of the Knickerbocker Club. Sleeveless and knee length underwear was unknown, and the outing shirt for summer wear was of a substantial flannel favorably regarded as an absorbent of perspiration.

Ready made clothing was regarded as plebeian. Strangely enough, the creases which always betrayed the ready made clothes, became afterwards the sacred emblem of the custom-made garment and are now meticulously renewed by "snappy" dressers throughout the life of a suit. *Costume de rigueur* for an afternoon call was a plug hat, a diagonal Prince Albert, Congress gaiters, check trousers, a heavy watch chain and a locket containing family portraits.

Old Fifth Avenue—The Daniel Parrish House,
Corner of 16th Street

About this period Fifth Avenue, below Madison
Square, contained perhaps the most important group
of socially prominent families ever before contained
in a similar short stretch of territory. Beyond the
Square were perhaps wealthier families but not quite
as old or so well known.

On the west side of Fifth Avenue and Washington
Square was the large Georgian house of the Misses
Julia and Serena Rhinelander where they lived for the
last forty or fifty years of their lives. It is now an
apartment house. The family were always held in
high respect and were very benevolent and public
spirited. The Church of the Holy Trinity on East
Eighty-ninth Street was erected by them in memory

of their father and they were very generous in their patronage of the Church of the Ascension on the corner of Fifth Avenue and Tenth Street.

The Howland family, likewise very prominent in the social history of New York, lived for a lifetime in the house adjoining the Rhinelander home. The older Howland in connection with William H. Aspinwall founded a very great business connection with China and the firm of Howland and Aspinwall for reputation and wealth stood at the head of the commercial houses in New York at the time of which we are writing. Mr. Howland, Sr., married twice. By his first wife he had a son, the Reverend Robert Howland, who built the Church of Heavenly Rest at Fifth Avenue and Forty-fifth Street. His second son made his home chiefly in Paris. His second marriage was to a Mrs. Merideth of Baltimore and three sons were born—Gardiner G. Howland, Merideth and Samuel Shaw Howland, and a daughter, who subsequently married Mr. J. W. Clendenin. The younger branch of the Howland family were very prominent in many ways in the city, Mr. Gardiner Howland being for a long time manager of the *New York Herald*. Mr. S. S. Howland married the daughter of August Belmont and associated himself very closely with racing and sporting interests in the country, having charge at one time of Mr. August Belmont's stables.

The Langdon family in Washington Square, at the time of which we write, was connected by marriage with the Astors. Mr. Walter Langdon, spent most of his time on his beautiful estate at Hyde Park on the Hudson River. He had a town house at Lafayette

Place. Mr. Eugene and Mr. Walter Langdon were sons of the older branch.

Directly opposite was his brother-in-law, Mr. Wilkes, a Canadian, who married another of the Langdon sisters. Mrs. Kane was a Langdon. The next generation of Langdons was represented by Col. de Lancey Kane, Walter, Woodbury and Nicholson Kane.

Mr. Graham was on the north side where today a very comfortable apartment house is a notable feature of that part of the square. The name of the Grahams was well known in the city and highly esteemed. During the Civil War the firm of Schuyler, Hartley and Graham were purveyors to the U. S. Government of military material of high grade. Dr. Wilkes' home, next to Mr. Langdon's, was the headquarters for many years of musical and intellectual gatherings. Dr. Wilkes had lived for many years in St. John's Park. He was closely allied by marriage to Governor Colden, so well known in the history of New York. Miss Grace Wilkes was extensively identified with St. Mary's Hospital in West Thirty-fourth Street.

In Washington Square was also the home of Alexander Hamilton, one of the younger sons of the celebrated General bearing that name. Mr. Hamilton was a lawyer of distinction. He spent a very large portion of his time during the last years of his life at "Nevis," his home at Irvington on the Hudson which is now occupied by Coleman Dupont.

Mrs. John Minturn, who was Louisa Aspinwall, was one of the last residents to move from this attractive neighborhood. So likewise was W. D. Morgan who had married a Miss Hoyt, closely connected with

Old Fifth Avenue—A May day at 59th Street Plaza, 1890

A bit of old Fifth Avenue—The Marshall O. Roberts and Hezron A. Johnson houses, corner of 18th Street

the Livingstons and other well-known families of long standing in the city.

On the north side of Washington Square, from Fifth Avenue eastward, was University Place. The corner was occupied by James Boorman, also by Butler Duncan, afterwards by Edward Cooper, the son of the philanthropist, and who was Mayor of New York for two terms. It was occupied by his daughter Mrs. Lloyd Brice after his death, and subsequently by Eugene Delano and lastly by Rodman Wanamaker who is its present tenant.

Facing eastward is the residence of Edward M. Tailer, who married Miss Suffern, a descendant of the old Suffern family. Mr. John C. Green occupied the house next adjoining, Mr. Green being a retired merchant of the firm of Russell & Co. of China and Hong

Kong. Mrs. Green had been a Miss Griswold from the family in Lymne, Connecticut. No. 8 was the home of Philip M. Lydig, of a very old family connected with the Suydams and Mesiers. Mr. Lydig lived first opposite the City Hall, removed to St. Johns Park and ultimately to Washington Square. To the east of No. 7 North Washington Square the house was occupied by the widow of John Johnston and the mother of John Taylor Johnston, well known in the New York social and art world. No. 6 was occupied by Mr. Redmond and his family who were closely connected with families of distinction in the social life of the city. No. 5 was the home of Mrs. Woolsey, the sister-in-law of Mr. Wm. H. Aspinwall and a widow of wide activities and distinction.

Between Washington Square and Broadway, in Washington Place, lived Francis R. Rives, who married the daughter of the British Consul, George Barclay. Then there were General James I. Jones of the Jones' Wood family; Matthew Morgan who had large business interests in New Orleans; Commodore Vanderbilt; William Remsen; James Seldon and David Wagstaff.

In University Place, going north, many prominent families resided. At the corner of Tenth Street was the house of Mr. Aspinwall with its great art gallery, one of the show places of town. Admittance was by card on application. On the northeast corner of Twelfth Street was the residence of Mrs. R. Tilden Auchmuty and Col. Auchmuty.

Turning toward Fifth Avenue we find on the southwest corner of Eighth Street the home of John Taylor Johnston, now occupied by his daughter, Mrs. Mali. On the northeast corner of Eighth Street is the

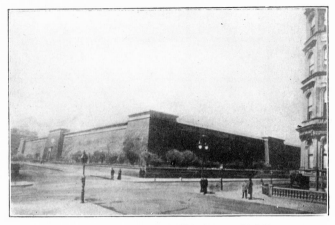

The old Reservoir, corner of Fifth Avenue, 42nd Street, where the Library now stands, 1885

Brevoort House. History is replete with anecdotes of interest about this house for many years previous to the Civil War and up to the present. Diagonally across on the northwest corner of Ninth Street was the old Brevoort home. Charles de Rham was the owner and a respected citizen. He was an importer of goods from Switzerland and France. On the northeast corner of Ninth Street, General Daniel E. Sickles settled after coming from the battles of the Civil War. Like Sherman and Grant, he liked New York.

On the southwest corner of Tenth Street lived Paul Forbes, a native of Boston. He made a large fortune in the China trade, and made his home in New York on retirement. He had three daughters, two of whom married into the French nobility. He also had a son, de Courcey Forbes, who was a great horseman and authority on running turf of this country as well as in Europe.

On the southwest corner of Eleventh Street lived Robert Lenox Kennedy. Subsequently Mrs. Kennedy occupied the house on the southeast corner. The First Presbyterian Church extended from the northwest corner of Eleventh Street to Twelfth Street and is still a landmark of the city. Directly opposite to it were three large brownstone houses occupied by Charles Burrell Hoffman on the corner; next Dr. Wood, and subsequently, going north, was George Hawley, prominent in the social life of the city. Henry Bergh, who organized the Society for the Prevention of Cruelty to Animals, lived at No. 17.

The New Yorker of today has only the slightest conception of the splendid work performed by Mr. Bergh and his associates on behalf of the animal world. In a city which only recently suggested that after 1927 no more horses are to be allowed on the streets of New York, it

Stewart's Marble Palace, corner Fifth Avenue and 34th Street, 1875

may be difficult to realize just how important was the horse in the domestic economy of our everyday lives in the Seventies. Everything was horse-drawn. You could transport no goods, or go anywhere without the aid of this indispensable animal. So utterly dependent were we on the horse that when a mysterious epidemic called the "epizootic" afflicted these animals, so that temporarily we were without the services of our dumb friends, the business of the entire city was paralyzed. Instead of street cars we walked. Such goods as had to be delivered were moved by hand-carts and wheelbarrows, often by the merchants themselves. The following lines were typical of the regard in which Mr. Bergh was held by all except those whose abuse of the horse caused him to be feared and hated.

"BERGH ON THE LINE"

Two-and-twenty street cars standing in a row,
Horses in, drivers there—why do they not go?
Cross and sulky men-folk grumbling up the street,
Cross and sulky women looking at their feet,
Or asking the policeman, with an angry sign,
"What's the matter?" "Well, madam, Bergh is on the
    line."
"What a nuisance!" and with scorn Beauty walks away.
Says a little foreigner, "Who's dis Bergh, Sar, pray?
Some great generale, no doubt?" "Yes, he's had some
    fights—
Hard-won fights for horses, Sir, and for horses' rights."
"But I understand not it." "That's your care, not mine.
Move forward, Sir—crowd enough: Bergh is on the
    line."
Grumbling, praising, on all went; but I heard one say,
"Gentlemen, we're proud to walk in the snow today—
Proud to think our mother-land has so great a heart,
She can stoop, with love and law, to take a wronged
    beast's part;
For the 'good time coming,' Sir, 'tis a gracious sign
We may well afford a cheer for *'Bergh upon the line!'*"

From an old print issued by Dr. Gardner's private school for Young Ladies

, ABOUT 1876. NOTE VACANT LAND WHERE TWIN
ANDS IN FRONT OF GARDNER'S SCHOOL.

Mr. Bergh arresting a cruel driver

On the northeast side of Twelfth Street lived James
Lenox, the house occupying a front of 60 feet. North of
him, on the corner of Thirteenth Street, was the home of
Charles Heckscher and his beautiful daughters. Mr.
Heckscher had married the daughter of Mr. Costar, one
of New York's oldest merchants, and his home was
always full of gaiety and attraction. On the northwest
corner of Twelfth Street was the home of Robert Minturn, a member of the firm of Grinnell, Minturn & Co.,
in the China trade and with the Island of Cuba. Mr.
Minturn's family consisted of two sons, one of whom
married Miss Shaw, daughter of Francis G. Shaw, and
the other married Louisa Aspinwall, whom we have just
spoken of as living in Washington Square.

[225]

Mrs. William Coles lived in the large house just north of Mr. Minturn. She was celebrated for her entertainments which were given frequently at Delmonico's and were largely attended.

On the lower corner of Fourteenth Street, on the west side, lived John Van Schaick. It was a large and attractive house, with stables in the rear. On the southeast corner lived Paul Spofford, a merchant prince of great wealth and high reputation. On the upper corner of Fourteenth Street and Fifth Avenue was the home of Moses Grinnell. He was a partner of Mr. Robert Minturn. He was a most distinguished gentleman, being a founder of the Union League Club and the American Geographical Society. Grinnell Land in the Arctic is named after this family. His home in later years was the scene of great gaiety and pleasure. Delmonico created there his well-known Delmonico Restaurant. Fourteenth Street, both on the north and south sides, between Fifth Avenue and University Place, held many people of importance—Mr. McCurdy, Henry A. Smyth, and others. On the southwest corner of Fifteenth Street and Fifth Avenue was the home of Mr. James Benkard, a merchant of the firm of Benkard & Hutton. He married a Miss Horton from Boston, a noted beauty of her day. They were very prominent in the social world of New York. On the southeast corner lived Mr. Haight, of the firm of Halsey & Haight, likewise very distinguished. On the northeast corner lived Daniel Fearing with his large family of children, most prominent in New York. Henry S. Fearing married Miss Jones. The eldest daughter, Amy Fearing, married Mr. Frederick Sheldon, member of an old Connecticut family. He was a distinguished Har-

vard man and left that University his fortune. Another
daughter married the eldest son of Moses Taylor, the
banker.

On the south corner above Mr. Fearing's house, at
Sixteenth Street, lived Daniel Parrish. He was the President of the New York Life Insurance and Trust Co. On
the northwest corner of Sixteenth Street lived Mr. Gibbs,
a man of great repute, and later Edwin Post, his son-in-
law. On the northeast corner lived Lorrilard Spencer. This
house was later occupied by Gov. Levi P. Morton.

On the southwest corner of Seventeenth Street were the
two homes of George and William Kingsland, houses of
great dignity. On the northwest corner of Seventeenth
Street lived Robert Winthrop who had married the daughter of Moses Taylor who lived in the adjoining house on
the north. Mr. Taylor's son married Miss Fearing and
he had a very beautiful home at Newport now occupied
by their descendants. On the southwest corner of Eighteenth Street lived Gordon Webster Burnham. He was
very public-spirited. Through him the statue of Daniel
Webster, now standing in the park, was erected. He
assumed the name of Webster, although it was not his
own, because of his great admiration for this statesman.
Directly opposite, on the lower side of Fifth Avenue,
lived Marshall O. Roberts. He had an extensive picture
gallery in the rear. Adjoining his house was that of
Mr. Hezron A. Johnson, a prominent member of the
Union Club, who married a Miss Whitney of Boston. He
was a leading member of the best social circles. On the
northeast corner of Eighteenth Street was a large red brick
house. Originally built by a Mr. Gihon, a man of Irish
extraction. He made his fortune by the importation of

Irish linens and other British goods. Upon Mr. Gihon's death, Mr. August Belmont acquired the property and added a picture gallery in the rear. Mr. Belmont had married a daughter of Commodore Matthew Galbraith Perry, who had opened the ports of the Hermit Kingdom to the commerce of the world. The imposing service of silver, presented by Congress to the Commodore for this great achievement, was kept in the Belmont mansion and used on special occasions. A reception to Japanese envoys held in this house was a nine-day wonder. No one had ever seen a Jap before in New York, and great crowds followed them wherever they went.

On the upper corner of Nineteenth Street east, lived William G. Read. The Presbyterian Church, under the pastorate of the famous Dr. John Hall, was on the southeast corner. On the block between Twentieth Street and

Fifth Avenue looking south from 42nd Street, 1884

Twenty-first Street, on the west side, was the palatial home of Robert L. Stuart, a merchant who made his fortune in sugar in connection with his brother, Alexander. They were born in Scotland, coming to this country from their home in the vicinity of Edinborough. Mr. John Steward lived on the corner of Twenty-first Street.

The well-known Union Club was on the northwest corner of Twenty-first Street. On the east side, between Twentieth and Twenty-first Streets, lived Clarence Seward, the lawyer, son of the famous Secretary Seward in Lincoln's Cabinet and purchaser of Alaska (then called "Seward's Folly"), from Russia. Next to him lived Robt. L. Cutting. Mr. Bradish G. Johnson was on the upper corner of Twenty-first Street.

On the east side, near Eighteenth Street, lived Edwards Pierrepont, ambassador to the Court of St. James. Also George Griswold of the old shipping firm of N. L. & G. Griswold. The Griswold flag was well known throughout the China trade.

34th Street looking west from Fifth Avenue

IN the following pages I offer a series of portraits showing a few of the men eminent in the commercial and financial world of New York toward the close of the 19th Century. They are taken from the wonderful collection owned by the Chamber of Commerce and reproduced by their courtesy. So far as we know, the Chamber is probably in possession of what is more nearly like a National Portrait Gallery than any other institution in our country. They have nearly two thousand portraits, most of them painted from life, representative of the highest commercial development of our City. While these men are called New Yorkers, the proportion born in the City is, of course, surprisingly small. This is true of every great metropolis so that while this collection is local, it is also National, in its best and truest sense. We would advise our readers to visit this collection. It is a credit to the Chamber as well as an honor to the City.

J. PIERPONT MORGAN

COMMODORE CORNELIUS VANDERBILT

WM. H. VANDERBILT

ALEXANDER T. STEWART

PETER COOPER

WILLIAM B. ASTOR

D. WILLIS JAMES

COLLIS P. HUNTINGTON

Moses Taylor

Andrew Carnegie

JOHN D. ROCKEFELLER

Morris K. Jessup

Alexander E. Orr

JOHN SLOANE

ISIDOR STRAUS

George A. Hearn

Until the torpedoing of the *Lusitania* it had been the proud boast of the Cunard Line that it had never lost a passenger. It did, however, lose a fine ship in the sinking of the *Oregon*, off Fire Island in March, 1886. This was a most mysterious maritime disaster. It occurred on a calm, starlight night and was declared by the first officer in charge of the ship, as due to a collision with a three-masted schooner which was running without lights. The schooner struck the huge liner twice, and then disappeared. That a small schooner could remain afloat after a double impact with a steel steamer was regarded as extremely unlikely, yet no sign of wreckage was ever discovered, nor any report ever made that would give a clue to the identity of the mysterious vessel. Many curious conjectures were made regarding the loss of the *Oregon* and one at least bears a rather odd relation to the loss of the *Lusitania*.

About the time of the sinking, Lieutenant Zalinski of dynamite gun fame, was experimenting with his big gun at the Narrows. It was said by those who favored the theory, that an unexploded shell might have been washed out to sea and been struck by the *Oregon*. The *Sun* stated, "The efforts to discover the identity of the lost schooner have been unavailing. The utter absence of any trace of the wreck of the schooner has puzzled a good many people and was the origin no doubt of the dynamite story."

The *Oregon* was one of the finest vessels of her time. She was bought by the Cunard Co. from the Guion Line, and until the advent of the *Etruria* and *Umbria*, held the record for the fastest crossing of the Atlantic.

The *Sun* closed an editorial on the *Oregon* thus: "Weep for the unfortunate sailors of the schooner, and weep for the *Oregon*. She was, taken all in all, the proudest boat on the sea. She was the culmination of the shipbuilder's art—an unsurpassed mark of engineers' and modelers' skill. Hers was a most mournful end, but fortunately she lies at the bottom, all bloodless, and without a single body of the thousand who had crossed on her, shut up within her sides. Peace be to her ashes."

The *Oregon,* 1886

The ship news reporters never failed to interview the skipper of a crack liner when she made port, and many a good story came from him.

A great many habitual travelers would choose a ship because it was commanded by a favorite captain. "What Captain sails on Tuesday?" a lady passenger would ask at the company's office. "What, that horrid Captain Dash? I would rather swim it than cross with him again. And who leaves next week? Capt. Blank? Oh, that's splendid! I'll wait and sail with him."

One of the "Dash" school was Capt. Judkins of the Cunard Line. He was highly esteemed by the com-

The departure of the largest trans-Atlantic liner of her day, *The City of Rome*, 1883

pany, but the bane of nine-tenths of his passenger list. He was once approached by a lady passenger who said, "Oh, Captain, do tell me, is it always as foggy and nasty as this off the Banks?" "How the devil do I know, Madam, I don't live here," was the reply.

Capt. Lott of the same line was another of the same type. He was a jolly looking man and usually wore a pleasant smile which frequently emboldened passengers to address him. "I tried it once," said a passenger, "I thought I would sail into the Gulf Stream, but found I had struck an iceberg." Capt. Cook of the *Etruria* was similarly gaited, but McKay, of its sister ship, the *Umbria,* was the line's social star.

Capt. Hains of the *Aurania* was a ladies' man, wherefore he was dubbed the "calico captain." On one trip he had as passengers the Mother Superior and several nuns of an American convent and did what no man, perhaps, ever did before—he kissed the venerable Superior and all the younger nuns, and from that day became a great favorite in their convent.

Captain Price of the *Alaska* was a human curiosity. He had led a sea life for forty years and he neither drank liquor, used tobacco in any form nor gave vent to profane language. A more genial officer never entertained a ship's saloon. One story he told with inimitable drollery. It concerned a German whom fortune had stranded in New Orleans. Though ignorant of the duties, he shipped as deck hand on a Mississippi steamer. All went well until the mate told him to heave the lead. He had heard the other hand give the depth of water in a sing-song tone, but he did not understand the marks on the line. But he had common sense. He dropped the lead over the side of the boat, gauged the depth of water and drawled out, intoning his voice thus:

```
                wa-       he-
            dy      dher
        blen-
"Deres                      ar"
```

He kept up his song at every cast of the lead until the water began to shoal when he sang out:

```
            you       ow-
        dher      look
      bed-                  id."
"More
```

A second and a third time he gave the warning. Suddenly the boat went high and dry on a sand bank. The German kept his place and sang to the pilot in the same strain:

```
          dold
        I           zo-
    didn't      you
"Oh                   oo?"
```

On one of the voyages when Price told this story the *Alaska's* engines gave out and she stopped. This was the signal for a universal chorus of:

```
          dold
        I           zo-
    didn't      you
"Oh                   oo?"
```

And finally when the *Alaska* anchored at Sandy Hook, waited eighteen hours for high water and daylight to get over the bar, the jolly old captain was bombarded by the gang with:

```
                wa-       he-
            dy      dher
        blen-
"Deres                      ar"
```

Other well-known old-time captains were Watkins, of the Inman Line; Irving, Perry, and Parsell, of the White Star; Brooks, of the Guion, who crossed the Atlantic 540 times and was a great favorite of Adelina Patti, Henry Irving, and Mrs. Langtry.

They were one and all of the Hearts-of-Oak-Britania-Rules-the-Waves type, and all of them were reeking with gold watches. Every time a wave smacked the side of a ship the young ladies in the first cabin would get up a meeting of praise and thanksgiving at which the captain would listen to a lot of bunk from passengers about his undaunted courage in saving the ship and their lives. Frequently this would be the first time the captain had heard about it, but a small detail like this was of no consequence. These meetings were usually presided over by G. Whatawad, the Glue King, or some other of the line's best customers. Resolutions signed by the cabin passen-

"All aboard!" Closing the gangway, 1876

gers and the inevitable gold watch were then presented to the captain and a collection taken up for the Liverpool Seamen's Home. It was great stuff.

A very decided impetus was given to American Art and Letters due to the success achieved by the *Century* and *Harper's* magazines. Mr. Roswell Smith, founder of the former, was the pioneer in a movement which placed the American magazine in a class by itself. The art of wood engraving reached its highest development during the reign of the *Century* and the beautiful pages of the *Century* were at once the envy and despair of European critics, who up to this time had practically usurped the field of art as applied to illustration. The new era in magazine printing, however, was on a scale of excellence never before attained by a publisher, and the fame of the *Century* and its printer, Theodore L. De Vinne, spread to the uttermost parts of the earth.

Smith also introduced another innovation into the business. He sought and secured advertisements for the back portion of his magazine, and for years this proved a most lucrative source of income. It had one serious drawback wholly unrecognized at the time. It created no end of competition. Other men, quick to perceive the emoluments possible from the advertising department, had less to fear in a venture of this kind. With so plethoric a source of income at hand, the element of risk was greatly reduced. Under the old dispensation, an enormous outlay of capital was necessary before any returns were possible and competition was, naturally, slow to develop. Under the new conditions magazines of all sorts shortly began to appear, and all much cheaper than the leader. In all probability had not this advertising element come into being, the

Century, Harper's, and *Scribner's* would have enjoyed a practical monopoly of the field for many years.

The rapid growth of population, particularly in the Middle West, provided a fruitful field for illustrated periodicals at a cheaper price. The invention of a mechanical process of engraving, which appeared at this time also, greatly reduced the cost of this most important item and made their production practical. The first break in the time-honored price of 35 cents charged by the *Century* and *Harper's* occurred when Scribner entered the field at 25 cents. S. S. McClure startled the world with a good magazine at as low a price as 15 cents. It subsequently attained a tremendous circulation and became one of the great publication properties of its day. McClure was rightly considered one of the great editors of his time. He had begun life with a new idea in publishing—that of syndicating—in other words, selling the same article to a number of papers in different parts of the country for simultaneous publication. The works of high-priced writers were thus made available for publishers who could never attempt them alone, and the cause of good literature greatly advanced. Much of his syndicated articles went to make up his magazine at the beginning, followed soon after by important exclusive undertakings, such as his "Life of Lincoln," "Life of Napoleon," etc., etc.

But perhaps the magazine which enjoyed the greatest prestige, if not circulation, was undoubtedly *The North American Review,* owned by Allan Thorndike Rice for a few brief weeks prior to his sudden and wholly unexpected death. It was then purchased by Lloyd Brice and edited by Wm. H. Rideing, whose abiding fame was achieved in a similar capacity for the *Youth's Companion* in Boston.

Can you imagine that New York depended on Fire Towers as late as 1874 to detect the first sign of a fire as Forest Rangers do today? This tower stood at the corner of Spring and Varick Streets. An early sketch by Winslow Homer, while a "Kid" on *Harper's Weekly*.

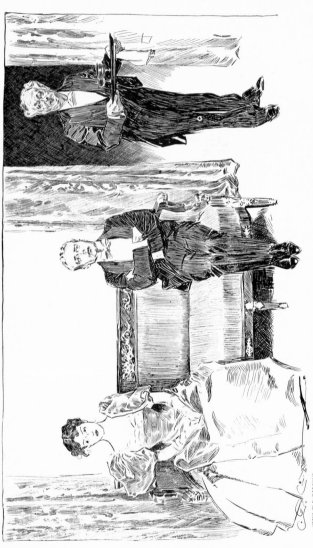

A LITTLE STORY
By A. BLACK

"BIG GAME"

"THE GIBSON GIRL"

In the early Nineties the famous "Gibson Girl" was the toast of the town. The gifted young artist, Charles Dana Gibson, was then at the beginning of his distinguished career. His brilliant cartoons, in *Life*, were the rivals of Du Maurier of *Punch* and each number of this popular periodical was eagerly awaited. Leading figures on the stage and in society aped the pose and the style of the 'Gibson Girl'. and every college had its devoted band of admirers. These two pictures give a slight idea of the beauty of these wonderful drawings, and of the styles of that day

In those days theology was a subject of great interest and it was Mr. Rideing's delight to have three such opposite stars in one issue as Wm. E. Gladstone, Cardinal Manning and Bob Ingersoll, all of whom discussed Faith, and from entirely different standpoints. The *Review* attained wide celebrity during the publication of this series and not a little circulation for a publication of its scholarly standing and high price, 50 cents. This was further increased by an article on "Home Rule," also by Gladstone. These articles were widely read on both sides of the Atlantic. I might mention in passing that this small sum according to our present-day reckoning was quite formidable in the Seventies and Eighties. Another *Review,* introduced later by Wm. T. Stead, the famous London publicist, entered the lists against *The North American.* Its lower price (20 cents) and the additional attraction of illustrations speedily brought it to the front. Stead subsequently disposed of the property to one of its young editors, Dr. Albert Shaw, who has conducted it ever since. Under Shaw's management it grew to be a magnificent property and remains so to this day.

The ten cent magazines did not appear till the early Nineties. Frank A. Munsey, present proprietor of a string of newspapers, was the first to enter the field and also the first to jar the complacent sides of no less a personage than Patrick Farrelly, czar of the American News Co. In order to get his magazine into the hands of the retailer at seven cents per copy, Mr. Munsey was obliged to organize practically a rival to the American News, which he did successfully. The original ten cent magazine appeared in England under George Newnes, and its immediate success directed the attention of American publishers to the possibilities of a similar field here.

Few fields are more closely competitive than the magazine field of today. They have multiplied amazingly and there seems no end of newcomers. But the high standard of the old *Century* and *Harper's* no longer exists.

The introduction of photo engraving, which revolutionized the magazine business, began in the late Seventies. The process was simple and inexpensive. At first it applied only to drawings made with a pen and India ink. These were photographed on a piece of sensitized zinc and an acid bath etched everything but the picture to be preserved. Gradually the art improved so that in time the wash drawing made by the artist was capable of the same treatment, and once this was accomplished the art of the wood engraver was doomed. Several years elapsed ere this was accomplished, but when the high-class magazines began to adopt the process the beginning of the end was in sight. For a long time, however, the *Century, Harper's* and *Scribner's* had the half-tone plate of the photo-engraver gone over by the wood engraver and finished by him. Even this could not save the situation. The process men developed such skill in finishing their own work that no further refinement was necessary. So disappeared the delightful art that gave us those entrancing blocks by Timothy Cole, of the old Italian masters and other work of this beautiful character. It is now almost as extinct as the Dodo.

Not content with the obliteration of wood engraving, the process men now set sail for the lithographer. It was not long ere he was able to reproduce in four colors the same effect that required the lithographer to use nine or ten. The immense saving in press work still further cheapened the cost of publishing and the news stands were soon groaning beneath the weight of the rapidly growing number of periodicals that seemed to spring up almost out of thin air.

In the meantime the daily press began to see the value of illustration in the news of the day. Joseph Pulitzer was the first to adopt the idea in New York. He had just acquired the *World* and it was sadly in need of circulation. He had already tested the value of the idea in St. Louis, where he published the *Post-Despatch,* so he was more fully alive to the advantages of the new idea than his contemporaries. Beginning with portraits, he soon added wrecks, fires and, in fact, everything possible to give spice to his columns and his paper grew apace. The present-day Sunday issue, with its wealth of half-tones, colored comics and other special features, was wholly unknown before the day of the mechanical process of making pictures, and our Sunday papers were solid looking, unattractive pages compared with the Jacob's coat of many colors which comes to us now on our day of rest.

Few things seem to illustrate the immense difference the fifty years have made more dramatically than the subjects which were discussed in the daily papers as part of the day's news. As an illustration of the point we append a clipping from the *Herald* which gives a picturesque account of a meeting between the Indians and the Commission of the Government regarding the purchase of the Black Hills. The names of the delegates from the Indian tribes recall Jack Harkaway and Mr. Beadle's lurid dime novels. Here are a few names: Red Dog, Spotted Tail, Spotted Bear, Red Cloud, Lone Horn, Young-Man-Afraid-of-His-Horses. The correspondent is at pains to telegraph as a special dispatch a colorful incident. "Long Horn rode into the council on horseback and claimed he owned all the country. The Indians felt insulted by Lone Horn's conduct and after the council attempted to kill him. He is hid in the bush along the White River. The closing handshaking was most friendly." These Indians afterwards came East to consult the Great White Father and conclude the negotiations. They stopped on the way at Cooper Union. It had been many years since any Indians were seen on the streets of New York. Shortly after the item quoted above, came the disastrous massacre of General Custer and his brave troops, all of which made spectacular reading in our daily press.

The papers were singularly destitute of original humor. Of course there were good stories in the news columns but there were no "columnists," "comic strips" or other professed incentives to laughter. It seemed that New York had to go West like Greeley's young man, to get a good laugh. Old readers will remember the liberal exercise of the scissors and paste pot in the New York papers; the good things credited to the *Detroit Free Press* (Mr. Quad's Bowser series were eagerly awaited), *The New Orleans Picayune, Texas Siftings, The Laramie Boomerang, Toledo Blade, The Danbury News, The Oil City Derrick, The Burlington Hawkeye,* and the Sparrowgrass papers in the *Brooklyn Eagle,* to name only a few. There was a breeziness and a rural humor to these sources which just suited the period that enjoyed "The Old Homestead," "My Partner," "M'liss" and "Mulligan Guards" on the stage, and Mark Twain, Bret Harte, Eggleston and Whitcomb Riley, in the library. Dialect stories abounded in the magazines and the "b'gosh" school of humor was still an article of faith in the popular mind, only slightly shaken by extracts from *Punch* in the Harper publications. How local taste has changed in this respect may be observed by the copious borrowings of European humor in today's comic weeklies. The recently defunct New York *Globe* also ran a humorous section that contained a daily average of seventy-five per cent. from British sources.

There was in the old "hayseed" character a mingling of astuteness and stupidity that made him a favorite subject of journalistic humor and the New York public enjoyed his antics to the full. The following is a sample of the stories from the *Detroit Free Press* that continually amused New York readers:

"A Detroit bobtail car overtook a man with a hand trunk of ancient make walking in the middle of the street. He inquired if the car went to the railroad station and then got aboard. There were several passengers in the car and as he stood in the door he looked from one to the other and said:

" 'If I'm intruding, don't hesitate to tell me so. I like people to speak right out and I am used to plain talk.'

"No one objected and he took a seat, crossed his legs and said to himself:

" 'I'll bet they never built the car for less than fifty dollars! I'm glad the old woman isn't here. If she should see how it's fixed up she'd never let up on me till I tacked one to the house. I'll never ride on a wood wagon again when I can jog along in a chariot like this. It's got more windows than a bee-hive.'

"As he made no move to pay his fare the driver rang the bell.

" 'Got bells on here, eh?' mused the plain man. 'Now who'd athought they'd have gone to such an expense as that! Folks here in town are right on the style no matter what it costs!'

"The driver rang again and again and seeing that it did no good he finally opened the door and said:

" 'You—man in the corner there—you didn't pay your fare!'

" 'My fare! Why, that's so! Hanged if I hadn't forgotten all about it! Were you ringing that bell for me?'

" 'Yes.'

" 'That's too bad! Why didn't you open the door long ago and say to me, "Here you old potato-top if you don't pass up your ducats I'll land you in the mud!" I'm a plain man and I never get miffed at plain talk. Take the damage out of this half dollar.' "

Of course the great blizzard of 1888 will always be New York's classic example of its climatic eccentricities, at least, until "Old Boreas" or "Old Sol," as they are familiarly known to newspaper readers, choose to provide the metropolis with a rival sensation. The blizzard of '88 was more than a local snowstorm. It was a national topic of interest. Some of this interest makes curious reading today:

"Mayor Hewitt, N. Y.

"Huron, Dak., under a mild spring sun, sends her sympathy to blizzard-stricken New York. If need, you may draw on us for $50 at once.   "F. H. Kent, Chairman."

"Bismarck stands ready to give substantial aid to blizzard sufferers of New York. Let us know your needs.
                "M. R. Jewell, Chamber of Commerce."

"Subscription papers reported passed throughout Dakota for aid of storm sufferers in New York and surrounding county. Would you prefer clothes or food or both?
                "Jhn. Quinn, Bismarck Tribune."

The blizzard which started on Sunday night, March 11th, with a rain storm brought New York to a standstill. Wednesday evening papers contained the following items:

"There was a general resumption of business downtown today. The handshaking between employer and employee who in many cases had not seen each other since Saturday was cordial in the extreme."

"At 11 o'clock a big truck on runners and loaded with pigs was driven down Broadway and by the Produce Exchange. When the boys on 'Change spied this, they set up a great shout of welcome, and dealings in the pork corner received a fresh impetus."

"The elevated roads and bridge cars were the salvation of the town and never till now was their value appreciated. The surface roads during the morning were making herculean efforts to clear the way for resumption of business before night, but the outlook at the time of going to press is, to say the least, gloomy.

"At the Signal Service office Sergeant Dunn tried to hoist his northwest offshore signals this morning, but the halyards were frozen stiff to the sheave of the block, and the pennants couldn't be raised."

"Roundsman Brophy of the bridge police came up smiling today after eighteen continuous hours of duty yesterday, and last night stroked his ambrosial whiskers and remarked, 'It's the biggest crowd of tramps I ever saw on the promenade, because they are all going one way. I'll be mighty glad when the ferries are running again.' The 'all going one way' alluded to the marooned Manhattan workers, who had spent the previous night reposing on billiard tables, barber chairs, and hallway mattresses in the Astor House, French's Hotel, Smith & McNell's and other downtown hostelries filled to overflowing."

Frank K. Sturgis was one of the few New Yorkers who ventured out on this eventful day. Following his usual custom he walked from his home on 33rd Street down Broadway to the Stock Exchange and repeated this strenuous performance in the evening. Upon his arrival at the Exchange he found seven members present instead of the usual four hundred and only one doorkeeper on guard. With the exception of the one private wire connecting Mr. Sturgis' office with his Boston correspondent

Scenes in the City during the great blizzard of 1888

there was no other communication between these two cities. As a consequence the office was besieged all day long with persons anxious to communicate on matters of urgent business with friends in Boston. Accordingly the private wire was burdened with messages of every description and this service was of course of the greatest convenience and comfort to a great many people.

There have been a good many tempestuous snow storms in New York since then, and certain statistics have been referred to by wiseacres, in the way of inches of snowfall and velocity of wind in susbequent storms to at least rival if not surpass that classic hurricane, but nothing that New York has experienced since has been a marker to it in spectacular devastation. Some of its details are worth recalling. The Staten Island ferryboats had their flagstaffs snapped off the instant they put out their noses in the morning. A Sixth Avenue elevated train loaded with passengers, consumed six hours and twenty minutes in covering a distance of two blocks. This train finally came to a stop between Eighteenth Street and Fourteenth Street. Many of the passengers effected their escape after hours of waiting by means of a ladder reared against the "L" structure by private enterprise. It cost fifty cents a head to go down the ladder into the comparative freedom of the blizzard and the drifts. Roscoe Conkling, an athletic man, of a powerful frame started to walk up Broadway from Wall Street. The electric lights had failed and the great thoroughfare was in darkness. After a walk of two miles in the storm Mr. Conkling reached Union Square. It was unlighted and in trying to cross it he sank into the snow to his armpits. For twenty minutes he put forth his utmost strength in order to work himself free, and he was at the point of

LITTLE BISMARCK TO FATHER KNICKERBOCKER.

"To Mayor Hewitt, New York:—
"Bismarck stands ready to give substantial aid to blizzard sufferers of New York. Let us know your needs.

"M. R. JEWELL, Chamber of Commerce."

exhaustion when he finally succeeded and managed to stagger to the New York Club at Twenty-fifth Street. It was as a consequence of this experience that Mr. Conkling's death not long after was attributed. Mr. Barremore, a merchant, was found the next morning dead from cold and exhaustion in a drift at Seventh Avenue and Fifty-third Street, within four blocks of his home.

The Sandy Hook pilot-boats fared badly. Nine of these sturdy vessels—one-third of all that were in commission—were driven ashore, or sunk, or abandoned, between noon and midnight and the crews of all fortunately escaped.

In Brooklyn the roofs of five houses were blown off. There were serious hurts in consequence, but no loss of life. The day following—Tuesday—was the day of the shovel. Great heaps of snow from six to sixteen feet in height, rose in the gutters. There was an eruption of runners—groceries, coal, wood, meat, everything except milk, of which there was none, were delivered in sleighs. Chief McCabe went to a fire on West Forty-second Street on horseback.

In the morning an ice bridge formed over the East River and several thousand persons crossed on foot between New York and Brooklyn. The floe broke with the turn of the tide and a tugboat was essential to the rescue of five men who were drifting to sea on small cakes.

Wednesday was bonfire day. All over town fire was brought into play to assist the sun. The idea originated, it is said, with a Vesey Street storekeeper, who dug a hole in a snow heap and started a bonfire in it. Soon there was fire leaping up from snow heaps everywhere and the gutters and sewers were flooded with the melted snow.

On Thursday the bonfires were continued and the sun came out strong. The horse cars broke into Park Row and the gutters sang merrily. On Friday the crosstown cars were running and the town returned to "normalcy."

The aberrations of the city's climate were not confined to blizzard conditions as any old-timer's recollections will attest. The heat of summer was a trial both to man and beast in the old pre-gasoline age. There was no such thing as an electric fan, no electric cars or motor vehicles. When a "hot spell" hit the town, the town wilted. Dray horses appeared on the streets with wet sponges and odd looking bonnets on their heads. The poor car horses suffered dreadfully and might have been seen at relay points drooping and perspiring, waiting for the merciful bucket of water. The S. P. C. A. exercised special vigilance during the season and if the car companies did not deem it policy to conserve their horseflesh, the Society promptly convinced them of the error of their ways.

Indeed, the mortality among other work horses is incredible today. All over the city scores of prostrated animals would lie in the streets where they had finally collapsed, to the further menace of public health. In a city which has recently decreed that within two years all horse-driven vehicles will be prohibited on the island, no conception now exists of New York's former utter dependence on man's best friend, for the transportation of commerce. The mortality has reached as high as two hundred cases in a few days of a hot spell.

Hardly half a dozen theaters were open throughout the city, there being no modern cooling equipment to render them tolerable. About the middle nineties electric fans appeared in some of the theaters, but their whirring and buzzing was so distracting to the audience that they were only turned on during entre-acts.

A great deal of discomfort was due to sheer stupidity both in dress and in food. A small minority wore linen seersucker clothing with white waistcoats, the majority stuck to black clothes and other heat absorbing colors. Tan shoes were a frivolity of the early Nineties. About the only previous deviation from black shoes being a canvas "baseball" shoe. Male "sport clothes" comprised a flannel "outing" shirt, a blazer and a gorgeous multi-colored silk belt, almost a foot and a half wide, with a tassel. Female ditto was a tam-o'-shanter and a snug-fitting jersey. Heavy meals were in popular demand—only millionaires and bank presidents lunching on crackers and milk.

There are few things more pleasant in retrospect than old songs. The songs of childhood are never forgotten. Nor are the songs of youth. Who can forget "Sunday Night When the Parlor's Full," where, at the piano, the dearest girl in the world played the accompaniment to "Sweet Violets," or "Only a Pansy Blossom," while at her nod one turned the pages of the "Album of Song" with its lithograph portrait of the queens of song. Ah, my dear sir, you are stouter now, your hair is a bit thinner in front and more grizzled at the sides, but perhaps as you read this, you steal a glance at the matronly lady—who hasn't divorced you—who is reading the page devoted to "Woman and the Home," and see her again at the piano and hear her warbling the tender ballad that was "Sung with Great Success by Anna Louise Cary" or "Clara Louise Kellogg" or "Parepa Rosa." You will agree with me, I warrant, when I say that they were better songs than the illiterate doggerel that we get via the air in today's "living room."

Nor were all our old favorites of this tender nature. There were jolly ditties, too, sung by the street boys, and whistled about town. Why do you hear so little whistling today? Is it because there is so little melody in the crazy dance jazz tunes? How the boys used to whistle the "Skidmore on Parade" or "Dem Golden Slippers" or "After the Ball." And the organ-grinders played them. There were not many piano organs then, most of them being the one-legged variety borne on the back, some with monkeys, to the great delight of the kiddies. Not until the coming of the piano organ did the children "trip the light fantastic on the Sidewalks of New York."

I could devote many pages to these old songs, but I have space for only a few of the most widely popular. Among these were many of what were known as "drawing-room songs"—ballads of a superior character in diction and composition, including such classics as "Let Me Dream Again," "Just a Song at Twilight," and Tosti's famous "Bid Me Goodby, and Go" and his "Goodby," still a standard favorite.

Sentimental songs that reached a climax in the assurance that "Love Me and the World Is Mine!" were very much the vogue before its advent. One of the tremendous favorites was "Call Me Back Again" inspired by Hugh Conway's popular novel, "Called Back":

"Call me back again, call me back again;
Ah! when your love has conquered pride and anger
I know that you will call me back again."

This, however, was eclipsed by the famous "In the Gloaming," one of the greatest favorites ever written. Other songs of this type were "Afterward," its words by Mark Lemon of *Punch*, and "Some Day" also widely popular. Almost all of these were English ballads of a superior class. The domestic output was represented by songs like, "With All Her Faults I Love Her Still," "Say Au Revoir but Not Goodby," "When the Robins Nest Again," and "Wait Till the Clouds Roll By, Jennie."

Of a still more popular type were songs like "Little Annie Rooney," "Sweet Marie," and "Where Did You Get That Hat." It used to be the custom on the variety stage to sing medleys of the popular songs of the period; as an example:

> "Listen to my Tale of Woe, in Paddy Duffy's Cart,
> Sweet Katie Connor sang That is Love, The Song
>   Reached my Heart,
> Little Bunch of Lilacs, what can the matter be?
> Father was killed by the Pinkerton Men, singing
>   The Irish Jubilee.
> What a difference in the morning, no more does
>   Kelly slide,
> I stood on the Bridge at midnight, with Danny by
>   my side,
> Then down to Maggie Murphy's we all did call
> When she wouldn't rush the growler, we turned her
>   picture to the wall."

Minstrel songs were the rage, and they had a quaint "Hallelujah" quality about them, entirely lacking in modern coon songs:

> "Oh hear dem bells aringing, they're sweet I do declare
> Oh hear dem darkies singing, a'climbin' up de golden stair."

There was no lack of ribald "coon" songs, however. "There's a New Coon in Town," and "Get Away from Dat Window" echo their melodies down the corridor of time.

Contemporary conditions and events were closely reflected by the popular song. The bicycle craze, for instance, is commemorated by:

> "Daisy, Daisy, give me your answer true
> I'm half crazy, all for the love of you,
> It won't be a handsome marriage
> I can't afford a carriage
> But you'll look sweet, upon the seat
> Of a bicycle built for two."

Hard times, strikes and business panics also had their metrical echoes:

> "The savings of a lifetime of a mother for her child
> The fortunes of the sick, the great, the gay,
> The reward of great careers, and of labor's thrifty years
> Are gone at last—the bank has failed today."

Drawn by C. Kessler

"A Bicycle Built for Two."

And another in the same vein was:

> "Oh, what are we to do, dear wife
> I cannot get my pay,
> The grocer's bill is overdue
> The mills shut down today."

The two types of comic song most common to the variety stage were the nigger minstrel and the Irish dialect ballads. The "Brigadier Brannigan" was an imported type of the latter, interspersed with a spoken monologue of a rather more extended character than usual.

> "Soon into battle we went, where the bullets were shooting
> and flying sure,
> Where many a poor fellow lay killed and many another
> lay dying sure,
> A bombshell came flying o'er me, I was thinking of
> Judy O'Calagan
> With the Brigadier's head it made free, faith, it finished
> the Brigadier Brannigan."

Then would follow a long interpolation spoken in an ordinary conversational tone of voice:

"Yes, there we stood, Murphy on one side, I on the other and the Brigadier in the middle, when along came a bombshell, taking the head clean off the Brigadier. 'Hurrah!' cried Murphy raising his hand, 'We're free at last!' when along came another bombshell, taking the hand right off Murphy. 'Arrah!' cried Murphy. 'I've lost me hand! I've lost me hand!' 'Hould your gab, you blackguard,' says I, 'there's the Brigadier lost his head, and divil a word he said about it.'

"I went over to where he was lying. 'Are you kilt,' said I; he didn't condescend to speak to me. 'If you have any request to make,' said I, 'If you tell me what it is, I will do it for you.' 'Paddy,' says he, 'I'm not kilt, but I'm murdered and spachless, and if you have any regards for me, you'll be afther going over the field and looking for my head, place it on my shoulders, and see me buried decently.' 'I'll do that same,' said I, so over the field I went, looking for his head; at last I came to it, trying to roll over to a canteen full of whiskey. I knew it was his head for he had a big pimple on the side of his nose. I brought it over to him. 'There's your head,' said I. 'No, Paddy,' that's not my head.' 'Yes it is,' said I. 'No, it's not,' said he. 'Well head or no head,' said I, 'divil another head you'll get from me!' So I threw his head in his face and I ran off sing-ing—"

and then the chorus would continue.

History repeats itself, and some of the foregoing humor was current not long ago as World War facetiae.

While Charles Hoyt's famous "Bowery" song is no doubt, the established epic of that thoroughfare, it had its precursors, among them the following, which is prefaced by the announcement:

"This song has been called for nightly for months in succession, having been sung by Mr. Pastor in his own inimitable style, and been received with *thunders of applause.*"

> "Some say that Central Park's the place,
> For fun of every kind;
> On Broadway and Fifth Avenue
> Much pleasure others find
> But I'm a difficult sort of chap
> No fun in that I see
> For when I want enjoyment
> The Bowery for me.

"SPOKEN—Yes, you may talk about your Broadway belles, your Fifth Avenue swells, your exquisitely dressed crea-tures, with their lavender kids, and their la-de-da's. Now, what do they know about enjoyment? They are afraid to go in for a little fun for fear of disarrang-ing their toilets, and then what would Mrs. Grundy say? 'Charles Frederick Augustus is getting decidedly vulgar; Seraphina Emelia is positively shocking!' But here in the Bowery people enjoy themselves, just when they feel like it. They don't care a curse what others may say for that's the custom.

> "In the Bowery, in the Bowery
> For beautiful girls with bright eyes
>   and dark curls
> In the Bowery, in the Bowery
> That's where I reside when I'm home."

English music halls furnished a considerable quota of the popular songs of the New York stage—of the "Cham-

pagne Charley" periods. "The Man in the Moon is Looking" was one of them:

> "You all know what this feeling is
> When at some quick shot
> All around you may be ice
> But true love's burning hot
> Of course her hand so tight you squeeze
> As you both gaze afar
> Yes, while the moon is laughing at you
> Knowing what fools you are.

"SPOKEN—When you are in love, and sitting on some
romantic cliff, by the light of the moon you gaze in the
girl's face, and imagine how much powder and rouge she
has been putting on; and she's thinking at the same time,
what expressive eyes—how his nose turns up—and I
think I should love him a little more if it was a Roman,
and the moon is winking at you and seems to say—
> The man in the moon is looking love,
> He's winking love, he's blinking love,
> And each little star can tell where you are
> The man in the moon is looking."

An imperishable ditty was the famous "Johnny Morgan" song, reciting the adventures of an itinerant musical
family:

> "Johnny Morgan played the organ
> The father beat the drum
> The sister played the tambourine
> The brother went pom, pom, pom.
> All alone on the old trombone, the music
>   was so sweet
> They often got a penny to go into
>   another street."

Johnny, it may be remembered, played the organ to such
good purpose that he won the heart of a lady of title and
lived happily forever after.

A good many old variety hall songs also had a short
spoken monologue between the stanzas. Harry Kernell,
of Tony Pastor's, one of the most popular comedians of

his day, was particularly glib in effusions like the following:

"If you listen to me for a while
I'll tell you a tale,
You all know Mrs. Casey down
The Street that sells the ale.
She gave a raffle for a store
And to have a dance as well
And I being floor manager
Had tickets for to sell.

"SPOKEN—Mrs. Casey is a particular friend of John Mc-Swegan, and her husband Sam Casey, alias Gas House Sam (he was once employed in the gas house at $60 a month wheeling smoke out in a pushcart), he went to the war and never returned and Mrs. Casey raffled off the old store.

"The raffling then did commence
As you may understand
McGriffin threw forty-four
And O'Donnell called his hand
But Mrs. Casey got vexed then
And ordered them all out
When the fiddler played St. Patrick's Day
Then you had ought to hear them shout.

"SPOKEN—Such shouting you never heard in your life; but when the supper was announced all became quiet. They had a splendid supper. There was mackerel and ice cream and molasses and oysters. Bradley went to wait on the ladies. He asked one girl what she would have? Says she, 'I'll have quail.' Says Bradley, 'You will have bean soup or you will give your seat to Biddy Doyle.' Then Barney Conklin wanted to make a speech. Says he, 'Would I were an eagle that I might fly over the sea and spread the liberty of my country.' Says Bradley, 'Sit down; you would be shot for a goose before you got half way.'

"But oh! what a row, etc."

It was Harry also who told, in one of these "spokens," of the inmate at Bloomingdale whom he met rolling a wheelbarrow along upside down. "Why don't you turn it the other way round?" said Harry. "Because," answered the other, "I did that yesterday and they filled it full of bricks."

Surely there is no other church in all New York that holds the affectionate regard of its whole public as does "The Little Church Around the Corner." It recently loomed large in the newspapers, upon the dedication of a memorial window to Joseph Jefferson, whose story of the refusal of a fashionable pastor to officiate at the obsequies of George Holland, caused a great stir at the time. He referred the genial "Rip" to the "little Church around the corner," and hence the name. The incident was responsible for a number of songs from the stage, of which the following is one of the lesser known:

> "When from the stage of real life
> George Holland made his *exit*
> To rest until the final 'call'—
> The trumpet *'Resurrexit'*
> He left no blot upon his name
> No wrong had he done to man,
> But laid, with his good life aside
> His well-played part of 'Trueman.'

Chorus

> "Upon his tomb write 'Honest Man'
> And cry with 'Rip' blind mourner
> 'All honor to the little Church
> The Church around the corner!'
> Stern, bitter word of strong rebuke
> Might we speak to that Pastor
> But leave him—as he should have left
> The dead man—to his Master.
> We will not judge as he hath judged
> Nor sit with him—the scorner!
> But say 'God bless the little Church
> The Church around the corner!'"

There were others of the school known as "weepers"; they usually depicted some heart-breaking domestic tragedy of which the following is a good example:

WE NEVER SPEAK AS WE PASS BY

The spell is past, the dream is o'er
And though we meet we love no more,
One heart is crushed to droop and die,
And for relief must heavenward fly.
The once bright smile has faded—gone—
And given way to looks forlorn,
Despite her grandeur's wicked flame,
She stoops to blush beneath her shame.

Chorus.

We never speak as we pass by,
Although a tear bedims her eye;
I know she thinks of her past life,
When we were loving man and wife.

In guileless youth I sought her side,
And she became my virtuous bride;
Our lot was peace—so fair so bright;
One sunny day, no gloomy night.
No life on earth more pure than ours
In that dear home midst field and flowers
Until the tempter come to Nell,
It dazzled her—alas! she fell!

We never speak, etc.

In gilded hall midst wealth she dwells;
How her heart aches her sad face tells;
She fain would smile—seem bright and gay
But conscience steals her peace away.
And when the flatterer casts aside
My fallen and dishonored bride,
I'll close her eyes in death—forgive!
And in my heart her name shall live.

We never speak, etc.

Others recall those days when a man with fifteen dollars in his pocket at one time was rated by his envious neighbors as nothing short of a plutocrat. The following song was a real heart-breaking expression in those days, considering the stupendous sum involved:

I HAD FIFTEEN DOLLARS IN MY INSIDE POCKET

Chorus

I had fifteen dollars in my inside pocket,
  Don't you see, to me it is a warning;
Saturday night I made a call on a friend of Tam'ny Hall,
  And the divil a cent I had on Monday morning.

But the song that has attained something of the dignity of a national anthem, or at least is in the class of "Dixie" and "Maryland" is undoubtedly "The Sidewalks of New York." At the last Democratic convention it was recognized as peculiarly a New York product and is apparently destined to rank in future as a classic.

Let us do honor, said a writer in the *World* recently, to Charles B. Lawlor, who wrote this now famous song and who has just died. And let us not honor him as a minstrel who just hit a good tune, but let us do full credit to his genius. For he caught something in this song which is precious—the spirit, the pathos of New York. It is our fate here to be gay under handicap, and the children in the street, playing there because there are no yards, inventing queer games because there is no space for regular games, bring our fate home to us. All of this, and the lyric spirit which laughs at the handicaps and still manages to sing "London Bridge is falling down," Lawlor caught in his song, and he said it in the homely language of the people. The music is as unforgetable as the words. It runs through your head, but softly, with a haunting wistfulness: it seems always just around the corner, like the children's voices, the blind fiddler and the hurdy-gurdy man. It is no accident that the song has lived thirty years after its time. It is an immortal song.

THE SINGING WAITER PULLS A "WEEPER"

"The spell is past the dream is o'er
And though we meet we love no more.
One heart is crushed to droop and die
And for relief must Heavenward fly.

Cho. "We never speak as we pass by.", etc.

I will close my recital with a specimen of the melo-dramatic with a happy ending. One cannot read these verses without considerable misgivings as to the sanity of the author. Yet they were highly popular. And strange to relate many of our present-day compositions have no more literary excellence than this:

MY MOTHER WAS A LADY

Two drummers sat at dinner in a grand hotel one day,
While dining they were chatting in a jolly sort of way,
And when a pretty waitress brought them a tray of food,
They spoke to her familiarly in a manner rather rude.
At first she did not notice them or make the least reply,
But one remark was passed that brought the teardrops to
  her eye,
And facing her tormentor with cheeks now burning red,
She looked a perfect picture as appealingly she said.

Chorus

My Mother was a Lady like yours you will allow,
And you may have a Sister who needs protection now,
I came to this great city to find a brother dear.
And you wouldn't dare insult me Sir, if Jack were only here.

It's true one touch of nature it makes the whole world
  kin,
And every word she utterd seemed to touch their hearts
  within,
They sat there stunned and silent until one cried in shame,
"Forgive me Miss, I meant no harm, pray tell me what's
  your name?"
She told him and he cried again, "I know your Brother too,
Why we've been friends for many years and he often
  speaks of you,
He'll be so glad to see you and if you'll only wed,
I'll take you to him as my wife for I love you since you
  said."

Chorus, etc.

Few there are who do not recall the great excitement produced by Henry George and his "Progress and Poverty." It appeared at a time when there was a dearth of employment and all the "get rich quick" men were hailed as saviors of the race.

The "Toothpick" Shoe.

There was something unusually appealing about Mr. George who was by no means the charlatan which his opponents described. The extraordinary vicissitudes which attended the publication of his work no doubt added an additional glamour to his quickly won reputation. He was a typesetter by trade. His efforts to find a publisher for his book were unavailing. At length it was arranged that if he would do the composition himself, the Appletons would print and bind a few hundred copies and more if the demand warranted. George obtained permission from his employers to use their type and for more than two weary years he spent his evenings in his self appointed task. At last the forms were ready for the press. Under the circumstances George became practically the sole owner of the work; the publisher receiving only a reasonable sum for the printing and distributing. Aside from this slight expense all the proceeds of the sale reverted to Mr. George. In some inexplicable manner the subject of his book—the single tax theory— made a tremendous appeal to the public and although the work sold at $7.50—an enormous price in those days—it went like wildfire. Edition after edition was called for and I am told the total for the first year reached the unheard of number of nearly two million copies. With such a large sale and no advertising expense, the profits were staggering, and George speedily became a man of property himself.

His followers were largely among the laboring classes and in a subsequent Mayoralty contest he accepted the nomination for that office on the labor ticket.

Joined with Mr. George in his labors was Father McGlynn, a priest attached, I believe, to the Church of St.

Xavier. They had a very small office in Ann Street just off Broadway and at noon when they sallied forth for lunch were followed by great crowds. The newspapers were filled with their comings and goings and when George entered the political field a splendid opportunity was afforded for the propaganda of his peculiar doctrines. He was a forceful speaker and it was soon seen that unless Tammany could check the stampede into the labor camp the election would be lost and the peculiar ideas of Mr. George on taxation might possibly be tried out in the wealthiest city in the Union. While all admired his unquestioned ability—his speeches quickly proved that— there was a general feeling of apprehension that his election bode ill for the community.

In no campaign that I can recall was there ever so much repressed excitement. Meetings were held every night by all the candidates before huge audiences. Mr George labored twenty-four hours a day for weeks without pause. The terrible strain was more than mortal man could endure. In the middle of a sentence, before a tremendous crowd, Mr. George suddenly stopped; he sank to the ground before the agonized eyes of his admirers and was instantly carried from the platform. Doctors reached his side immediately but they could do nothing. He was carried to the Union Square Hotel. A sudden stroke of apoplexy had laid low the champion of the poor and needy as his party said, and the next day came the sorrowful intelligence of his death.

It was one of the most tragic happenings in all the dramatic history of New York local politics. Interest in the campaign collapsed with the death of Mr. George and the Tammany candidate was safe.

There was much to admire in the life and work of Mr. George, and his monumental book continued for a long time, the object or relentless criticism. A perusal of its pages, especially of its footnotes, revealed Mr. George as a profound and widely read student of political economy; had he been spared, no doubt the world would have heard much from him on this subject. He had at least succeeded in reaching the ear of the public and his every utterance was greeted with widespread comment. There are many persons who believe in his peculiar doctrines and certainly the proposal to tax unimproved property in a fully improved section in keeping with its acknowledged value, is not unfair or visionary. The phrase, since then so generally used in our vocabulary, "the unearned increment," originated with Mr. George and bids fair to be a permanent addition to our language.

The uniformed police force of recent years has been the subject of many deserved enconiums, among them from such a talented observer as Conan Doyle who declares that the New York policeman of his first visit was a comic object compared with the spruce, smartly disciplined London "Bobby" of the time. He was then either a huge corpulent Irishman or German, distinguishable with unerring certainty, in "plain clothes," by a pair of Brobdignagian feet, shod with incredible solidity. His uniform included a helmet, constructed with a view of gently breaking the fall of descending bricks in the gangsters' districts, a tunic, liberally brass-buttoned, a starched white collar of the "white wing" variety, and as a final accoutrement a stout and dependable locust "nightstick" carried in a leather belt. Aid was summoned by rapping the nightstick on the pavement, no whistles being then provided the police. This formidable truncheon

Mounted police at about 145th Street, Washington Heights,
capturing burglars

was an irresistible symbol of authority, especially in the
suppression of the gangster, who flourished in well defined
districts, and was not, as today, a free lance in crime.
The experienced "cop" used this weapon with discriminating fervor. When a captain of police ordered a neighborhood to be "cleaned up" it meant no arrests, but a
literal clubbing out of offending parties. The famous
"Tenderloin" Williams earned the sobriquet of "Club-
ber" Williams by his penchant for this form of exercise.
Of course, many policemen exceeded the bounds—some
indeed in their cups committed atrocious assaults on
citizens, but the ferocious rabble that has always been
New York's heritage from the days of the Five Points
to the present taxicab bandits, have met, for the most
part, with a most effective resistance by the police.

There existed in these days also a number of well organized gangs composed mainly of the alumni of the House of Refuge and Elmira Reformatory with a sprinkling of mentors from the more advanced schools of Sing Sing and Auburn. These gentry were to some extent supported by political organizations that found their services useful on occasions. They formed a sort of local banditti, preying on shopkeepers and passersby, in addition to occasional forays on the outer world. Some of these gangs were the "Whyos," "Gas House," "Dry Dock," "Corcoran's Roost" and "Hell's Kitchen."

The police courts of New York have always been an unfailing source of human interest. The character of the cases they handle is a faithful reflection of the seamy side of local life. Forty years ago "drunk and disorderly" cases predominated, enhanced by a goodly number of "tenement house rows." These cases were adjudicated by men of peculiar competence in such matters though they might have been open to criticism on legal and cultural grounds. They were fond of double negatives and had a supreme contempt for Lindley Murray.

Prior to legislative enactments requiring incumbents to be members of the bar, appointments to the police bench were political rewards bestowed on saloon keepers, campaign orators, shyster lawyers and numerous other benefactors of the "machine." Their redeeming quality was their native familiarity with the conditions presented by the vast majority of cases brought before them. A sort of rude justice was meted out, wherever political influence was not cast into the balance. In many respects the system served

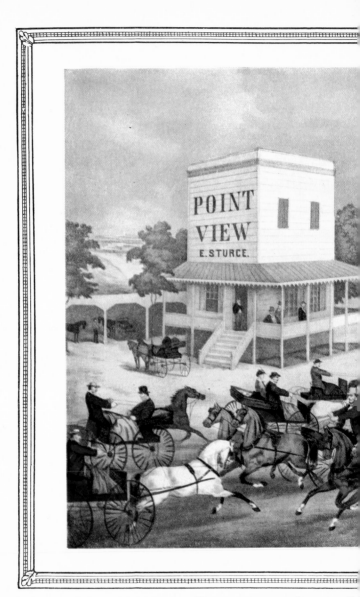

POINT
VIEW
E. STURGE.

o Gabe Case's, up Seventh Avenue.

the needs of the community most adequately. It certainly kept the bench clear of some of the theorists and prigs that were not unknown in its later period.

The great drawback, however, was the unsavory atmosphere surrounding the proceedings. Rough, arrogant officers and clerks, who handled the unfortunates present like cattle, and who seemed incapable of the common courtesies of the street, were the executive forces. A plaintiff come to press a charge, or a bewildered witness answering a subpoena, were the recipients of the same brand of politeness accorded a recognized thug. To the onlooker there was always an undefinable sensation that conditions were about to be reversed and the plaintiff held on a counter-charge of interfering with a burglary, or that the judge, like the fabled Turkish Cadi, would fine the plaintiff, imprison the defendant, and bastinado the witnesses.

The occupant of the bench was often a "judicial humorist," prone to exercise his facetious bent on the sodden wretches awaiting judgment. The infliction of a ten-day "bit" was often accompanied by a convivial jest that convulsed the red-nosed guardian of the "bridge"—as the dock was called—and other by-standers. These "bon mots" were duly reported in the newspapers, and were a source of great amusement to readers around the evening lamp.

As for the judge's decisions in the multifarious disputes at bar, weight of evidence was no match for strength of "pull." A word from the seats of the mighty turned the scales. "Abandon hope, all ye who enter here without a pull," should have been chiseled over the doorway of the police court of the day.

Not all of the humor of the police court came from one side of the bench. Irish women who had "felt a little cauld, your honor, and had only taken a thimbleful," exercised a native fluency in their transactions with the court. "Sure, Judge, such a noice lukken man as yourself, ain't goin' to send me away." "But, Mary, the officer says you jabbed him with a hatpin. I'll have to give you a month." "You murtherin ould villun wid yer munkey face—sure Judge O'Brien wud niver do that. Wait till I get out! Wait till I get out! You ———"

The whole scene was an accurate reflection of the worst side of New York's teeming polyglot population. Our present Ellis Island restrictions were unknown and Castle Garden poured its hordes, liberally sprinkled with the vicious and the criminal, without restraint into the streets of New York, to become in due time desirable or otherwise, members of the community.

One of the best known of all New Yorkers to newspaper readers and a perennial source of "copy" to the reporters was "Farmer" Dunn, the Government weather sharp who held forth on the roof of the old Equitable Building.

It was one of the tenets of newspaper men to hold the "Farmer" responsible for the distressful conditions of the climate on the street below. An item that never varied was "Farmer Dunn declares the temperature at three o'clock to be 94, but the thermometer at Hudnut's at the same hour stood at 101." There was some resentment at "Farmer's" airy nonchalance in giving out these reports and some simple folks regarded him in the light of an unfeeling Jupiter. The "Farmer," on the other hand, had a system of statistics intended to be consoling to that vast populace who are affected by statistics. "If you think it hot here, you ought to be in Yuma, Arizona, where the mercury reached 126 this noon," or "It is not so very cold here when you consider that Medicine Hat recorded 40 below at 12 o'clock last night." Of course a citizen reading this cheery news was more than ever convinced that New York was either the best summer resort or winter resort in the country.

"Hudnut's," here mentioned, was the drug store in the old Herald building at Broadway and Ann Street. Its thermometer was gazed at by more people than any other object ever displayed in New York.

Almost opposite Hudnut's was another popular attraction, the old Time Ball on the Western Union. This was affixed to the top of a tall flagstaff and was dropped every day promptly on the second at noon. Hundreds of citizens lined the curb opposite, watches in hand to compare with the Western Union Time Ball.

Another popular indoor sport was fortune telling and kindred amusements. The *Herald* contained as its most conspicuous public announcement the ads of a numerous fraternity of soothsayers, astrologers, prophets, palmists, necromancers and sundry commercial medicine men willing and anxious to exert their occult powers for the benefit of suffering humanity at prices ranging from 10c. at Coney Island to $10 on Fifth Avenue.

One of the largest of these ads read:

> He gives advice on business, speculation, love, *Court-ship, Marriage, and Divorce.*
> Settles lovers' quarrels, reunites the separated, causes a speedy and happy marriage with the one of your choice. The earth reveals to him the hidden treasures buried in her bosom. He locates mines, interprets dreams, tells of your friends and enemies, removes evil influence, gives advice pertaining to law suits; everything.

Another announces that

PROF. JOSEPH RIES

Is the only clairvoyant ever having been accorded receptions by the European sovereigns, to whose courts he has been invited. He has successfully penetrated the secrets of the Monarchs, Princes, Diplomats, Statesmen and the most distinguished in the philosophic and scientific world.

One of the most eminent of these practitioners had quarters in a brownstone mansion where he held forth to an exclusive clientele. The door was opened by a flunky in livery who ushered the prospective customer into a waiting room of sumptuous splendor. This, however, was a mere ante room to the real business quarters which were furnished with due regard for all the legendary necessities of the situation. A dim religious light pervaded the Oriental magnificence of the apartment, an incense burner sent out a langourous perfume, and the entire *mise en scene* would have done credit to the stage of the "Green Goddess." The particular exponents of the mysteries, who did business here, had a following of women who, besides the regular professional fees, pressed jewels of price upon him, and held him in exalted esteem. In fact the proverbial Indian potentate had nothing on this Western sorcerer in the matter of the little luxuries of life.

About thirty years ago, however, the "real thing" in soothsayers, invaded New York in the person of one

"Cheiro," a specialist in palm reading, with headquarters in Bond Street, London, who opened a branch on Fifth Avenue. Cheiro was a tall handsome young man with glossy locks, an Oxford accent and testimonials from Duchesses, Countesses and any number of the landed gentry of Great Britain. Cheiro established quite a vogue among the "400" and if I am not mistaken published a book on palmistry. Numerous imitators sprang up under similar sounding titles, such as "Chiro," "Chero," etc., but they were crude quacks with none of Chiero's social graces. He flourished in New York for some time, but suddenly vanished from the scene leaving at least one disciple who practised on West 43rd Street under the aegio of "Cheiro's certified pupil."

Lower in the professional scale were such as "Countess Zingara," gipsy palmist, who told fortunes in the Sixth Avenue shopping district for 50c. and $1.00 with an occasional advance in price when the future was foggy; and Gonzales, who combined palmistry and astrology with daily "readings." In fact nearly all of the craft were general practitioners of black magic, equally proficient in palmistry, astrology, crystal ball reading, clairvoyancy, spiritualism or whatever happened to be the caper of the hour. Some even had the hardihood to lecture to congenial audiences on Sunday nights in numerous small halls throughout the city. One notorious affair of the kind occurred in Chickering Hall, where a discourse on spiritualism became such a ludicrous farce that the audience got its money's worth in laughter instead of in the anticipated scientific instruction.

There was a vast public to support these charlatans, even among the poor of the tenement houses. Knavish women sold love philtres to hard working German and

Irish servant girls who had conceived attachments to butcher's boys. Voodoo doctors terrorized the Thompson Street and Seventh Avenue darkies with incantations and spells.

Every small stationer and bookseller kept a stock of dream books. "Napoleon's Dream Book," "The Gipsy's Dream Book," "How to Tell Fortunes," "The Egyptian Oracle," etc., were always part of the decorative scheme in the windows of penny toy and candy shops where they commanded a ready sale, and were bought not alone by benighted housemaids but in many cases by their mistresses.

The business of public rag picking was an institution that flourished most prolifically as pursued years ago, by ancient Italians in the streets of New York. The figure of a wretched male or female tatterdemalion poking with an iron hook in the ash barrels which in those days contained the promiscuous refuse of households was a familiar one. This method of salvage is now under Street Cleaning supervision. There were some surprising reincarnations as a result of the old system in the way of resuscitated hats that found their way to Baxter Street, there to be offered for sale as fruit plucked from the hat stands of the Fifth Avenue Hotel and other noted hat bearing arbors.

Before the consolidation of the railroad ticket offices, most of the important roads had their own branch offices, located principally on Broadway from Chambers to Canal Streets. Interspersed with these were any number of "ticket scalpers," who dealt in unused railroad and steamboat tickets and passes. In those days the railroads did not redeem unused tickets and there was a lucrative trade driven in them by dealers. There was also a large

The only woman in town who smoked

Scene from the famous Black Crook, which doesn't look so naughty to us as it did to our daddies.

excursion business done by the railroads, which used to sell round trip tickets for the price of a single fair or a little over. It was customary for the "wise ones" to travel on these tickets and to sell the return stub to "scalpers." Excursion tickets in those days were good for an extended period and this made the practice possible. Railroad rate wars were common, one of the most bitter being that between the N. Y. Central and the West Shore.

Where, oh where, is that ancient darky or his female consort who used to make the quiet summer nights musical with the cry of "Hot Corn?" Where is his steaming kettle, and the paint brush wherewith he would anoint the golden kernels with butter? Of all the cries of Gotham, his were by far the most melodious, and the notes of that black nightingale were of such potent persuasion that one must have dined well not to pause for at least a moment at the call. There was also a sable vender of cold soft shell crabs whose notes were dulcet, and in the middle "Nineties" a white garbed figure visited the glimpses of the moon selling "Hot Tamales."

Little boys used to sell penny cylinders of lozenges "lemon," "peppermint," and "wintergreen" flavored, in Central Park, and a great favorite with juvenilia was the "bolivar" sold on corner fruit stands. The "bolivar" was a tasteful, but usually stale, cake of gingerbread, yet was nevertheless considered a delicacy by the hungry youngsters.

Another delicacy was the penny cup of ice cream sold by the Italian venders. This was sometimes varied by a dab of ice cream licked avidly off a piece of brown paper. When "brick" ice cream made its appearance it was immediately translated into miniature slabs for youthful consumption and sold under the name of "hokey-pokey."

It was during the Eighties than an attempt was made to introduce that classic British institution, the barmaid, in connection with a theater, in the basement of Wallack's at Thirtieth Street where a barroom was opened with the maids in attendance. The venture bid fair to be a success, as many people liked the idea of barmaids mixing their drinks; but the police would not permit it to continue, as there was a stairway to the barroom leading from the lobby of the theater in violation of the excise law. The first English barmaids ever seen in New York were introduced by Alex. Henderson, husband of Lydia Thompson, of "British Blondes" fame, in a saloon in New Street, near the Stock Exchange. There were eight of them but the venture was a failure as the "boys" so guyed them that they soon after returned to the congenial atmosphere of Lombard Street.

That distinguished patron of the drama, the old-time gallery god is for all practical purposes an extinct species. The gallery in the modern theater that still caters to the social extremes, finds an extremely tame and undemonstrative patron compared with the "boys" of the old "Bowery," "Windsor," "Peoples," "Miners," and "London" theaters. The thrills obtainable at these temples of the drama are now conjured in the "movies" and the old gallery god is now slicked up in the "New York manner," mixes in with the connoisseurs of the stalls, and gazes enraptured at scenes of carnage, violence and sudden death that would turn "Sure Shot, the Demon Avenger" of

Just in time to be too late—a daily scene at any of our ferries

the old Bowery boards, greener with envy than any calcium tint cast down upon him could do.

The real old-time gallery was furnished for its elastic seating capacity. It was supplied with benches in which there was always room for one more. Its social code was also elastic. Pandemonium reigned before the rising of the curtain and between the acts, quelled only by the sharp demand "Order, Gents!" supplemented by the resounding blows of a rattan stick on the woodwork. Tobacco chewing was universal and "Hey! Mike, chuck us your plug" was a familiar cry. Spitting was performed *ad libitum,* but the unpardonable sin from the managerial standpoint, was to expel tobacco juice upon the occupants of the orchestra. This, if detected, meant sudden, painful and ignominious ejection down an incredibly steep stairway, probably by a boot. On the other hand, no apology was offered for the same delicate attention bestowed on a neighbor, said neighbor's only redress being to "put up his dukes." Among the other innocent pranks of the gallery boy was the surreptitious hurling of "spit balls" at some objectionable figure in the boxes. A dress suit with an "open face shirt" was sure to draw the fire of the gallery marksmen. I may here mention that dress suits on the East Side were frequently worn with four-in-hand ties, tucked in the shirt bosom, and ornamented with horseshoe scarfpins.

One of the most picturesque characters New York has ever known was P. T. Barnum, whose benign countenance was the greatest attraction in the great parade which marked the formal opening of the annual circus in Madison Square Garden. He lived for many years at 484 Fifth Avenue and in his younger days was quite a noted figure in the everyday life of the growing city. At the request of Washington Irv-

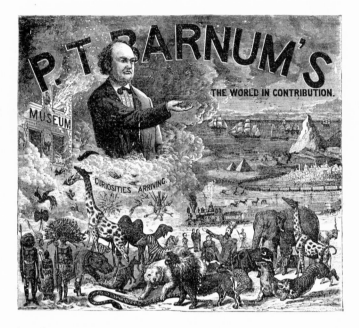

ing he became president of the first of the industrial exhibitions ever held in this country—the well-remembered Crystal Palace erected in Bryant Park. He was also one of the committee which created Central Park, also in association with Irving who was President of the Commission.

His life, written by himself, achieved an enormous circulation and of late he has been the subject of other books depicting his career so that the details of his spectacular career are quite well known to my readers. As he occupied Madison Square Garden at the period of which I write—more than twenty years before the structure built by Stanford White and which is the only Garden the present generation knows about, I want to recall one incident of this period which I am sure will be eagerly read by the boys and girls of that day. I refer to Jumbo—the most interesting, lovable, popular and fascinating wild animal ever shown in captivity. I cannot possibly depict the wonderful fascination this great elephant had for the little folks not only in our country but in England as well. It was from the London Zoo that Barnum got him. The two countries were plunged in grief at the news of his untimely end.

No animal ever existed, it is safe to say, that was so universally beloved. He was of enormous size and in proportion to his strength and his bulk so was his exquisite tenderness in caring for children. He had human intelligence in this direction. If a child happened in his path the huge beast would stop and carefully nose the little figure to a place of safety. It is quite impossible to describe the affection that children had for this amazing animal and this affection was cordially returned by Jumbo. Even at this late date I am conscious of the pain the sad news brought to me, a feeling that was shared wherever a boy or girl existed.

Even his death was in keeping with his life. Always on the lookout for the safety of others he saw an approaching train about to crash into the baby elephant of the troup. In a vain attempt to push the threatened youngster to a place of safety the huge beast received the full impact of the train himself and in a few minutes expired from his injuries. His skin is now stuffed and rests in Tuft's College.

Barnum's most famous attraction—"Jumbo" the greatest
elephant ever shown in captivity

The news of his death created the most profound
sadness that had overtaken childhood in many a day.
Even the staid old London papers announced the
tragedy in three column headings—a hitherto unknown performance. We append herewith an account of
Jumbo's life. The skeleton of this noble animal is now
preserved in our own American Museum of Natural
History.

"Jumbo was known to everybody in this country east of the
Mississippi River and had probably been seen by more persons
than any other animal that ever made the tour of the land in
captivity. If not the largest elephant in the world, he was certainly the most massive animal that was ever exhibited, and in
this respect he stood alone in the brute creation. His weight
was 7½ tons. His trunk, for a distance of two feet from its

base, was as large around as the body of a stout man, and when he raised it aloft to catch the apples, cakes, and other dainties which his admirers were constantly tossing into his gaping mouth, the end was 26 feet in the air. His length was out of all proportion to his height, so that he looked short and stubby, and a front view gave almost as good an idea of the massiveness of his body as a place at his side. He was a native of Africa and supposed to be about 22 years old when he first stepped on American shores in 1882, so that at the time of his violent death he was still a young elephant, probably not over 25 years of age.

"The giant elephant was captured by a party of Arabs when a calf presumably about 2 years old, and by them carried on camels across the desert to Zanzibar. At this time he was a small animal, showing no points of difference from other elephants, and giving no signs of the tremendous proportions into which he was to develop. The Arabs sold the young elephant to an agent of the Jardin des Plantes, of Paris, for a trifling sum, and the future monarch of his race was transferred to France. Here he remained for a time, attracting no more attention than the other animals in the garden, until finally an exchange of a number of specimens was made between the Jardin des Plantes and the Zoological Garden in London. Jumbo was one of the animals sent from Paris, and was turned over to Keeper Scott, who has ever since attended him. Scott has a picture of Jumbo taken at this time, with the keeper standing by his side, and this shows that the keeper was then a head taller than his charge. Nobody dreamed at this time of the immense height to which Jumbo would attain, and the beast was looked upon with languid interest by the frequenters of the Gardens, as were the other live curiosities.

"The elephant was always kind and gentle, and he gradually became a great favorite with the children, who were never tired of riding on his back, and he in turn seemed to take naturally to the little ones, and never to weary of rocking them on his back. In the meantime, however, he was growing rapidly, and his keeper and the Directors of the Gardens soon found that he was getting much larger than the other elephants. He continued to expand until he had reached the height of about 11 feet, and the other animals of his species appeared like lilliputians beside him. He continued tractable, however, and his fondness for children seemed rather to increase than diminish with his rapid growth. He was the great feature of the Gardens, and the Queen herself did not scorn to pay him many a royal visit.

"The elephant's immense size suggested the name of Jumbo to Keeper Scott, and the name soon became a household word all over the United Kingdom. Children instead of asking their parents to take them to the Gardens would plead for permission to visit Jumbo, which to them represented all that there was of interest in the institution. To ride upon Jumbo's back, to feed him with apples and candy, and to stand gazing at the huge brute by the hour was the great ambition of every true British boy and girl, and men and women were inspired with a good deal of the same ambition. Foreigners on business or pleasure trips never failed to visit Jumbo, for not to have seen the gentle brute was not to have seen one of the sights of the great city.

"The fame of Jumbo could not be confined to the United Kingdom. It naturally crossed the Atlantic, and P. T. Barnum as naturally made up his mind to secure the largest and best advertised attraction in the world for his great show. Early in 1882 he sent an agent to London to negotiate for the purchase of Jumbo. The time was auspicious, for notwithstanding the brute's proved gentleness and tractability a fear that he might suddenly be seized with the species of insanity which usually attacks every captive elephant at some time in his career had arisen in England, and as Jumbo advanced in years British mothers were less disposed to trust their children within reach of his ponderous trunk. The Directors of the Gardens felt the same uneasiness, and were well disposed to relieve themselves of all responsibility for trouble in the future if they could sell Jumbo for a good round sum to the American showman. The result of the negotiations was that a contract was made between the Directors and Mr. Barnum for the sale of the monster elephant for $10,000, and Mr. Barnum began to make preparations for bringing Jumbo to America.

"The moment it was known in England that Jumbo had been sold all fear in regard to his future conduct disappeared, and a universal cry of indignation went up from one end of the United Kingdom to the other. Jumbo was looked upon as a national pet, and his removal was denounced as a national disgrace. The newspapers, not only of London, but of other large cities, and even of provincial towns, were filled with column after column of protests against the execution of the bargain. The Directors of the Gardens were assailed with an avalanche of abuse for daring to part with the elephant, and the news of the controversy about Jumbo was cabled as regularly all over the world as the reports of other national events. John Ruskin wrote a long letter, which was widely published, protesting against the sale of Jumbo, and declaring that England was not in the habit of parting with her pets.

"Mr. Barnum's agent, however, had paid the purchase money, and the Directors were powerless to annul the contract. Mr. Barnum was appealed to in vain to renounce his claim on the giant. The Queen and the Prince of Wales declared that the elephant should not be allowed to leave England, and the Queen advised the counsel not to deliver him up, but allow Mr. Barnum to sue for damages. 'Great Britain can pay him his damages,' she was reported to have said. Meantime, a suit was begun in Chancery for the annulment of the sale on the ground that the Directors of the Gardens had no right to make it. It took five weeks to decide this suit, which was finally declared in favor of Mr. Barnum.

"The result of all this excitement was that crowds rushed to the Zoological Gardens to see the cause of it. The Directors had Mr. Barnum's $10,000, and it was estimated that they cleared $30,000 more while the fight over Jumbo was going on. When the court finally rendered a decision in favor of Mr. Barnum, Parliament passed a law forbidding any passenger of a steamer to be on the same deck with Jumbo on his passage over. As two decks of the steamship *Assyrian Monarch* had to be used for the accommodation of the elephant, his purchaser was obliged to pay the passage money for all the passengers which the steamship company thus lost, and this brought the expense of bringing Jumbo to America up to about $30,000. He was transported in a large iron-bound box, which, with himself weighed $12\frac{1}{2}$ tons. Thousands gathered at the dock to wave a farewell to the London pet, and the scene at his departure was like that at the sailing from home of some great man. Children cried, and men and women cheered as the steamship moved away. Mr. Barnum had promised to take Jumbo back to England at some future time, and the newspapers printed this promise for the consolation of the mourners after the giant elephant was well on his way to the shores of America.

"The *Assyrian Monarch* arrived at New York with Jumbo on board safe and well April 9, 1882, after a voyage of 14 days. Keeper Scott accompanied his charge, and never left Jumbo until his death. The great box and its precious cargo was lifted from the steamer by a floating derrick and drawn to Madison Square Garden by 16 horses, where Barnum's show was then exhibiting. Within three days the extra receipts at the Garden more than covered the amount which it had cost to bring Jumbo from London. New York went wild over the monster elephant, who soon accustomed himself to his new surroundings and method of life. Jumbo was exhibited during four seasons to over 4,000,000 children and over 16,000,000 people. He was the great feature of Barnum's show, and the little ones of America took as kindly to him as did those of England. Jumbo was never so docile as when his back was covered with children, and during the whole time of his American experience he showed no symptoms of the insanity which the Directors of the Zoological Gardens had feared would afflict him. He had become as much the pet of America as he had been of London, and many a child in this city will hear of his death with mournful regret."

Barnum, who knew the value of publicity as well as any man, made his two-a-day appearance the same as any of the other attractions. He said, and it was true, that he was as much of a "card" as any of his performers. At all events his regular appearance on these occasions was greatly enjoyed by his immense audience, and there is no doubt that a "close up" of the greatest circus man the world has ever known, was one of the greatest satisfactions his patrons knew. The annual opening of the Circus at Madison Square Garden was distinctly an event of the Spring and it was eagerly anticipated by the old as well as the young.

Notwithstanding the peculiar business in which he was engaged and the rather nebulous reputation which he enjoyed as a result, the fact remains that Mr. Barnum was a man of the highest integrity and of the most scrupulous honesty. Although he was fond of saying that the people liked to be humbugged he was exceedingly careful not to humbug them himself. No matter how he got you there you always came away more than satisfied with what you'd seen.

Reading an advertisement in a country paper that a cherry colored cat was for sale for fifty dollars Barnum, scenting at once a rare attraction, sent the man a check for this amount. When pussy arrived she was black! "There's a sucker bórn every minute," was his only comment when he finished laughing.

Immediately however, he caused the town to be smothered with huge posters advertising the great natural freak—a Cherry Colored Cat. Crowds flocked to his Museum and soon the cost of the cat was returned many times over.

In the rear of the first floor was the sign "This way to the Egress." It led to the street and it cost 10c to get in again. His Museum, which in the Sixties occupied the corner of Broadway and Ann Street, was burned to the ground. This was also the last fire at which the volunteer fire companies were called into action, the paid fire department taking their place within a few days.

Perhaps the most engaging attraction that Barnum ever possessed was the little midget, Tom Thumb or General Tom Thumb as Barnum pleased to call him. Tom was a remarkable freak of nature; of bright wit and a sunny disposition he became an idol of the American public. When Barnum announced the midget's approaching marriage to another diminutive specimen—Miss Minnie Warren—there was not room enough in the spacious Museum to hold the crowds who wanted to witness the ceremony.

Mrs. Tom Thumb survived her husband many years and it is not so long ago that I read of her demise. She had gone to live in a house in Medford, Mass., I think, where the rooms, furniture and everything had been built to accommodate her particular size. It was a veritable doll's house.

Old Blind Tom, a wonderful negro pianist, was also a marvelous success. After once hearing a piece played, Blind Tom could duplicate the performance to the last note. He was wonderfully well liked and made a nice fortune under Barnum's management.

There were other attractions equally great—the White Elephant and last but by no means least—Jumbo—the greatest drawing card for a circus that was ever brought to these shores just described.

Early in the Eighties a great craze for picture cards struck the city and every storekeeper was beseiged by children crying, "Say mister, will you gimme me some picture cards?" They trooped from one store to another and reaped a rich harvest.

I think it was E. C. Burt & Co., the shoe manufacturers, who started the craze. They imported a lot of cards from France made by Vallet Minot & Co. They were at once a tremendous hit. Nothing like them had ever been seen before. The excellent designs, the brilliant coloring, combined to produce an effect that was at once fascinating and attractive. As they were distributed free, the demand was enormous. The idea was contagious and soon every lithographer in town was running his presses day and night.

The idea was not exactly new, for the shipping people had used colored cards as far back as the Clipper days. But the new cards were far more beautiful in execution, much more attractive in design and were easily obtainable. The ship men confined their distribution to only a few customers. The craze assumed enormous proportions and finally became a great nuisance to the retail merchant so that in self defense he was obliged to discontinue it. While it lasted, these pretty conceptions were printed by the hundreds of millions, and some handsome fortunes were made by those engaged in the business. It would be of great interest to have a complete collection of all those published though I presume it would take a good size building to hold them all. The boom lasted several years and was followed by a development of other card ideas which, strange to relate, have attained a place of permanency in the business world while their progenitor is practically forgotten.

The Christmas card is perhaps the oldest member of the family. It had already appeared but was not in general use. It made rapid strides after the original craze and is now a staple article. Greeting cards, Easter cards and Birthday cards have been added to this line. The Picture Post Card, the greatest publishing idea in a generation, was the thought of an English school boy. It also is a permanent addition to the publishing business and in the vastness of its output probably represents more money than all the others combined.

The business card was followed by an enormous development of lithographic advertising in the way of fans, cut-out figures, artists' palettes, and other novelties given to each purchaser in a store, followed by posters, window displays, and a hundred other methods in which highly colored designs were the dominating idea. The cigarette people in particular made wide use of this new school of advertising. They have preserved for posterity a long list of ladies distinguished mainly for their contour. One good result was to perfect the color printing process in this country to a point where it compared favorably with the best in Europe. The line of work covered by the lithographer embraced almost every possible grade and a high degree of artistic excellence was attained. So in a perfectly unintentional way Mr. Burt called into being one of the greatest industries of our country today and he ought to be enshrined in the hearts of the Lithographers Union.

One of the allied trades which greatly benefited by this improvement in the graphic art was the Bill Poster. He was a picturesque figure in these days and bore no resemblance to the millionaires in this line today. His chief aim in life was to cover the town, especially the curb stones, with gutter snipes. Ash barrels, which stood on every corner, were also the recipients of his delicate attentions. Rival bill stickers each had a religious duty to perform and that was to cover up the paper of his competitor. This led to many an appearance of the belligerents in police courts with their heads artistically swathed in bandages. There was nothing sacred to the bill sticker. Anything that would stand still long enough for him to wield his paste brush was sure to be covered with a bill of some kind.

On the beach at Coney, 1876

The formal opening of the Metropolitan Museum of Art became an accomplished fact in the spring of '79 with Mr. John Taylor Johnston as first president. Up to this time such works of art as were of transcendent interest were housed in the private galleries of a few well-known citizens—Aspinwall, Marquand, Belmont, Johnston, Stewart and Vanderbilt. Admission to these galleries was by private card which was sent upon application through the secretaries of these various owners. All the guide books carried a note to this effect. Mr. Johnston was rightly entitled to the honor conferred upon him by his election as first President. For years his house at the corner of Fifth Avenue and Eighth Street contained an annex which he had converted into an Art Gallery. It was his custom to open the gallery to the general public who were welcomed without the formality of a card. In this way public taste was fostered for the creation of the Institution which was shortly to follow.

Begun in '69, years were to elapse ere the Museum was finally in its own building. Meantime it occupied several temporary locations—Dodsworth's Dance Hall at 681 Fifth Avenue being the first and the Douglass Mansion on Fourteenth Street near Sixth Avenue, now the Salvation Army storehouse, the second. Boss Tweed had a good deal to do with the starting of this Museum. He was all powerful in the Legislature and when the matter was brought to his attention it received his hearty approval and shortly thereafter the necessary legislation was enacted and the funds granted for the erection of the building and a section of land in Central Park added for a site. All in all there was the lapse of ten years between the first agitation for this Museum and a final realization of the plan. Mr. Johnston subscribed $10,000,

Mr. A. T. Stewart $5,000 and Mr. W. T. Blodgett $5,000, and their generous example was imitated in a great or less degree by many other gentlemen. The new American Wing, recently added to the Museum, is also the benefaction of the Johnston family, Mrs. Robert W. de Forest being a daughter of the first President of the Museum.

In its early days the Museum was closed on Sunday and for many years the Trustees were bitterly assailed for their continued refusal to open its doors on the one day of the week when the average citizen could find the time to pay it a visit. The late J. A. Mitchell, the cultured and scholarly editor of *Life,* led the attack of the liberals. He brought to his aid such powerful cartoonists as Charles Dana Gibson, then a young man and not yet known as the creator of the Gibson Girls but as an exceptionally talented young artist of the Du Maurier school; F. G. Attwood whose biting satire was delicious; Frank P. Bellew ("Chip") an irresistibly funny fellow; John Kendrick Bangs; E. S. Martin and a score of others. Keppler in *Puck* added to the ensemble and Keppler knew how to draw.

The controversy raged for many years. The number of converts to the Sunday opening idea among the Metropolitan's Trustees gradually increased and finally with the resignation of a few "die hards," the way was at last open for a move which placed it in the van of all the artistic educational forces in the country. No step that the Metropolitan has ever taken has done so much to enlarge its usefulness as the decision to open on Sundays.

Before the coming of the Metropolitan Museum (1878) such works of art as were of transcendent interest were housed in private galleries. This is Mr. Aspinwall's Gallery, corner Tenth Street and University Place

Henry Ward Beecher
As he appeared in 1859

CHAPTER V

RELIGIOUS ACTIVITIES – THE Y. M. C. A. – GREAT PREACHERS – HENRY WARD BEECHER – MOODY AND SANKEY – CAMP MEETINGS – BEGINNING OF THE DEPARTMENT STORE – FAMOUS BEAUTIES IN THE PETER MARIE COLLECTION OF MINIATURES.

LOOKING back to those old days, it seems to me that the ministers—not of one but of all denominations—occupied a more prominent place in the public eye than they do today. They did not have to compete, however, with radios, movies and other modern distractions and their intellectual influence in everyday life was much greater.

Dean Hoffman was then in charge of All Angels Episcopal Church and John Cotton Smith held forth at the Church of the Ascension. Right Reverend Horatio Potter was Bishop of the Diocese. Dr. Henry C. Potter and his renowned sexton, Isaac H. Brown, were then at Grace Church. Dr. Potter's elevation to the bishopric in later years marked the beginning of what might be called the Golden Age of Episcopalianism. He conceived and set in motion the idea of building a great Cathedral and lived to lay the cornerstone of that magnificent edifice on

Morningsic 'eights, the Cathedral of St. John the Divine. It is doubtfu whether any other minister of the Gospel in New York at that time excelled Bishop Potter in influence and popularity, not only as a great force in the religious life of the city but also as a mighty power in its civic affairs. He graced every occasion and became a formidable rival of Joseph H. Choate, a contemporary, in the field of gastronomic oratory.

Dr. Samuel Cooke of St. Bartholomew's; Dr. Tyng of St. George's; Dr. Rylance of St. Mark's; Dr. George J. Geer of St. Timothy's; Dr. George H. Hepworth of the Church of the Disciples; Dr. A. Cleveland Coxe of Calvary Episcopal Church, later Bishop Coxe, and his successor Dr. Henry Y. Satterlee, later Bishop Satterlee; Dr. Haight of St. Paul's; Dr. George H. Houghton of the Church of the Transfiguration, more popularly known as the "Little Church Around the Corner," of which many romantic tales are told; and Dr. Morgan Dix of Trinity—these were among the outstanding figures of the Episcopal Church.

St. Patrick's Cathedral on Fifth Avenue was still unfinished and services were yet held in its old location, Mott, corner of Prince Street. His Eminence, Right Reverend John McCloskey was Archbishop. There was as yet no Cardinal in New York.

In Old St. Peter's in Barclay Street, the first Roman Catholic Church in New York, the Rev. Dr. Edward McGlynn preached.

Among the Evangelical denominations Dr. Henry W. Bellows of the Unitarian Church of All Souls, Dr. Taylor of the Broadway Tabernacle, Congregationalist, and Dr. E. H. Chapin of the Fourth Universalist Church are well remembered. Dr. Chapin in particular. He was a man of great force, tremendous eloquence and brought the Universalist Church into the forefront of religious bodies. The Sixth Universalist Church was presided over by Dr. James M. Pullman, brother of the famous parlor-car builder. There was also Dr. Charles F. Deems of the Church of the Strangers, and Dr. Collier of the Universalist Church in Thirty-fourth Street, was the Community Church.

The most noted and revered preacher of the Presbyterian denomination for over a quarter of a century was the Rev. Dr. John Hall, pastor of the Fifth Avenue Presbyterian Church. This church being one of the largest and by far the most influential in the United States of that faith, Dr. Hall became a figure of national importance and was greatly beloved by the people of all denominations. His sermons were always gospel messages delivered in clear, concise and simple language and appealed to the heart as well as to the head. He rarely touched on topical subjects, but nevertheless he attracted a great congregation from the beginning to the end of his ministry. He was a man of large calibre, physically, and his intellectual equipment was of such an order as to fit perfectly his powerful physique. He died in the harness and was mourned sincerely by all the people.

A feature of Trinity Church which we cannot overlook is its daily midday services—an essential need for the business section of the city known as "Wall Street." These services are particularly good at Easter time and the preachers always prominent men. Bishop Phillip Brooks will be remembered as the most notable speaker at these midday services, occupying the pulpit daily.

Across the river, however, our sister City of Brooklyn led, both in eloquence and in influence, the religious life of the comm... ... Henry Ward Beecher, an old Amherst grad., fresh f... m the great reputation which he had acquired in his famous visit to England during the Civil War, was greeted every Sunday in Plymouth Church by enormous audiences. Strangers crossing to Brooklyn would inquire the way to this noted edifice and were told to get off at Fulton Ferry and follow the crowd. It is doubtful if the equal of Mr. Beecher as a public orator ever existed. It was said that a great actor was lost to make a great preacher; but without the spiritual background and the emotional atmosphere of a religious gathering the eloquence of Beecher would never have risen to such heights of fervor and power. On the political platform he was a past master. To Beecher, more than to any other single influence, President Cleveland owed his election. The line of strangers seeking admission to his church extended all the way from the doors of his church in Orange Street clear down to Fulton Street, where a double line of cars were unloading the hundreds of people who came from far and near to hear this great preacher. Our enterprising friend, Edward W. Bok, then a young man, commenced his brilliant publishing career by reporting the sermons of Mr. Beecher and syndicating them through the country. He thus also introduced a new idea in journalism.

It would be difficult for the present generation to understand just the unique position attained by Mr. Beecher. In all probability he was the most eloquent preacher that has graced the pulpit in modern times. His voice was singularly sympathetic and yet, at times, it rang through the building like a clarion call. In softer passages it would sink almost to a whisper. Yet it would be distinctly heard in every part of the room, so closely did he hold the attention of his audience   e man himself presented an attractive picture. He ad a lion-like head which was crowned by heavy silver locks, almost reaching to his shoulders. His face was smooth-shaven and the features heavy and rugged. He was slightly undersized but possessed a rugged frame and enjoyed robust health nearly every moment of his life. It was his wont to boast of his superb constitution which had come to him through a long line of hardy ancestors.

Preaching was a natural attribute of the Beecher family. Descended from Jonathan Edwards, the most important divine in his day, his talents were perfectly natural. His father, Lyman Beecher, was also a noted figure in religious circles but was wholly lost in the greater things that came to his son. His sister, Harriet Beecher Stowe, occupied a prominent place in the literary world, "Uncle Tom's Cabin" having contributed almost as much as any single influence to the overthrow of slavery. In every way nature had created in this man her perfect specimen of the orator. Mr. Ingersoll, upon one occasion, remarked that the world had waited many centuries for a Beecher and would wait centuries for another. This is probably true as no such unique character has appeared since his death and it is certain that none existed before.

The emotional atmosphere of the pulpit was undoubtedly a necessary background for the fullest display of his marvelous oratory. His audience would be moved to tears and laughter almost at the same time. His running comments on Bible stories, delivered on the spur of the moment, were wonders of beauty and grace. He seemed never at a loss for the right word in the right place. He himself frequently remarked that, while preaching was his work, he loved it so that it became his pleasure. Dur-

ing the summer in which he was absent from his church
for three months, he was by no means idle. Wherever
Beecher was, there he preached. Being a great sufferer
from hay-fever, he summered in the White Mountains.
Visitors there were always sure of the beautiful experience of hearing a sermon from the pastor of Plymouth
Church.

It was, of course, to be expected that a man who had
taken such a prominent part in the abolition movement
and had identified himself with public efforts all his life,
would naturally be found on the political rostrum in presi-
dential and occasionally local campaigns. Upon these
occasions his addresses were usually in a much lighter vein
and his fund of repartee and sarcasm, inexhaustible.
I remember, on one occasion, when Joseph C. Hendrix,
a totally unknown young man, was suddenly projected as
a candidate on the Democratic ticket for Mayor of
Brooklyn. It turned out that Mr. Hendrix was only
a reporter for the *New York Sun* and it was a well-known
fact that the *Sun* was a bitter opponent of Mr. Beecher
and Mr. Dana seldom permitted an opportunity to pass
without a scurrilous attack on the great Plymouth pastor.
At a political meeting when the whole city was wondering
who Hendrix was, Mr. Beecher seemed to divine their
thoughts. Picking up the Bible he opened it apparently
at random. "I was somewhat puzzled," he began, "to
know who this remarkable young man was. In perplexi-
ties of this kind I find it a great solace to consult the Good
Book and there in Isaiah, First Chapter, 14th Verse, I
found the solution." And he read, "Behold! An angel,
stood in the *Sun*."

When James G. Blaine was nominated for the Presidency, a great schism was produced in the Republican

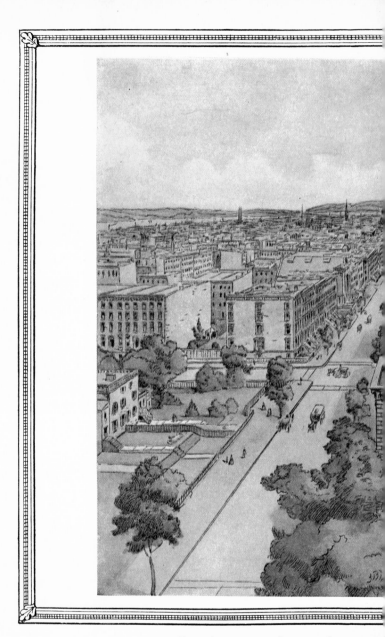

FIFTH AVENUE IN THE SEVENTIES. LOOKING SOU
FOREGROUND. RESIDENCE OF E. D. MO
SIZED

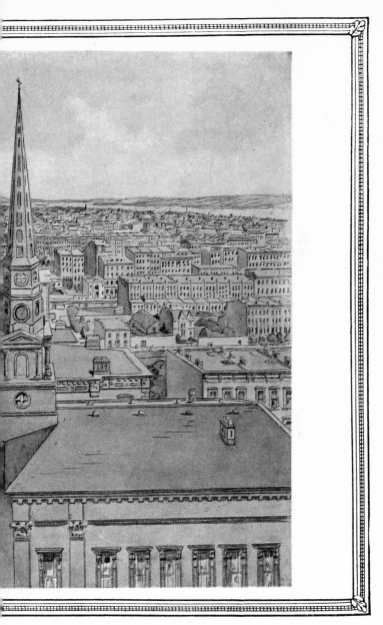

8TH STREET. BRICK PRESBYTERIAN CHURCH, RIGHT
ITE AND OTHERS STILL POSSESS GENEROUS
1873).

Party. The *New York Times,* the leading party organ, flatly refused to support the candidate. *Harper's Weekly,* the second influential publication, followed suit. It was hoped that the defection would not spread to King's County, at that time the most potent force in national politics. All eyes were turned toward Mr. Beecher. It was known that his Church was supported mostly by men high in the councils of the Republican Party and of great weight in national affairs. Their influence was counted upon to keep Mr. Beecher in line, although the gentlemen knew better than to make such a request of Mr. Beecher. In due time Mr. Beecher announced his position and it was in favor of Cleveland. The excitement which followed and continued during this campaign was something that was long remembered in our vicinity. During one of his stump speeches Mr. Beecher gave utterance to a remark which was largely a slip of the tongue. It was, however, most unfortunate, coming from a minister of the Gospel. Had Blaine been elected no doubt the matter would have ended there, but with Cleveland triumphant, the Republicans of Plymouth Church took their defeat very much to heart. There were many reports regarding their hostile attitude toward Mr. Beecher and remarks spread far and fast that their financial support had been withdrawn and that Mr. Beecher would be unable to continue at Plymouth Church.

It was my good fortune to be present when Mr. Beecher took cognizance of these reports and at once plunged into the heart of the subject by speaking of them in his own peculiarly touching manner. "I am told," he said, "that I have forfeited the friendship and the good-will of Plymouth Church. I am told that I have utterly destroyed its power for good in the world and that the support of its friends is to be withdrawn. My own salary is said to be far beyond the means of those who are left. I merely want to say that I have never known very much about my salary. Mrs. Beecher attends to all that. But I want to simply ask you to reduce that salary to whatever sum you feel you can pay—but don't send me away from Plymouth Church. If $20,000 is beyond your means let's make it $10,000, and if that is still unreasonable, let us make it $5,000—but don't send me away from old Plymouth. I could not stand it to be sent away. I came here a very young man from Indianapolis and my whole life has been spent here in Plymouth. Things have not changed much with me in my personal wants and I could still stay and preach for you at $1,500, and I would rather do it than have you send me away from old Plymouth."

By this time the congregation was in tears and all over the house there were suspicious sounds that proclaimed how deeply touched were the hearts of his hearers. When he closed his last plea and begged them not to send him away from Old Plymouth, it was a foregone conclusion that no more allusions would ever be made either to his salary or to the unfortunate remark that was at the bottom of the trouble, and so it proved to be.

About this time the Y. M. C. A. took possession of their imposing new building on Twenty-third Street and Fourth Avenue. This was a very noted structure and probably the most pretentious building in the country at the time. It had many special features and was designed with the single thought of meeting every condition pertaining to the work of the Association. No such elaborate and meticulous care had ever been bestowed upon any building in New York. The completion of this undertaking gave an immense impetus to Y. M. C. A. work and

The Y. M. C. A. Building, Twenty-third Street and Fourth Avenue, 1880.
National Academy of Design opposite

from this building might be dated the present nation-wide influence which this extraordinary organization now possesses. It was scarcely a decade before, that they occupied but two rooms in the Bible House at Ninth Street, of a most unpretentious character. Into these modest quarters, however, wandered a young man destined to become a powerful factor in the development of the work.

Like President McCosh of Princeton, he came from the north of Ireland and engaged temporarily in the hat business. He would undoubtedly have reared for himself a name equal to Stetson or Knox had he chosen to remain in that field, but the work in the dingy little room in the Bible House appealed to his spiritual nature and, although his remuneration was only five dollars a week, his liking for the work was so great that in a very few months he determined to consecrate himself to its furtherance. Such is the entrance of Robert M. McBurney, a figure that was to be dominant for more than thirty years in the councils of the Y. M. C. A. To his indomitable courage and limitless patience the affairs of the Association were satisfactorily guided through these early days. The new building was largely erected under his supervision and its success, architecturally and structurally, was the result of his planning. When one passes in review the vast number of buildings and the enormous clerical force now required to administer the business of this Institution, it seems hardly possible that within the life-time of men now living the entire work was performed by one man. For several years Mr. McBurney was the only salaried executive possessed by the Association.

Closely following Mr. McBurney, came another picturesque figure in the person of Richard C. Morse. Mr. Morse, now in his eighty-fourth year, still possesses an optimism and a capacity for work that would do credit to a much younger man. He has, however, the great advantage of coming from a line of ancestors who, with one exception, declined to lay down life's burden until they were well within striking distance of the century mark. He is the last surviving member of that brilliant group who originally took over the idea from England—service for young men. They developed it on this side of the world on a scale so gigantic as to utterly dwarf the parent body. Speaking of this interesting period, Mr. Morse has this to say:

"It was a threefold work—spiritual, social and educational—that had come to us from London under the leadership of George Williams, but it was in New York, under the leadership of such Christian laymen and Association members as William E. Dodge, Jr., D. Willis James, C. R. Agnew, Morris K. Jessup, Wm. F. Lee, John Crosby Brown, J. Pierpont Morgan, Cephas Brainerd, James Stokes, Jr., with Robert M. McBurney as their General Secretary, that the new departure of a fourfold work, with gymnasium and bowling alley attachment was so happily accomplished. It was by this extension that the leadership of the World Y. M. C. A. Movement passed from London to New York."

Among these early workers in this great movement was one figure destined to attain great eminence in his chosen field, Dwight L. Moody, one of the most eloquent evangelists this country has ever produced.

Mr. Moody came from Chicago where he was engaged as a salesman in a retail store. He was one of that brilliant group of young men who, following the lead of Robert M. McBurney, abandoned secular work for the more congenial atmosphere afforded by the newly

organized Y. M. C. A. movement. From the beginning
Mr. Moody revealed surpassing qualities as an exhorter.
It is said that he knew every sentence in the Bible and was
so thoroughly versed in its lore that he had an answer or
a simile for every possible contingency. In the possession of this peculiar knowledge he was invincible in argu-
ment and irresistible in logic. Upon his own initiative he
made a trip to England in company with Mr. Sankey and
scored a tremendous success as an evangelist. Upon his
return to America his great London reputation opened a
wide field for his talents in America and at the time of
which we write he was holding a series of revival meetings
in the great Hippodrome, where he preached to enormous
audiences. The effects of the Civil War were still seen
in the groping of the people after some consolation in a
spiritual sense, very much as it was in our own time directly after the Armistice.

Ira D. Sankey, Mr. Moody's associate, possessed a very
sweet tenor voice and to hear him sing the first verse of
a hymn which became very popular, "There were Ninety
and Nine," was a soul-stirring experience. Indeed the
music was a large factor in the success of these services.
Everybody joined in the singing and the effect was inde-
scribable. Thousands to this day remember "Hold the
Fort," "Beulah Land," "Pull for the Shore Sailors,"
"The Shining Shore," "Sweet Bye and Bye" and other
favorites. There was a peculiar Mason-and-Hamlin-
parlor-melodeon atmosphere about these Moody and
Sankey meetings which now seems to me not the least
delightful of the memories that linger around these old-
time exhorters. For many years after the revivals ceased,
their hymns were sung in Sunday Schools throughout
the country and undoubtedly accomplished great good.

Mr. Moody preaching at a great revival meeting. Mr. Sankey at right

In the summer time the religious fervor of the city was transferred to the country and many well-known fashionable resorts of today had their beginnings at that time as Camp Meetings for various enthusiasts. Sea Cliff was quite prominent and was the headquarters of a great temperance movement.

The chief drawing card at these gatherings seems to have been reformed drunkards whose delicate allusions to their lurid past formed the *piece de resistance* of these performances. One in particular, a Mr. Murphy by name, did not spare himself in any respect whatever. According to this gentleman's unvarnished account of his bibulous career, his chief recreation was to beat up the missus, kick the children around the house and add any other diabolical treatment which his gentle soul might suggest. Mr. Murphy was evidently an artist in his line and enjoyed the somewhat dubious distinction of a headliner in this business. He added quite a few other ghastly details which I need not repeat here. There is no accounting for the taste of some people and certainly to read Mr. Murphy's delightful reminiscences was to absorb as distressing an account of human degradation as is possible to imagine. It does not seem to me that such a story told today would have any other result than to cause a wave of indignation such as would drive the speaker from the platform. Mr. Murphy, however, was only one of a long list of popular attractions, at that time known as "horrible examples."

Another great seat of religious enthusiasm was Ocean Grove. It was the headquarters of the Methodists. They started with a modest collection of tents which gradually grew until it became quite a city. After a while they built a huge tabernacle and each season the crowds increased in number. I remember standing on the beach one Sunday evening when the vast throng sang a popular hymn entitled, "May God Be With Us 'Til We Meet Again." To hear that huge audience singing with the utmost feeling, this wonderfully beautiful hymn was a strangely moving experience. It was peculiarly appropriate on that night, as it marked the last meeting of the season. Even to this day I recall how profoundly I was swayed by the emotion of the moment. This hymn afterwards became widely known through the late President McKinley's affection for it, and it was sung a great many times during the tragedy that removed this amiable figure from our national life. Ocean Grove became a permanent fixture and has practically created the beautiful resort which we know today. It still retains some of the Puritan aspect of these early days, especially in its local ordinances regarding Sunday observance. No motor cars are allowed to visit the Grove and the entire day is given up to a strict observance of its religious duties. At that time Ocean Grove marked the extreme limit of the summer resort region of the Jersey coast. Beyond that, scrub oak and pines occupied the beach without interruption clear down to Cape May.

"Martha's Vineyard" was another famous summer place wholly given up to camp meetings. The great growth of the vacation habit has now converted all these erstwhile religious retreats to the common, everyday, garden variety of summer resort, in which the one-piece bathing suit has usurped the center of the stage and the song of the psalmist has died in the land.

There were many other devout and able men in the field of church work and perhaps it will be interesting to recall a few of the many who made New York an important religious center in those days.

One of the best known was Dr. Charles Parkhurst, minister of the Madison Avenue Presbyterian Church. His fame arose more from his civic activities than his preaching. Alone and single handed he fought the powers of evil at a time when they were rampant in the so-called tenderloin district. He ruthlessly exposed the graft, gambling and frightful immorality which were rife at that time and from his pulpit made specific charges against the authorities, supported by affidavits of his own personal experience. Dr. Parkhurst's exposures created the wildest excitement in the city and his fame spread over the entire country. He had all the great qualities of the Hebrew prophets—bold, fearless and even fierce and he accomplished work which may be classed with theirs. How much better conditions have been since his day! After these stirring events a new church was built for him opposite the site of the old. It was designed by Stanford White and was considered one of that great architect's finest works; but it has passed away and the city lost one of its very few classics in moving picture architecture, as applied to churches.

Dr. Edward Eggleston was a picturesque figure among the clergymen of Brooklyn. He had been a circuit rider in the Far West for many years and enjoyed considerable literary fame. He had a large head covered with a shock of long, thick brown hair which had a habit of falling over his face when he was animated and talking, but there was a softness in the eye and a charm in the voice which captivated his hearers and made him many friends. He came to New York in the early Seventies and was associated with Theodore Tilton as editor of a religious pub-

The Flower Market in Union Square, 1880

lication. He conceived the idea of establishing a church entirely free and independent of any denominational ties and for this purpose accepted the pastorate of the Lee Avenue Dutch Reformed Church, which then became the Church of Christian Endeavor. Dr. Eggleston was a prolific writer, the *Hoosier Schoolmaster* ranking as one of his best works. He was also a contributor for many years to the *Century Magazine,* then in the zenith of its influence. Dr. Eggleston retired on account of ill health when he was still a comparatively young man but lived long enough to produce his greatest work, the *Household History of the United States and Its People.*

In the Congregational body the influence of Plymouth Church began to decline after Mr. Beecher's death and the Central Congregational Church gradually rose to a leading position. Dr. Behrends, its pastor, was widely known for his biblical scholarship and his Sunday evening discourses drew large and interested audiences. His morning sermons packed the church to its fullest capacity and for many years he was looked upon as a worthy successor of the great preacher of Plymouth Church.

The successor of Dr. Behrends is the present pastor of the church, Rev. S. Parkes Cadman, who has made this church the leading influence in the Congregational body and has become not only the most widely known preacher but also one of the most eloquent speakers on public questions in the United States. He is the only minister whose Sunday addresses are broadcast regularly over the radio to every part of the country. He has a clear carrying voice, a very energetic and forceful manner and a magnetic personality and has become by far the most noted clergyman in our city, or in fact in the country.

Another of the noted divines of long ago was Dr. Theodore Cuyler, the minister of the Lafayette Avenue Presbyterian Church. He was a hard worker in the cause of temperance at a time when people did not take prohibition seriously, but Dr. Theodore Cuyler was a rock of strength to the earnest souls who worked so faithfully for abolishing the saloon. Old residents of Brooklyn will remember the good old doctor when he became quite deaf and shouted from the pulpit in stentorian tones driving home the telling points of his discourse. He lived to be a very old man and became pastor emeritus of the church when his day of activity was over.

Another of the noted clergymen of Brooklyn in the Eighties was Dr. R. R. Meredith of the Tompkins Avenue Congregational Church. He came from the City Temple, Boston, and at once became a popular figure in our sister city. He will be remembered chiefly for his Tuesday evening lectures to Sunday school teachers which were undoubtedly the most careful and helpful expositions of the lessons that have ever been given. The large auditorium of the church was always crowded long before the lectures began and to many the most interesting part of the services after Dr. Meredith had finished his discourse was the leading questions he put to his audience and the answers they brought forth. When all was over every teacher acquired an abundance of information about the lesson for the coming Sunday. Those who were not teachers had a most inspiring time. Dr. Meredith left Brooklyn on account of poor health and went to Pasadena, Cal. He returned once to his old church when he was well over 80 years of age and preached to a great audience. It proved to be his last sermon as he lived only a short time after his return to his home in California,

St. John's M. E. Church was the principal one of that denomination in the Eastern District in those days. It boasted the largest Sunday School in Brooklyn for many years. Its congregation was made up largely of old families who had originally settled in Williamsburgh before it was incorporated with Brooklyn. The ministers of this church were usually leading men in the Methodist denomination, notably Dr. Warren, who became a bishop immediately after his transfer from St. John's to a western diocese.

Among the Episcopalian churches of Brooklyn, Holy Trinity is the chief. It is many years ago that the kindly and well beloved Cuthbert Hall preached there and those who do remember him will recall the large and devoted following he had. Dr. Hall was an admirer and intimate friend of his neighbor, Henry Ward Beecher, and they spent many an hour of good-fellowship together.

St. Ann's on Clinton Street stood next to Holy Trinity as a church of great influence in Episcopalian circles of Brooklyn, and St. Luke's ministered to the more aristocratic element in the Clinton and Clermont Avenues section.

Over in the Eastern District, Christ Episcopal Church will be remembered for the earnest and able men who ministered there. Perhaps the most noted was Rev. J. H. Darlington who for many years attracted large congregations, more perhaps from his personality than his eloquence and who carried on a great work among the young men of the congregation. He was the most beloved clergyman of his denomination in the Williamsburgh district and his fame spread beyond the limits of Brooklyn. So successful was he in his work and so much appreciated by the dignitaries of the Episcopal Church that he became, while still a young man, Bishop of Harrisburg, Pa., and is the bishop of that diocese at the present time.

St. James Episcopal Church in Lafayette Avenue and the Church of the Messiah in Greene Avenue are of more recent date but of no less importance in the religious and humanitarian life of the city.

The Baptist Temple was always a center of great activity in the social as well as religious affairs of Brooklyn. In a way it followed Dr. Parkhurst's methods. When Rev. Cortland Myers directed its activities the officials of Brooklyn were constantly attacked for the immoral conditions that existed and the Temple was ever in the public eye. Nevertheless much good was accomplished and the loss of Cortland Myers when he went to Boston was felt by the entire city.

The Metropolitan Temple, Methodist Episcopal, in Seventh Avenue, Manhattan, is one of New York's old institutions. When that section of the city was a select residential quarter the Temple was the center of the social and religious life of the people for miles around including Greenwich Village and Chelsea. Its most noted period was during Grant's presidency. Bishop Newman was then its pastor and he and Gen. Grant were intimate friends. It was at his instigation that Bishop Newman was sent on a mission around the world. Another famous pastor of the Temple was Dr. S. Parkes Cadman who preached then and directed its many activities for several years before he was called to his present charge in Brooklyn.

Calvary Baptist Church in Fifty-seventh Street was the leading church of that denomination in those days and has held that place down to the present time. Fifty years ago when the population of that neighborhood was rather sparse Dr. MacArthur came from Canada to take charge and make his life work here. He served the church for 50 years when the responsibilities of such a large church became too heavy for him and he resigned. He was succeeded by Dr. Stratton whose ministrations attract large audiences and constantly keep the church in the public eye.

Of the Episcopal Churches St. Thomas' and St. Bartholomew's occupied the same relative position of influence and dignity they do today. Each of them had their share of the great financial and industrial magnates of the day. "The poor ye have always with you" and these so-called swell churches had their share of the poor too, and let us add that the generosity of these churches was beyond praise. They have both undergone great changes from an architectural point of view. St. Thomas' has been almost entirely reconstructed and beautified, and St. Bartholomew's rebuilt on a new site on Park Avenue—a magnificent edifice which has no equal except the great Cathedral of St. John the Divine.

We cannot pass over the old and venerable church in Varick Street, St. John's Chapel, which only a few years ago passed from the scene. It was a great church fifty years ago and at that time was famous for its fine musical services which drew great crowds but even that could not keep the congregation from dwindling. The population in that neighborhood changed in character so rapidly that this splendid old church became only a memorial of a bygone age. Almost a century ago the surroundings of St. John's Chapel and Park were the finest residential portions of the city. The transformation to its present condition is one of the heartrending changes of modern

"Announcing the death of Mr. Stewart at the Tenth Street Store"

industrial progress, and to the Old New Yorker who remembers St. John's in its palmy days, the change is a sad one.

Of the Roman Catholic Churches none is better known than the modest little church of St. Andrews that stands at the corner of Duane Street and City Hall Place. It was ministering to the toiling masses long before the subway and the bridges began pouring out their stream of human beings almost at its door and continues its work to the present day. Here in the very midst of workshops and factories it provides a place of rest and quiet and helpfulness to anyone who may need. The church is open at all hours—night as well as day.

The merchants of that day are also worth recalling. Many of them were closely allied with church and Sunday school work and served as superintendents, trustees, and in other offices, and were from every branch of business.

There were no such aggregations of capital or business at this time as we are familiar with today. A. T. Stewart and Horace B. Claflin were of such prodigious size compared with the others that they were in a class by themselves. So that when a Cleveland oil firm moved to New York with a capital of one million dollars it was an event to be noted. This was Rockefeller & Company, Exporters, afterwards the famous Standard Oil Company, which opened its New York offices at 181 Pearl Street. The building is still standing, half hidden by the elevated. The place where Mr. John D. Rockefeller had his personal desk can still be seen on the second floor. The building is now occupied by an army of tenants, but many of the partitions originally put in by the Standard Oil still remain. The imposing new building on lower Broadway is a far cry from the modest quarters in Pearl Street, and I suppose No. 26 is probably the best known location in the world.

Not long after the arrival of the Standard, a tobacco firm came from North Carolina and opened a factory over on the East Side. Mr. James B. Duke, then a young man, was in charge of the New York office. They prospered, and an old-time lithograph issued by them in the early Eighties proudly boasts of their capital—enormous for those days—of $600,000. Early this year (1925) Mr. Duke shipped back to a College in his own home town the trifling sum of forty-six million dollars as a souvenir of his affection, and I understand that he has enough left to eat all he wants in the automat any time he feels like it.

Enormous as this sum is, it does not begin to rival the incredible benefactions of Mr. Rockefeller or of Mr. Carnegie. The sad part of the story is that we who were born here and have lived here all our lives have somehow or other failed to see the vast sums which apparently have been lying loose around our own streets—for an owner. We have left the prizes for the stranger within our gates including the Pole, the Russ and the Scandinavian. Maybe we have been like the artist who searched the world over, neglecting his home town, for a face that would express his idea of the Madonna. After years of fruitless search he returned home disappointed and dejected only to have the model of his dreams walk past his doorstep. She had been living on the next street all the time!

The names of the old-time wholesale dry goods merchants of fifty years ago are almost forgotten now and the entire district from Canal Street to Duane Street and Broadway to Chambers Street, where the large wholesale houses were located, has completely changed. At that time A. T. Stewart and H. B. Claflin were the two great names in the wholesale dry goods business. There were other large firms, such as E. S. Jaffray & Co., Halsted Haines & Co., John F. Plummer & Co., Calhoun, Robbins & Co,. and Kayne, Spring & Dale; but they did not approach Stewart or Claflin in the enormous output of goods. A. T. Stewart was said to be doing about fifty millions yearly and Claflin only a little less—a tremendous turnover in those days. There were no other concerns in any part of the world to compare with these two in the magnitude of their business. It was quite a sight at the height of the season to see the throngs of buyers from every town in the country in Stewart's or Claflin's selecting their season's supplies. New York was then the great market for the entire United States and the hotels were crowded with these buyers making their spring and fall purchases and every house of any consequence had its representative drumming up trade at the hotels where the buyers put up. Of course this class of business had to be done chiefly at night when the buyers were to be found at leisure and were naturally disposed to enjoy themselves. The drummer's task in the buying seasons was no easy one but it was lucrative and to the man who could spend night after night in hilarity and amusement until the small hours of the morning a great business was assured. All the hotels downtown were full to their capacity and the buyers usually returned to the same quarters from year to year. The Metropolitan Hotel was the most popular, and the others on Broadway, the St. Nicholas, the New York, Broadway Central, and Sinclair had a large patronage. The Earle House on Canal Street and the Astor House downtown were also great favorites.

Not one of these famous hostelries remains today, but many a good tale could be told of the merrymaking of their patrons, intermingled with some good big business deals. The great panic of 1873 brought a tremendous crowd of buyers to New York for the purpose of picking up the bargains that were offered for cash by the big wholesalers in order to get the absolutely necessary ready cash to save them from bankruptcy. H. B. Claflin & Co. offered their entire stock at such reduced prices for spot cash that their immense first floor was like a bee hive for several days and the firm gathered in sufficient cash to tide them over the most precarious and difficult period that they ever had encountered. Other firms adopted the same means, but many in every line of business succumbed. To walk down Broadway during the height of the panic was a sight never to be forgotten. Scores of business houses, especially insurance companies, were closed up and notices on the doors and windows that they were in the hands of receivers. It seemed as if the end of all things had come, but New York rose like a phœnix from the ashes and began its new career of prosperity which has brought us to our present wonderful development. Our present great retail establishments were only in their infancy then. Every one of them was small compared to their size today, and they did business very differently from what they do now. Only the more important ones delivered goods and only to those near at hand. People used to talk about R. H. Macy & Co. when they had about a score of delivery wagons—how wonderfully progressive. And then, too, those retail dry goods houses were all clustered together in certain sections, the largest section being between Fourteenth and Twenty-third Streets, Broadway and Sixth Avenue, where were located Macy & Co., Altman & Co., Richard Mears & Co., Simpson, Crawford & Simpson, H. O'Neil & Co., Adams & Co., Stern Bros., Ehrich & Co., J. McCreery & Co., Arnold Constable & Co., Aitken Son & Co., Le Boutilier and J. & C. Johnston. Another important retail dry goods district was Grand Street, below the Bowery, where E. Ridley & Sons, Lord & Taylor, Lichtenstein and others were located. Both of these districts have been completely obliterated so far as dry goods or department stores are concerned. They have all gone uptown and scattered to different parts. But in the fifty years we are considering what immense strides they have made—that is, those who still remain with us. Quite a number of them have disappeared—names that were household words in the Seventies—Simpson, Crawford & Simpson, H. O'Neil & Co., Adams & Co., Ehrich & Co., and that great East Side store, E. Ridley & Sons together with their neighbor, the Lichtensteins. Fifth Avenue, Forty-second Street and Thirty-fourth Street, which were then quiet and beautiful residential quarters, are now the homes of large palatial department stores which have been developed from the small and insignificant stores of the Seventies. Going downtown again we find that in the Seventies the wholesale grocery business was located below Canal Street and chiefly in the neighborhood of Chambers Street where West Broadway and Hudson Streets lead into College Place. Here the leading grocery house of H. K. Thurber & Co., now only a name, was doing a great business. From morning till night the retailers from all parts of the city were coming and going, for at that time the retailers had to carry their own goods and it was many years later that the system of delivering goods was introduced. Near them in Chambers Street was F. H. Leggett & Co., and on the opposite side Austin Nichols & Co., both still in business in different parts of the city and doing a business now immensely greater than at the time of which we speak. William Welsh and E. C. Hazard & Co. were left behind in the rapid march of affairs and are no more, but the old firm of Pupke & Reid, now Eppens Smith & Co., still remains in the old location, also B. Fischer & Co., both houses now dealing principally in teas and coffees. R. C. Williams & Co. were then on the East Side and had much of the business of the Long Island towns, but are now one of the great grocery houses of New York located in Hudson Street.

An interesting development of the grocery business was the beginning of the retail chain stores. One of the earliest and most successful was Thomas Anderson who began in the humblest way by peddling teas and coffees from a wagon which was his only store. He was simply an honest, hard-working man, ambitious and very thrifty. As soon as he was able he opened a small store on Eighth Avenue and there his business increased steadily for several years until he got capital enough to spread out. He was a most conscientious man and had a strong religious cast to his mind. While his neighbors in the same line of business opened their stores on Sunday for half a day, Mr. Anderson closed down on Saturday night and nothing under the sun could move him to open the door of his store for any purpose whatever until Monday morning. He spent his Sundays in church and in religious work. Bye and bye he became the great retailer of teas and coffees with a chain of stores extending to all parts of New York and Brooklyn. Although he has passed away himself his business still goes on and the spirit of the founder continues to direct it.

Among the great grocery houses were many kindred businesses contemporaneous with and dependent on them. Several firms which supplied paper and paper goods of all kinds used by both wholesale and retail grocers and by the drygoods merchants are still in business—one of the most widely known being Robert Gair Co., now of New York and Brooklyn, but fifty years ago known as Gair & West. Robert Gair had been through the Civil War and emerged from that struggle as Capt. Gair of the 79th Regt. He was still a very young man when he commenced business in the wholesale grocery district. His business grew rapidly and in a very few years he was joined by George West who had large paper mills in Balston Spa and represented that district in Congress and the firm of Gair & West became the chief purveyor of grocery supplies in New York City. Robert Gair's integrity of character, his Scotch perseverance and conscientiousness won him the confidence of all the big grocery firms. It used to be said of H. K. Thurber that he would buy no paper goods from any other man than Bob Gair, and none of his subordinates dare depart from that rule. But a time came when Robert Gair wanted to control the business alone, and he bought out George West's interest and then branched out into other channels that were then opening up for the extension of the business in paper goods. Mr. Gair was the pioneer in the folding box business—an industry which has grown to be one of the largest in the country—and the Robert Gair Co. now has seven factories manufacturing all kinds of goods made of paper, with branches in most of the large cities of the country. Mr. Gair himself, although a very old man, is still the head of the concern, but his son George West Gair, who has inherited his father's wonderful business capabilities, is the active and inspiring force that keeps it going and growing.

The great paper market centered in Beekman Street. Henry Lindenmeyr was the largest, then there were Harrison Bros. & Co., Coffin & Lyon, G. W. Millar & Co., Vernon Bros., Louis Dejonge & Co., Miller and Flinn, Clement & Stockwell, Jones & Skinner, Seymour & Co., C. B. Hewitt & Co., etc.

One of the most interesting reminders of the social glories of New York in the closing years of the last century is the wonderful collection of miniatures formed by the late Peter Marié and bequeathed by him to the New York Historical Society, where they now repose. The collection as an entity would bring back to mind practically every social leader of that period. Something like two hundred portraits are represented in this work and every picture is the work of one of the most noted miniaturists of his day. Taken as a whole they are of extraordinary interest. The artistic work is exquisite in coloring and the mounting of the miniature is likewise a work of art. Seldom, indeed, has any city been left such an historic group of portraits, and as the years pass by the collection will serve to preserve for us a glimpse of the city in its social side that cannot fail to be of ever-increasing interest.

Peter Marié himself was as near an approach to the beau brummel of our day as New York has produced. He was a Frenchman by birth and well connected. He made a modest fortune in Wall Street during and subsequent to the Civil War. He retired and lived just off the Avenue in West 19th Street, devoting his time wholly to social affairs. He entertained frequently, giving small, unique dinners which were famous at the time. These dinners were interspersed with musical receptions. Being himself a bachelor, he gave a Leap Year dinner once, that was long remembered. The centerpiece was of elaborate design, presenting a high tower of sugar candy, with all the most prominent bachelors of the time—Cutting, Redmond, Grey, Bruguer, Clendening and others—represented as jumping down to the outspread arms of a circle of debutantes.

Like his friend, Ward McAllister, he took his social obligations seriously and regarded the polite usages of society as one of the cardinal virtues in life. He was a man of rare personal charm, widely traveled, and his extensive acquaintance in society both here and in London and Paris, made him a charming raconteur. His fund of small talk was endless and he was a storehouse of information regarding the antecedents and the exact position socially of every family in town. The circle in which he moved at that time was, of course, much smaller than at present, and permitted a degree of intimacy wholly lacking in our present social structure.

And so, with the presentation of these delightful portraits, my little sketch of the City as I knew it in my youth comes to a close. A host of memories arise as I read the pages for the last time. In my old "McGuffy's Reader," which lies before me as I write, my eyes fall upon a verse of singular appropriateness for a finis:

> "Oh! would I were a boy again
>   When life was filled with sunny years,
> And all the heart then knew of pain
>   Was wiped away in transient tears!"

THE MISSES RIVES

Painted by Edw. Fesser

·· MISS MORRIS ··

Painted by Abendschein

MRS. JOHN R. DREXEL

Painted by C. & F. Weidner   Four Daughters of Robert Minturn

Painted by Meave T. Gedney

Mrs. Bradley Martin

Painted by Carl Weidner

Mrs. William Allen

Painted by Behenna   Mrs. J. P. Morgan, Jr.

Painted by Paillet
Mrs. Hamilton Fish Webster

Painted by C. & F. Weidner

FOUR DAUGHTERS OF HEBER R. BISHOP

Painted by Weidner

MRS. JOHN G. HECKSCHER

Painted by Paillet

Mrs. Royal Phelps Carrol

Painted by Behenna

Miss Choate

Painted by Paillet

MISS MARGARET CLARKSON

Painted by Paillet

MRS. VAN RENSSELAER CRUGER

Painted by Weidner

Mrs. Edwin Main Post

Painted by Weidner

Mrs. Charles de Rham, Jr.

Painted by Edw. Fesser

MRS. STANLEY MORTIMER

Painted by Paillet

MRS. ARTHUR HENRY PAGET

Behenna

MRS. FREDERIC GRAND D'HAUTEVILLE

Meare T. Gedney

MRS. OLIVER HARRIMAN, JR.

The Produce Exchange in 1883

EARLY DAYS OF THE NEW YORK
PRODUCE EXCHANGE

By George A. Zabriskie

SOME forty-two years ago, in May, the opening of the
New York Produce Exchange—that huge terra cotta
building which faces Bowling Green in the lower end of
the city—was an outstanding event, not only in the city's
history, but wherever there was commercial activity the
world over.

Not by accident, because those things are not accidental,
even though we call them so, the Produce Exchange stands
practically upon the site of the old market place, the first
on Manhattan Island, established by the earliest settlers
of New Amsterdam. Its immediate ancestors, however,
gravitated a little from the home base, for we find them

in about 1840 meeting at the corner of Broad and South
Streets, and on rainy days seeking the shelter of an awn-
ing, put up for their convenience in front of the flour
warehouse of Weeks & Douglas at 16 South Street; this
firm, later changed to Weeks & Parr, is still in business,
and Colonel Parr—a contemporary of Chauncey Depew—
is still hale and hearty, a fine example of American pioneer
manhood.

After ten or twelve years the gradual increase in the
number of flour and grain merchants who found it convenient to meet here to transact their business, suggested
an association, and so one was formed, which went by the
name of the New York Corn Exchange. This association
was duly incorporated, quarters were established inside
the buildings where formerly the members occupied the
sidewalk, and the institution blossomed forth like a green
bay tree.

Early days at corner Broad and South Streets

New York Produce Exchange. Laying the cornerstone of the present building, 1883

Those were happy days; apparently the Scotch took little interest in the flour and grain trade then, for in looking over some old Manuals I notice that their notions of trading were quite different from those of our merchants—probably more like the "go-getters" of the present time. Witness this in the early days of New York: "It has been noticed and observed, with great concern, that many Scotch merchants from time to time come out of their country with the ships, and are doing or aiming at nothing else than with their underselling and manners of trading to destroy trade; selling their goods very rapidly and having sold out, going home without leaving any benefit to the country, etc."

Ten years later saw another change in prospect for the Exchange, and this time history began to take a hand in shaping matters, for the site selected was the block bounded by Whitehall and Moore Streets, between Pearl

Corner of Whitehall and Moore Streets
in Governor Stuyvesant's time

Drawn by Thure de Thulstrup

Promenade Concert and Ladies' Reception, New Year's Eve,
at Produce Exchange, 1883

and Water, where, during Governor Stuyvesant's administration, some two hundred years earlier, it was ordained that "a fitt house be built and everyone admitted that had anything to buy or sell." This probably was the first expression of the idea of Exchange manifested in Manhattan, and it was very necessary at the time because of another ordinance in effect in the interest of the West India Company forbidding the inhabitants "from having the hardihood to go into the interior with any cargoes or any other merchandise; but they shall leave them at the usual place of deposit and there wait for traffic."

Flour men now operating on the floor of the New York Produce Exchange can remember when this was still true of their industry—when tables on the Exchange were filled with samples, each sample representing a quantity of flour, and purchasers from far and near came to examine them, make their selections and buy their requirements. Those days, however, like the days of the clipper ships "the roaring forties" and South Street sidewalk conversations are gone. Combinations of mills and baking companies have reduced the number of traders, and even the comparatively small mills have their laboratories now, standardizing their flour, and buying is done on an analysis of its color, protein and ash, rather than by the old method of examination of samples.

And so, on this propitious site of Moore and Whitehall Streets, was erected in 1860-61 a goodly sized building, and the name of the association was changed from the New York Corn Exchange to the New York Produce Exchange—the present charter being granted a year later. Business was carried on by the members of the Exchange with every port on the globe—three quarters of all the flour and grain exported from the United States was sold

How the neighborhood looked about the time the Produce Exchange opened.
Broadway north from Bowling Green

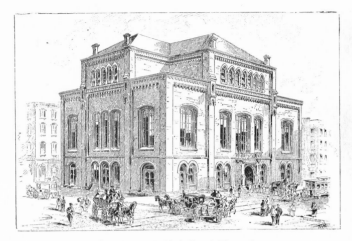

The Exchange at Whitehall and Moore Streets

and financed by them; the inspection and grading of flour and grain made under the supervision and guarantee of the Exchange were accepted everywhere, and, I may add, at no time has their accuracy or integrity been questioned.

Commodious as the building on Moore and Whitehall Streets was, it sufficed only twenty-five years, when it became necessary for the members, now nearly three thousand in number, to cast about for something still larger, so, with funds approximating $2,000,000, the present site was purchased, and a building housing the largest and finest trading floor in the world was finished in 1883. The tower of the Produce Exchange at that time was a landmark downtown—it was the natural observatory, overlooking the lower bay to the south, and the fast developing city to the north—only the steeple of Trinity Church compared with it in loftiness—its clock was the

Old-time holiday frolic at the Produce Exchange.
December 31, 1882

navigator's chronometer, its flagpole the tallest that had ever been stepped on any building, and the Exchange was a glorious monument to commerce and trade. So it was in 1883—now, after forty-two years, its structural prominence dimmed by the skyscrapers surrounding it, the old institution still represents all that is fine in commercial endeavor—proud of its cornerstone inscription "Equity."

The festivities attending the opening ceremonies of the Exchange will ever be remembered by those who had the good fortune to be present. It was on the evening of the fifth of May that the first welcome to the new building was extended; the Executive Committee, feeling that the families and friends of the members should grace the beginning of its career, suggested a May day gathering, and this was followed by a Promenade Concert and Ladies' Reception, such as downtown New York had never seen or will likely see again. Carriages thronged the streets from City Hall south, and the guests soon filled the great trading Hall, overflowing into the corridors, so that members, throwing open the doors of their counting rooms and private offices, added a unique feature to the hospitality and general entertainment.

The following day—May 6th—at 11 a.m. the members assembled in the old building at Moore and Whitehall Streets for the last time, and the President, Mr. J. H. Herrick, in calling the meeting to order, expressed sadness in saying goodbye to the old halls.

The valedictory address of Mr. James McGee, too, brought tears to the eye of many a member, recalling the small beginnings from which came the present grand success (many were there who remembered the open air meetings at the corner of Broad and South Streets) he urged that they forget not the principles on which success

FIFTH AVENUE IN THE HEYDEY OF ITS SOCIAL
DAYS OF HIGH STOO

. Looking south from 31st Street in the
    ʳ ɢᴀʀᴅᴇɴѕ. (1870.)

had been attained, nor the struggles which had been incident hereto. These struggles were the warrant of healthy growth, like the giant tree obtains its structure by the beating of the elements. Two friends looked into the faces listening to Mr. McGee—Memory and Hope—Memory bid them all not to forget their comrades, but cling close to each other, bound in one common brotherhood, that the Exchange might be powerful for grand things in the community. Hope said, "believe in the possibilities—be optimists. There are great resources in the future, our fathers did not have the telegraph, the telephone, the East River Bridge, we shall make the new Exchange grander than the old."

Tempered with a tone of sadness, the applause had scarcely subsided at the close of the address, when the glee club of the Exchange sang with fine effect "Goodbye dear Halls of old."

The ceremonies concluded with the Glee Club leading and the members joining in singing "Auld Lang Syne" accompanied by the band.

Under the direction of the Grand Marshall, the members then proceeded from the old Exchange to the new, and assembling in the main hall, under the inspiring strains of Cappa's Seventh Regiment Band, the members and invited guests filled to the utmost capacity the great trading room.

On a raised platform, emerging from supporting banks of flowers, and under the drapery of our National flag, in the midst of distinguished guests and prominent citizens, members of the Exchange, the President, arising, invited the Rev. Arthur Brooks to offer prayer. Then followed the address of Franklin Edson, chairman of the Building Committee, surrendering the completed building, as the result of their labors, and in witnessing its dedication "As a Temple of Commerce worthy of this commercial metropolis," he stated that his committee received their ample reward.

After President Herrick's address, receiving the building from the Chairman of the Committee, the Glee Club sang "Hail this Temple Grand" and the account of this says that "the volume of tone and the precision of enunciation carried the harmony and sentiment to the utmost limits of the Great Hall."

Then came the oration by Mr. Herrick—a masterful one—covering a history of the Exchange, after which addresses by the Hon. Chauncey M. Depew, Hon. Algernon S. Sullivan, Hon. Thomas White of the Montreal Board of Trade, Mr. Travo, President of the Pittsburgh Board of Trade, and officials of the New York Stock Exchange, Chicago, Toledo, Milwaukee, St. Louis, San Francisco, and other Boards of Trade.

Space does not permit a very comprehensive reference to these addresses, but one or two may not be amiss. Chauncey Depew, preliminary to his more formal remarks, said, "I think it incumbent upon me to extend to you two congratulations. The one is that on the occasion of the opening of this Exchange, with all that it signifies, in this commercial metropolis of the new world, the chairman of the committee, under whose genius it was constructed is also the Mayor of the city. The second congratulation is suggested by the address of your President, that this is probably the last time under your rules of arbitration that you will ever, in a business way, have occasion to call upon the profession to which I belong. The opening of this Exchange marks an important era in our National development. The wildest anticipation of the

The floor of the Exchange

The three buildings at left center show present site of Produce Exchange. Here also was located the first Dutch market-place. Building at right, old Government House—now site of Custom House

preceding generation would not have hazarded the prediction that in thirty years the merchants of this city engaged only in the handling of domestic food products would have required and possessed the resources to build a palace of commerce costing three millions of dollars. The modest rented room which met all your wants in 1860 expanding into this superb structure in 1884, illustrates the agricultural and commercial progress of this country in the last quarter of a century. The startling splendor of the facts reduces to ordinary experience the wildest imaginings of the Arabian Nights."

The Hon. Algernon S. Sullivan, whose eloquent and poetic address at the laying of the cornerstone was still fresh in the memory of many of those present, was then introduced, and describing the edifice said, "Fine in architecture and colossal in proportions—sprung from massive

cornerstones—ribbed with iron, and walled with bricks
burned in the hottest kilns—opening windows to every
sky, and, like a beetling cliff commanding the eye of the
homebound mariner. Oh, Tower crowned Trade Hall!
Thou standest imperial and complete. Look from thy
parapets down the bay where three arms of the ocean
meet and listen to the swash of their flood tides."

Very true was this description forty years ago, and
while time has wrought changes in the outside perspective,
and the Grand Canyon of lower Broadway takes on a far
different aspect than the highway dotted with white stage
coaches, the medium of approach in those days, the dignified impressiveness of the building remains the same, the
personnel of its members command the highest esteem and
its trading floor is still unsurpassed the world over.

Looking up Broadway from No. 1 to Trinity Church.
Bowling Green in Center. 1825

[385]

Liberty Pole Parade, Sons of Revolution. President Olyphant
leading. Governor Silzer, guest of honor, escorted by
George A. Zabriskie, following

Governor Silzer speaking at Liberty Pole celebration, City Hall
Park, New York. June 14, 1925

EDITORIAL

| No. 10 | New York, 1926 | Vol. 1 |

RETROSPECTIVE.   1916 - 1926

By the Editor

IT is now ten years since the first number of the *Manual* of the new series made its appearance before the public. This birthday number not only commemorates the three hundredth anniversary of the founding of New York but also the end of the first decade in an interesting venture.

Reviewing the past ten years there are some things the *Manual* has accomplished which we regard with great satisfaction, and in this my readers, who made it possible, are fully entitled to share. For example, in the first number we called attention to the neglect of the City Fathers in not printing the minutes of the Common Council from 1789 to 1831. Up to this time not a single copy of this valuable record, including as it did the early cradle days of our great city, was available to the general public. Many attempts had been made to rectify this unfortunate condition, Dr. Edward Hageman Hall in particular, having spent much time in this direction. Fortunately, Mayor Mitchel was then in office, and it took but little effort to convince him of the necessity of this work, and a long neglected duty was thus finally performed.

A second achievement of much satisfaction was the erection of the Liberty Pole in City Hall Park. Shortly after the *Manual* began work on this task, it was joined by the Sons of the Revolution and the New York Histori-

Print Room—Museum of the City of New York

cal Society, who carried the plan to completion. The Pole is now in the custody of the City of New York, but under the special care of the Sons of the Revolution. Each year this organization holds a celebration on Flag Day, in the Park. Around the base of the Pole it has been arranged that one stone from a Revolutionary battlefield in each of the thirteen colonies be placed in position each year. So far, three States are represented. Stones have been received from the Battlefield of Washington Heights in New York; from the home of General Nelson, headquarters of Lord Cornwallis during the battle and surrender of Yorktown, Virginia, and from the Battlefield of Princeton, in New Jersey. Not only has the erection of the Pole itself been important, but the yearly exercises, recalling as they do the significance of the Pole and of the events which led up to it, have inculcated lessons of patriotism the country over. Distinguished men addressed the people at these celebrations; U. S. Senator Willis, of Ohio; Governor Alfred Smith, of New York; Governor Lee Trinkle, of Virginia; and Governor Silzer, of New Jersey, each having already appeared.

The third accomplishment has been the founding of the Museum of the City of New York, in which the Legislature and the City government co-operated. The Museum is now established in the old Gracie Mansion, at the foot of Eighty-eighth Street and East River. It was duly opened November 7, 1924, and has made gratifying progress ever since. It numbers among its founders and trustees, such names as Mrs. Andrew Carnegie, Mrs. John Stewart Kennedy, J. P. Morgan, Archer M. Huntington, William Rhinelander Stewart, James Speyer, Henry Richmond Taylor, Edwin Gould, George A. Zabriskie, Henry R. Towne, Edwin C. Jameson, and Frank Bailey. Naturally, a venture of this kind is of slow growth; the Metropolitan and the Natural History struggled along for about ten years before they were able to open their own buildings, but since then their growth has been astonishing. It is hardly reasonable to expect that the City Museum will prove any exception to the general experience. It comes at an opportune time and has a rich field peculiarly its own. There is no other institution wholly and exclusively devoted to the task of preserving and collecting material pertaining to the great City of New York. In this respect it is exactly like the London Museum, and the Museé Carnavalet, in Paris, both of which are specifically charged with the duty of preserving the historical relics of their respective cities. Few persons, however, are as yet aware of the new Museum's existence. It goes without saying, however, that when our people become acquainted with it, the same generous support that has always been available for worthy purposes will be extended to the new venture.

As I write, we are rapidly approaching the three hundredth anniversary of the founding of the City of New York. This event will undoubtedly arouse public interest in the Museum to a larger degree than now exists. In short, I have every reason to think that it will direct attention to the necessity for a fire-proof building. As you perhaps know, our present structure is an old colonial home by no means fire proof. It is, however, isolated in a little 12-acre park and is adequately provided with fire

Early New York room—Museum of the City of New York

protection; but so important and wealthy a city as New York, requires, and should have, every safeguard for the preservation of such important material.

You ought to see this little Museum for yourself. Take either the east side, or the west side subway (or elevated), and get off at Eighty-sixth Street. A bus and street car connect with both. It swings around at 86th Street on its way to the Ninety-second Street Ferry. Ask the driver to let you off at Eighty-eighth Street, and the house is plainly in sight.

It has always been the policy of the *Manual* to create ideas and then find the proper custodian for their perpetuation. The same plan will be followed in the case of the Museum. It was my very great privilege to be elected Director for the first year and to play an active part in the important work of organization. The Museum is fortunate in having many members at once efficient and generous. Rapid and substantial growth may be expected.

*　　*　　*　　*　　*　　*

In the present issue the *Manual* has departed somewhat from its former selection of contents. Instead of the many interesting small items gathered here and there, I decided this year to concentrate on one long article, and the result is as you see it in the story—THE LAST FIFTY YEARS OF NEW YORK. I have not, of course, been able to record anything but the most outstanding features of this period and the text scarcely goes beyond the early Eighties. It seems to me that the time is already here when the closing years of the last century may be rightly said to have passed into history, so great has been the change in our civilization since the Great War. So stupendous and overwhelming an event, has in one sense almost wiped out the years that immediately preceded it, and there is no question but that we are now living in a wholly different era. It may be that I shall continue the narrative through 1880 in the next number. That I can decide when I see the amount of interest my readers take in the present instalment. Even then it might be that I shall substitute, "Old Broadway, the Main Street in Our Village," in place of a continuation. At all events my readers may look forward to a succession of articles descriptive of certain sections of the City. "Third Avenue, the Old Boston Post Road," is scheduled to follow Broadway. I want the next ten numbers to be of unusual interest, and each number distinguished for a special authoritative article on some particular part of our wonderful City.

*　　*　　*　　*　　*　　*

In reviewing these pages of FIFTY YEARS I am not able to convince myself that the city has improved greatly since then. In some respects it has advanced greatly and in others it has gone back. Coal used to be $4 a ton. Now it is $16. Saloons were four to a corner and now there are none. In their place are a horde of bootleggers and the vast majority of our people are lawbreakers.

The street cars and the subways are, however, no longer filled with women with shawls in place of hats, cheap skirts, and shoes in the last stages of exhaustion. Instead, we have the stylish high heels with nude silk stockings and the latest mode in headgear. There is still much poverty, no doubt, but its tangible existence is not so much in evidence.

The domestic servant has disappeared from among middle-class families. Community life has supplanted individual life. Labor-saving devices have mitigated the

Dutch Room—Museum of the City of New York

burden of labor in the house and the factory. Working hours are shorter. You get a great many more dollars in the pay envelope Saturday night but they buy little or nothing. Yet the people seem to have more and to live better. It is the day of the proletariat.

The City itself has none of its old-time sociability left. The old days when everybody in the block knew everybody else; when the church parade on Fifth Avenue kept you bowing and saluting friends and neighbors for an hour or more, has disappeared. It is the exception and not the rule to meet an old friend on the street. Our thanks are due to *Harper's Weekly, Frank Leslie's Illustrated Weekly,* the New York Historical Society, the Public Library, Mr. George A. Zabriskie, Mr. Simeon

Ford, Mr. A. J. Wall for the many contemporaneous pictures used in connection with FIFTY YEARS.

*   *   *   *   *   *

We still are able to supply back numbers of the first nine issues, to those of our subscribers whose sets may not be complete. A special discount is also made to those who purchase ten numbers at once. To those who complain of the high price of the *Manual,* we need only point to the vast number of engravings in each issue and the original research work involved in every number. Perhaps, if they would remember that as far back as 1866 the cost of this publication to the City, which was then its publisher, was about $125,000. The final number (which appeared in 1870) is said to have cost nearly a

Colonial Room—Museum of the City of New York

Marine Room—Museum of the City of New York

quarter of a million. In those days manufacturing costs were just about one-third of what they are today. We have always been at a loss to understand the staggering totals of the old *Manual's* cost. In our experience we have spent much less than either of these sums in each year. Nevertheless, the *Manual* is an expensive book to manufacture and probably will always so remain. We would be very glad to have our readers express their opinion of this number, particularly as compared with the ones preceding. Their opinions will unquestionably be helpful.

We repeat a cordial invitation to visit the Museum. We need your co-operation to make it a worth-while institution during the Three-hundredth Birthday Celebration.

INDEX

A

Abbey, Mr., 154.
Academy of Music, 91, 148.
Adams & Co., 350.
Agney, C. R., 333.
Aitken Son & Co., 350.
Albemarle Hotel, 100.
Albers', Thomas, Assoc., 127.
Aldine (horse), 120.
Allen's Bleecker St. Den, 127.
All Angels Episcopal Church, 319.
Altman Co., 350.
Amen Corner, Fifth Ave. Hotel, 134.
American Museum of Natural History, 306.
American News Co., 258.
American Wing, 316.
American Geographical Society, 226.
American Institute Fair, 10.
American Rifle Team, 107, 108.
American Mabille, 127.
Amherst, 110.
Anderson, Thomas, 351.
Appletons, 284.
"Assyrian Monarch" (ship), 309.
Ashland, The Hotel, 106.
Ashland House, 102.
Aspinwall, 315.
Aspinwall, Louisa, 214, 225.
Aspinwall, Wm. H., 213-217.
Astors, The, 213.
Astor, Mrs. John Jacob, 97.
Astor House, 98, 264, 348.
Attwood, F. G., 316.
Auburn, 288
Auchmuty, 217.

B

Backus, 159.
Bailey, Frank, 389.
Bangs, John Kendrick, 316.
Bangs Restaurant, 170.
Baptist Temple, 343.
Barclay, George, 217.
Barnum, P. T., 303-305, 308-311.
Barnum's Museum, 311.
Barremore, Mr., 267.
Barrett House, 104.
Barrett, Judge, 180.
Barry, John, 120.
Barrymore, Maurice, 174.
Bates, Blanche, 168.

Bay Ridge, 131.
Beecher, Henry Ward, 322-324, 329, 342.
Beecher, Lyman, 323.
"Beefsteak John's" Restaurant, 94.
Behrends, Dr., 340.
Bell, Alexander, 10.
Bell, Digby, 170.
Bellew, Frank P., 316.
Bellows, Henry W., 320.
Belmont, August, 213, 228, 315.
Benkard, James, 226.
Benkard & Hutton, 226.
Bergh, Henry, 219.
Bernard, Sam, 58.
Bibby, Mr., 116.
Bible House on 9th St., 332.
Birch, Mr., 159.
Blaine, Mr., 329.
Blaine, James G., 324.
Blashfield, E. H., 25.
Blodgett, W. T., 316.
Bloodgood, John, 179.
Bloomingdale Road, 15.
Bodine, Col., 108.
Bok, Edward W., 322.
Boldt, George, 83, 97.
Bond Street, 98.
Bonner, Robert, 25.
Boulanger March, The, 190.
Boorman, James, 216.
Booth, Edwin, 102.
Bowdoin College, 110.
Bowery Theater, 302.
Boynton, Capt. Paul, 116.
Brady, Jude, 180.
Brainerd, Cephas, 333.
Bremer, Frederica, 43.
Breslin, Mr., 103.
Brevoort, Home, 218.
Brevoort Hotel, 100, 218.
Brice, Lloyd, 254.
Brice, Mrs. Lloyd, 216.
Brignoli, 91.
Brighton, Beach, 136.
Brillat, 91.
Bristol's Oyster House, 82.
Broadway Squad, 4.
Broadway Line, 22.
Broadway Central, Hotel, 106, 348.
Broadway Theater, 166, 191.
Broadway Tabernacle, 320.
Brockway's, 96.
Brooklyn Bridge, 3.